A Tremendous Thing

A Tremendous Thing

Friendship from the Iliad *to the Internet*

Gregory Jusdanis

Cornell University Press

Ithaca and London

First published 2014 by Cornell University Press

Printed in the United States of America

Library of Congress Cataloging-in-Publication Data

Jusdanis, Gregory, 1955– author
  A tremendous thing : friendship from the Iliad to the Internet / Gregory Jusdanis.
      pages cm
  Includes bibliographical references and index.
  ISBN 978-0-8014-5284-0 (cloth : alk. paper)
  1. Friendship. 2. Friendship in literature.
3. Social networks. I. Title.
  BJ1533.F8J87   2014
  302.34—dc23   2014013454

Cornell University Press strives to use environmentally responsible suppliers and materials to the fullest extent possible in the publishing of its books. Such materials include vegetable-based, low-VOC inks and acid-free papers that are recycled, totally chlorine-free, or partly composed of nonwood fibers. For further information, visit our website at www.cornellpress.cornell.edu.

Cloth printing   10 9 8 7 6 5 4 3 2 1

For my friends

Contents

Acknowledgments

"Why did you do all this for me?" he asked. "I don't deserve it. I've never done anything for you."

"You have been my friend," replied Charlotte. "That in itself is a tremendous thing."

E. B. White, *Charlotte's Web*

It has been my good fortune to have tremendous friends. Julian Anderson, my wife, has painstakingly read every line I have written ever since we met one May morning by a Bavarian lake. I have been discussing these and other issues with Vassilis Lambropoulos for thirty years, profiting always from his insights. Artemis Leontis went over the manuscript with both rigor and compassion. Ric Rader read various drafts many times over, answering all my anxious queries.

My children, Adrian, Alexander, and Clare, have patiently humored my thinking out loud, sometimes at length, on ideas of empathy, sacrifice, consistency, and devotion.

As ever, Jim Phelan offered major changes, deletions, and additions to the original version. Yiorgos Anagnostou helped shape the work by pointing out strengths and weaknesses. Lou Ruprecht insisted that I push my thinking further. Peter Jeffreys read an early draft and suggested wider readings. Although I met Mark Roche only once, he sent me a long commentary on the manuscript.

Peter J. Potter, my editor at Cornell University Press, encouraged me to find a route I had not myself imagined and offered unstinting guidance along the way. The generous and learned comments of two anonymous readers urged me to expand my vision. For their help I will always be grateful. I appreciate the careful copyediting of the manuscript by John Raymond.

A fellowship from the American Council of Learned Societies enabled me to complete an initial version. The news of the fellowship came in the bleakest winter of my life and proved one more time that hope sustains us. The College of Arts and Sciences of The Ohio State University offered a sabbatical and much research support. Although not underwriting this project, the Onassis Foundation sent me to teach in Ann Arbor, Bogota, Cartagena, and Buenos Aires. As a result the manuscript breathes the air of these four unforgettable cities.

In the course of writing, I have witnessed the possibility of friendship in extreme old age. At ninety-three my mother moved into an apartment and came to know Eleni, a resident of the apartment twenty years her junior. Becoming immediate friends, they spent the better part of each day together over the next three years. When in April 2013 my mother had a heart attack and stroke, Eleni visited her every day in the hospital, combing her hair, feeding her, keeping her company. She continues to do so as I write these final lines.

This relationship demonstrates that people have sought bonds of affection and amity throughout history. Despite news about environmental devastation, internecine strife, and social partitions, friendship prevails. It is worth remembering that in life there are many more connections than divisions. We are an affectionate species. Our bonds are stronger than our bombs.

Introduction

He knows who has experienced it how bitter
Is sorrow as a comrade to the man
Who lacks dear human friends.
— *The Wanderer* (Anglo-Saxon poem)

Ours is the era of unprecedented sharing. Now, as never before, we are connected "virtually" by posts, messages, and tweets—all delivered instantaneously as beams from the sky. And the word we use to describe this new connected state of being? Friendship. Indeed, friendship has become the metaphor of the Internet age. We say "friend" when speaking of an individual we may have never seen nor are likely to meet. Responding to bids landing in our electronic devices, we join an amplitude of information and allow our tastes, interests, and needs to be transformed by algorithms of affection and profit. Friendship abounds.

Yet, if we dig deeper into the strata underlying the digital network, we discover glimpses of disconnection. The ubiquity of friendship as trope belies its very vulnerability. Friendship is the most unencumbered of our relationships. It is the most freely entered into and the least underwritten by legal or religious codes. Moreover, people may have hundreds of virtual friends yet lack the protocols for friendship. They may communicate with countless users while fearing that intimacy sidetracks them from practical goals. In a world of split-second velocity, friendship appears to dally and waste time. There is a disparity, in other words, between our elevation of friendship into an icon of digital connectivity and our experience of friendship in reality.

This paradox notwithstanding, it is significant that friendship is the word we use to designate communal life on the Web. For this choice expresses confidence in the potential of human communication and understanding. Friendship has always connoted the possibility of imagining the mind of an unrelated person. In friendship individuals arrive in someone else's house, step into unfamiliar corridors, and learn the layout of that person's life.

Friends are the first individuals we bond with outside of the family. As children, we learn to play and negotiate with boys and girls to whom we are not obligated by links of blood or law. In so doing, we begin to live socially, beyond the known world of relatives. Our initial playmates, later the buddies of adolescence, and the companions of adulthood help us transcend the familiar and imagine a larger neighborhood of camaraderie. Friendship, then, engages us with people outside of our house, in relationships not underwritten by law, religion, or the state, in attachments formed through love, pleasure, and possibility.

This capacity for imagination and invention is what makes friendship a natural ally of literature. In many ways, making friends resembles the process of engaging with fiction; both ask you to project yourself into the mind and heart of another. Is it a coincidence, therefore, that friendship and poetry took their first breaths together? Friendship witnessed the birth of literature, and poetry sang of friendship. Both the *Epic of Gilgamesh* and the *Iliad*, two of the earliest extant literary creations, tell stories of comradely love.

In *Charlotte's Web* E. B. White develops the special rapport between fiction and friendship. Charlotte, the spider-web writer, imagines herself in Wilbur's hooves, and then in a supreme act of self-sacrifice she spins her fiction to save his life. As author and reader, she projects herself on her friend while also apprehending her friend's own projection. In this, White proposes that the urge toward friendship reiterates the literary. Charlotte seems instinctively to understand the empathic link between art and friendship. The narrator stresses that "it's not often that someone comes along who is a true friend and a good writer. Charlotte was both" (White

1952, 184). The urge toward friendship and an engagement with fiction are two parts of the same impulse.

Although of a different species, Charlotte empathizes so much with the pig destined for slaughter that she devises a strategy for his salvation. What is it? Writing, of course—the enchanting words she fashions over Wilbur such as "Some Pig" or "Radiant" that persuade the farmer and then visitors to the fair of Wilbur's special qualities. To be sure, all of this is a ploy, a product of Charlotte's artistry, but it succeeds in rescuing her friend. When a grateful Wilbur asks Charlotte why she wove her webs for him, she answers that she did it because she wanted to "lift up" her life a trifle (164). It is the transcendence I referred to earlier.

The story of Charlotte and Wilbur proposes that friendship signifies meaningful fellowship between two individuals. It is a way of saying that somebody matters, that someone outside of the home is concerned for you, that she engages in a dialogue that's neither predictable nor scripted by familial obligation. Friendship is an attempt to forge a connection between self and other, to chisel a resemblance with what is different, to develop a reciprocal tie with someone outside the blood group. This emphasis on reciprocity is what ultimately distinguishes friendship from other types of relations. For you could be in love with someone who does not return your feelings, but a nonreciprocal friendship is hard to imagine.[1] Of course, people fashion other types of relations in the workplace, in courtship, and in marriage. But friendship can't count on the legal, religious, and social infrastructure that family can. Nor is it motivated by the endgame of sexual fulfillment and reproduction, like marriage. Finally, it does not rest on professional alliances. Even though you may become friends with your boss or your teacher, the inequality is likely to strain, if not hobble, the relationship.

Although *Charlotte's Web* chronicles a few short weeks in the lives of two creatures, it assigns this period of companionship a monumental intensity. If friendship is a relation, then the relationship has a temporal as well as a spatial delineation. People experience periods of profound friendship the way travelers, transfixed by the panorama unfolding before them, recognize a border between one domain and another.[2] A person entering a friendship is like the speaker in John Keats's "On First Looking into Chapman's Homer" (1816), who "had travelled in the realms of gold" but had not known what travel was till he heard "Chapman speak out loud and bold." Now he feels like a "watcher of the skies," fixing on a new planet, or like "Cortez" (Hernán Cortés) staring out to sea.[3] Exploration disorients the two individuals, demanding of them a new alertness to their surroundings. Friendship and literature similarly defamiliarize daily life.

In personal narratives as well as literary descriptions, the journey often serves as the trope for friendship. The friends not only undertake an adventure together but they also see their relationship as an odyssey in itself. They regard friendship as a departure from hubris and habit, a transition from certainty to reverie, and a plunge into the unpredictable.

My aim in this book is to reflect more closely on this link between our need for friends and our desire for fiction. I wish to examine how the capacity to appreciate someone else's position, to enter the mind of another person, closely resembles our ability to invent and enjoy alternative worlds. Literature and friendship both occupy structurally similar positions in society, each being nonessential and nonproductive human activities, squanderers of time. People engage with literature and make friends even though neither offers them much instrumental advantage.

Our First and Only Noncontractual Relationship

We embark on friendship for no other goal than the relationship itself. In other words, the arguments we give for the justification of friendship are circular. Again the comparison with travel is apt. For the longest period of human history, people moved from one place to another for a particular reason: to conduct trade, wage war, escape conflict, undertake a pilgrimage, or engage in a scientific mission. In the modern epoch, however, those with the means began to journey for the experience itself. In a letter from the Greek territories of the Ottoman Empire, Lord Byron (1788–1824) writes to his mother that his Turkish hosts "have no idea of traveling for amusement."[4] But for Byron the journey has become the purpose itself.

Friendship too posits its own worth within itself. It is a legally, religiously, and economically inconsequential affiliation. There is no fixed beginning or end of friendship, no rite celebrating its appearance, and no covenant sealing its existence. We are free to enter into and leave it without any social, legal, professional, or religious sanctions. For this reason I refer to it as *an institution that does not resemble an institution*. It is the important unimportant, the peripheral centrality, the tardy contemporaneity of life.

To a certain extent friendship has always been an incongruity—a social riddle, an evolutionary conundrum, and a personal tug-of-war. Why does it seem so contradictory? Primarily because friendship functions as an exchange between the self and the other, an interdependence that implies both cooperation and conflict. The friend is, as Aristotle says, another self. But it is precarious in more ways than Aristotle could have imagined. He presupposed a political and social foundation for friendship and a homogeneous society of citizens that no longer exists, if it ever existed. Lacking broad public or philosophical recognition, friendship roams in the passages of our social categories, the spaces between kinship and law, matrimony and professions, productivity and leisure. It is betwixt and between.

The time of life that casts friendship's ambiguity in starkest relief is the period between childhood and adulthood. Individuals passing through this transitional moment (or, as the anthropologist Victor Turner called it, an "interstructural situation") find themselves amid the different forms of regulations and conventions. Having an unclear status, they exhibit a blend of categories of male and female, the same and the different, of high and low. This merging of classification makes it, temporarily, a condition of confusion, paradox, and ambiguity. Not surprisingly, societies develop rituals—rites of passage—to help individuals through these transitional moments

As a dialogue of the similar with the other, friendship exhibits many characteristics of rites of passage. But the intermediary nature of friendship constitutes a permanent structural feature rather than a temporal marker. The neophytes are concealed, physically secluded during the ritual period before entering adulthood, whereas friendship is visible and invisible at the same time, socially significant and insignificant. It attempts to integrate the normative and the unconventional rather than being a stage between them, as the case of Charlotte and Wilbur shows. Finding herself in the company of a pig, Charlotte spins for him a companionship, even with her dying breaths. It is this attempt to bridge the normal with the extraordinary that makes friendship fragile. Thus, whereas the neophytes return to the community as adults, friends proceed always as a mode of comparison, first between self and social order, then between the friend and the other, and finally between an actual and imagined self. Friendship exists as a relation rather than an end product, a metamorphosis rather than a conclusion.

In this process of linking the "I" and the "You," two uniquely human functions come into play, the faculty of the imagination and the emotion of empathy. The friend has to envision an affective tie with another person in the absence of an institutional infrastructure. Lacking the scripts and maps available, say, to marriage or a business partnership, friends are forced to make up their own rules. They have to imagine how a situation should be and compare this with the way it is now. If structural paradox enforces a distance on the friend from the social order, empathy struggles to minimize this distance. Charlotte becomes a friend when she successfully imagines what a runt pig feels and needs.

This aspect makes friendship a prototype for all nonblood relationships, a testing ground for the possibility of voluntary links outside of blood and law relations. Whereas we are born into our families, races, nationalities, and religions, we choose our friends. Friendship is the one intimate and nonutilitarian relationship we have outside of kinship, as we can see again in children's literature. Children's books describe our first steps outside of the home, our testing the winds with nonkin, our initial betrayals, and, quite often, our first sacrifices.[5] From hundreds, I will choose two of my children's own favorites.

In his *George and Martha* series James Marshall writes about two hippopotami who are "two fine friends." Charmingly understated, they learn how to get along with each other, as boy and girl, but, more important, as two creatures biologically unrelated to each other. George accompanies Martha to a horror movie determined to protect her, only to have to admit that he's the one who is terrified. In another story, the ever-impatient Martha crashes into George's secret clubhouse and discovers, to her embarrassment, that it's the "Martha Fan Club" with George as president. The stories constitute, in essence, a kind of guidebook for friendship. In their undertakings, the friends confront their foibles—that George can be a "fibber," more cowardly than he thinks, or that Martha can be impetuous and lack tact. The faults, significantly, constitute the essence of the story line, and may destabilize but never undermine the friends' foundational affection.

William Steig's *Boris and Amos* tells of the extraordinary powers and resolve possible in friendship. Suddenly blown off his ship, the mouse, Amos, is rescued by the whale, Boris. In his odyssey back to North America on Boris's back, Amos gets to know a bit of the world, but more importantly he learns the difference between the two species. When asked what type of fish he is, Amos answers: "I'm not a fish. . . . I am a mouse, which is a mammal, the highest form of life. I live on land" (Steig 1971, n.p.). Along the way they "became the closest possible friends. They told each other about their lives, their ambitions. They shared their deepest secrets with each other." Trying to sense what a whale was like (and vice versa) must have required the same type of imaginative energy that Charlotte needed with Wilbur.

Rediscovering Friendship

As fundamental as friendship is to our lives as human beings (who among us doesn't experience it in one form or another?), it is astonishing how little we actually know about it. In 2009 Tara Parker-Pope, who reports on medical science and health matters for the *New York Times*, wrote about researchers who were just then beginning to pay attention to the importance of friendship and social networks in human health. She quoted one sociologist who admitted to being "baffled" by the lack of serious research on friendship, especially in comparison to the "scads" of research on families and marriage. In truth, she said, "friendship has a bigger impact on our psychological well-being than family relationships."[6]

Throughout Western history, few eras can be said to have truly embraced the notion of friendship; that is, if by "embrace" we mean that few of the greatest thinkers of the day thought it important enough to grapple with friendship and come to terms with its larger significance for the meaning of life. The classical world stands out, giving us some of the most profound explorations of friendship ever written—by Plato, Aristotle, some Hellenistic philosophers, and, of course, Cicero. After the fall of the Roman Empire, there would be nothing comparable in the way of serious speculation on the meaning of friendship until the twelfth century, and then the focus would be on a particular strain of friendship emerging from the cloisters of medieval France and England. Most notably, the English Cistercian monk Aelred of Rievaulx wrote with great fervor and enthusiasm about "spiritual" friendship, which he believed was largely possible only within the walls of the monastery. Indeed, it is fair to say that for those outside the monastery, Christianity has much preferred the family and filial relationships as organizing metaphors. As Søren Kierkegaard would later put it, Christianity thrust "erotic love and friendship from the throne."[7]

The first major philosophical statement on friendship does not appear until the sixteenth century with Michel de Montaigne's (1533–92) masterful essay, "Of Friendship." Other philosophers of early modern Europe, however, had little of substance to say on the subject. Niccolò Machiavelli (1469–1527), for instance, famously asked whether it is preferable to be loved or to be feared. One would like both, he admitted, but it is "far better to be feared than loved" ([1532] 1999, 54).[8] From this it is not difficult to deduce where in Machiavelli's eyes friendship ranks in the hierarchy of human relations. Friendship does not figure in Thomas Hobbes's (1588–1679) world either, where people seek honor rather than affective bonds. We enter into relationship with others, Hobbes believes, not for love but for glory and gain ([1651] 1991, 44, 45). Hobbes denies the autonomous existence of friendship as a good in itself. Although he cites in *De Cive* (*On the Citizen*) that the Greek maxim of man is a "zoon politikon," that is, a creature born for collective living, he believes we seek social interaction for selfish reasons: "All society, therefore, is either for Gain or for Glory; not so much for love of our fellows as for love of ourselves." Our motivation in entering civil society is not our "good will" toward others but our mutual fear of the other. He sees the friend here in purely instrumental terms as an ally against the enemy.[9] This is why in *Leviathan* Hobbes disagrees with Aristotle's comparison of human society with colonies of bees and ants: "Men have no pleasure . . . in keeping company, where there is no power able to over-awe them all" (1991, 88).

Although John Locke (1632–1704) was no Machiavellian or Hobbesian, he was no romantic either. He contended that forms of association such as friendship compromise the efficient, neutral, and goal-oriented norms of modern, commercial society. People lose their intellectual independence when they allow themselves to be influenced by vestiges of organic community such as friendship, nation, and neighborhood. These types of attachments, Locke writes, "captivate" our reason and lead "men of sincerity blindfold from common sense."[10] Not surprisingly, in this worldview friendship comes to represent a vestige of the past, inimical to the rational, self-interested discussions of the public sphere and the market.

Ever since Hobbes and Locke moral philosophy has largely been silent on friendship, seeing it as essentially outside the important claims that people place on one another.[11] In fact, by the late nineteenth century little of note was written on friendship. Nothing could be more telling than its physical disappearance from the *Encyclopedia Britannica*. The fourth edition (1810) devoted twenty columns to friendship, but the entry had all but vanished by the ninth edition of 1879. Nearly a hundred years later, *The Encyclopedia of Philosophy* of 1967 hardly mentioned it at all. Only within the last twenty years has friendship again become the focus of serious inquiry.[12] Today, however, it is social scientists and scientists who are doing the most salient work, especially research on social collaboration and empathic understanding.

A Need for Collaboration

Ever since Charles Darwin struggled to reconcile the existence of altruistic behavior with the process of natural selection, a key desideratum of evolutionary science has been to identify the source of cooperative behavior in animalkind. Is it genetic, physiological, environmental? In 2005, when the editors of *Science* listed the twenty-five most compelling puzzles and questions facing scientists today, one of those questions was, "How did cooperative behavior evolve?"[13] Central to cooperation, of course, is the notion of empathy, the ability to share another's experiences and emotions. The cognitive neuroscientist Simon Baron-Cohen has called empathy one of the most valuable resources in the world, a view shared by the popular writer Jeremy Rifkin. In *The Empathic Civilization*, Rifkin demonstrates the degree to which empathy is essential not just in interpersonal relations but also in the development of human society.[14]

It comes as no surprise that scientists have sought our concern for people outside of the family in our evolutionary history. On the face of it, empathy seems to contradict the idea of a selfish gene—the drive for survival at the expense of others—since it minimizes the chances of the do-gooder for sexual reproduction. Why should Charlotte care for Wilbur or Amos for Boris? Yet, they do. In fact, scientists have catalogued a host of altruistic behaviors from the amoeba, to bats, to humans that indicate the individual sacrificing itself for the good of the group.[15] Whereas cooperation may be common to many animals, from insects to apes, humans seem to be the only species (outside of children's literature) to extend this practice to strangers.[16] People collaborate and help others even when they have nothing to gain. Evolutionary theorists propose that our hunter-gatherer ancestors had to forsake short-term temptations since they lived in small, mutually dependent groups. Emotions developed as modes of transition from egoism to consciousness of community by establishing trust and eliciting reciprocity: "I will love and stay with you, if you promise to do the same."[17] Indeed, on the basis of archaeological, ethnographic, and demographic evidence, scientists propose that we have developed into a supportive species because our ancestors lived in natural and social environments in which individuals who tended to cooperate survived.[18]

Humans have grown over time to be community builders and to rely on automated sensitivities to faces, bodies, and voices in order to connect with other humans and animals.[19] Emotions, such as empathy, may have been adaptations that triggered loyalty and reciprocity in early humans and thus ensured their survival. The group's existence then entailed the suppression of the egotistical instinct for individual gain. Whatever the ultimate source of empathy, it is safe to say that individuals belonging to cooperative groups have a greater likelihood of reproductive success than those living in groups that fight one another.[20]

I cite this research into the evolution of cooperation for two reasons. First, to show how deep in our chthonic selves our tendency to cooperate is without at the same time wanting to reduce a complex phenomenon, such as friendship, into a function of genes. Second, I wish to push back on our current obsession with violence and conflict as inherent human features and as the sole instigators of social change. It has become conventional since Hobbes to regard self-interest as the motivating impulse in social change and to attribute societal stability to the unchallenged authority wielded by states. Although not denying rivalry, competition, or deception, I wish to emphasize cooperation as an important human trait. Even if there is "no empathy center with empathy neurons" in the human brain making people more altruistic, we cannot underestimate the social importance of empathy, the capacity to imagine somebody else's position. At the very least, when you enter someone else's vantage point you become aware that she has a consciousness similar to yours, a recognition that can moderate your own provincialism.[21] Empathy is ultimately a dialectical process, depending on our mutual acknowledgment that others feel and think as we do, that they have a concept of self like ours. As the Athenian drinking song put it, we can't cut open a person to see whether or not he is a friend.[22]

This connection between self and other is illuminated in *The Last Brother*, a novel by the French-Mauritian writer Nathacha Appanah (2010). Set on Mauritius during World War II, it describes the friendship between Raj, a native boy, and David, a Jewish refugee, who, along with other Jews, is imprisoned on the island.[23] Years later, Raj as an old man is haunted by the death of David at the age of ten. To relieve his guilt he tries to imagine how David would have told his own story. Until that point we have heard only Raj's side of the narrative: how he notices David's blue eyes and his curly blond hair and that he, a white person, is a prisoner. But at the end of the novel, Raj attempts to view himself through David's experience. He visualizes how David would have looked at him in their first meeting: "On the other side of the barbed wire I saw a dark boy with black hair, . . . his eyes as dark as billiard balls . . . his face like a savage's" (126). In seeing the world through David's eyes, Raj not only grieves for this friend but he also recognizes him as an autonomous being, with a separate outlook on life.

Although I am not qualified to speculate on the science behind altruism and ultimately friendship, I would venture to say that empathy, as both the capacity to understand someone else's position and the ability to feel compassion for that person, is essential for humanity's future. It may even be more essential now than when human beings first began exhibiting traits of altruism some ninety thousand years ago.[24] Teamwork may have been one of the key cultural traits enabling the rapid global spread of humans. In today's world, the stakes are even higher, connected as we are not only by technology and capitalism but also by warfare, viruses, environmental pollution, and climate change. We face a paradox: the growing interconnection of people, commerce, and communication means greater potential for empathy and collaboration among the world's peoples, but along with globalization comes the increased expenditure of energy, which in turn could lead to environmental collapse. In other words, the greater connectedness inherent in today's globalization contains within it the seeds of greater entropy—with the use of fossil fuels leading to imminent global destruction.[25]

Instead of just obsessing over war, economic competition, and the fight over resources, we should call attention to other, more positive sources of historical transformation, such as empathy, friendship, and cooperation. The goal here is not to strive for some unreachable global consciousness or a violence-free society. There will always be conflict and competition between individuals and groups. That an empathetic globalism may never be attained does not mean we should forsake it. "A man's reach should exceed his grasp / Or what's a heaven for?" to quote from Robert Browning's dramatic monologue, "Andrea del Sarto." As a literary and cultural critic, I wish to point to nonmaterialist factors in the development of society—such as nation, art, and, friendship—hoping to show how ideas, discourses, and concepts can bring about social change.[26] These "soft" or "feminine" features of life are often dismissed as secondary forces, acted on by the economy or the state, rather than actors in their own right. Few relationships have been so overlooked as friendship, a bond that mediates between the self and the other, between the individual and the universal. Perhaps the turn in the "hard sciences" toward the study of cooperative behavior and altruism may be lending credibility to what fiction writers and poets have been telling us all along.

Imagining the Other

"We must, we simply must be friends," pleads Nathan in Gotthold Ephraim Lessing's great but now little-known drama, *Nathan the Wise*. Lessing's work asks whether a Christian can be a friend with a Jew or a Moslem. The question seemed so controversial that Lessing had to set the work in the Jerusalem of the Third Crusade rather than contemporary Hamburg or Berlin. Published in 1779 and first performed in 1783, the play seems centuries ahead of its time in asking readers to imagine the religious and racial other as a friend

Lessing's decision to stage his play goes to show that literature has the courage and the capacity to pose incendiary questions. Whereas contemporaneous scholarship and philosophy ignored friendship, literature embraced the possibility of dialogue between a Jew and a Christian. In the play, Nathan, newly returned to Jerusalem from Babylon, has learned that a Templar Knight had rescued his daughter Recha from a house fire. Rushing to thank him, Nathan collides with the Knight's prejudices. Nathan, of course, knows of religious hatred, having lost his entire family in a house fire ignited by Christians. But the Knight rejects his entreaties. Blaming the Jews for having introduced into human history the concept of electedness and thus the idea of a national access to God, the Templar asks to be left alone. Nathan pursues him, however. "Are we our people?" he pleads. "What does 'people' mean?" And he asks further, "Are Jews and Christians rather Jews and Christians / Than human beings?" Shouldn't we say that "this is a man" (Lessing 2002, 101–2)? The Knight finally relents, persuaded that friendship trumps biology. "We must, we must be friends," he says, echoing Nathan's petition to him.

Nathan, the Knight, and Saladin (the Muslim ruler of the city) have to try consciously to be friends, fighting against the centripetal forces of their respective communities. In so doing, they discover that friendship is its own reward, rather than a means to an end. Not a *Ding an sich* (thing in itself), it is an exchange between self and other. This voluntary relationship forces us to think about our relationships to these involuntary truths.[27]

Lessing sacrifices the absoluteness of rigid identities to the unpredictability of dialectic. All around Nathan are people who are persuaded that identity determines life. The seal of your label is you. The Patriarch, for instance, holds to his belief that Nathan has unlawfully raised a Christian girl as a Jew. Nathan, however, knows that blood does not make either a father or a friend (178). He understands that friendship is not self-contained. And his wisdom helps both the Templar and the Sultan accept him as their comrade.

Lessing's play shows that there is no internal logic to friends and that friendship does not pose itself as a religious, national, or racial identity. Rarely asking "who am I," it does not narrate a story about self-discovery and consistency.[28] The tale friendship tells is less of the self's odyssey into the self than that of the self in dialogue with the other—Charlotte and Wilbur, Nathan and the Knight, Amos and Boris. In friendship we experience the conflict between self-protection and a desire for attachment. And friendship is the uncharted water we are tipped into once we abandon the raft of autonomy. Amos discovers Boris after plunging into the ocean. Similarly, the Knight gets to know Nathan only after opening himself up to hazard. In so doing, the characters experience a duel that goes back to the *Epic of Gilgamesh*, one between limits and the limitless—the familiarity of the self and the uncertainties of love.

We can rise above ourselves by exploring the wonder of existence. We are not alone, in other words, but bound in a chain of solidarity with others. This is so because we have the aptitude, both through our judgment and our imagination, to play roles, to get into someone else's skin, to perceive what she is thinking or feeling, and to guess her mind. In short, we create and enter the fictional world of the other person. This is what ties fiction to empathy, aesthetics to ethics, literature to friendship.

The first recorded epic, the Sumerian *Epic of Gilgamesh*, is a reflection on empathy through poetry. In its most basic form the story of Gilgamesh is that of a man conquering both solitude and death through love. The poem also sings about the place of the comrade in the new urban formations while all the time posing new questions: Now that we are living in new cities along with so many strangers, how do we get along? How do we create bonds of trust and affection? Can we succeed without cooperation? And can we get along without our capacity to imagine what others are feeling and thinking? These inherently social, cultural, and political questions were recorded for posterity first in poetry. If literature enables readers to enter the minds of characters that are not real and to identify with them, it also tells them that in their social relationships they try to "create" the friend by imagining her as another self. Friendship requires that individuals be both writers and readers of the other and of the self.

The process of making friends and that of telling stories—*philia* and fiction—necessitate imagination, invention, and the capacity to assume the perspective of the other. Both are exercises in invention and projection into the other. I am not, however, representing reading as friendship or friendship as reading. Rather I am proposing that the fictionalization of reality and the "realization" of the fictional are processes analogous to friendship. The very idea that we aestheticize the world may sound postmodern and poststructuralist. But what I have in mind is the interpenetration of both, something that is actually quite old.

Early in the *Epic of Gilgamesh* we learn that "Enkidu made Gilgamesh a shelter for receiving dreams" (Anon. 2001, 32). What could this possibly mean? I don't know whether we, as modern readers, can grasp this interlacing of the fantastical with the real. By the same token we may not be able ultimately to understand that the ancient Egyptians did not separate the world of the now from the world of the imagination.[29] It seems then that the dream comes to Gilgamesh from the outside, while also becoming part of him. The dream thus represents the story, something fictional, a thing unreal, and its passage has been made possible by the friend. In friendship, as in literature, we enter into the zone of fantasy and possibility.

Friendship in the Age of Facebook

This capacity for fiction and empathy is not reserved to literature majors, teachers, or book lovers. It is, as I have suggested, a hardwired activity that guides us in all aspects of our lives, from our enjoyment of a joke to our interactions on the Web.[30] Indeed, new technologies make it possible for individuals to pool their imaginative resources in a way inconceivable in the past, to create projects together in Wikipedia, YouTube, and the Apache Web server program.[31] There are thousands of other examples: readers provide advice to other travelers in "Trip Advisor," they judge their teachers in "Rate my Professor," and they sign political petitions and organize protests or strikes. Electronic media allow individuals to behave in a greater variety of generous and publicly spirited ways. It's not so much that technology enables action, in some deterministic fashion, but that it enhances a human inclination toward sociability. These material innovations, in other words, mesh with the human urge to connect.

Social networks have been ubiquitous in human history because they permit individuals to realize and profit from a shared synergy. People join them because they achieve in unison what they cannot alone. In short, people understand the benefit of being part of the longer chain of experience and sharing. In either their traditional or digital variety, social networks represent a utopian impulse toward coexistence.[32] They offer an altruistic explanation for human motivation, in contrast to the economic model that sees self-interest as the main agent of change in society.

If the Internet is indeed promoting cooperative behaviors and fostering ever-greater links among people, then it can be said that it is turning into a literary phenomenon. By literary I don't suggest that it converts the world into text, as the poet Stéphane Mallarmé desired, but that it fosters an empathic understanding of reality, based on imaginative links. The Internet promotes an aesthetic perception of the world insofar as it encourages people to seek out implied and invented links with others. In so doing, it points to the intersection of literature and empathy. For fiction promotes an empathic awareness, instilling the capacity in us to project ourselves into other situations, to imagine alternate realities, to change the world, to conjure up what other people are feeling, to be mindful of them, and to identify ourselves with others, real or invented.

This may partly explain why, disenfranchised though it may be, friendship has become a forerunner in the way we have come to understand our other social attachments. That is to say, we model all our social links, from marriage, to family ties, to Facebook connections, as friendships—as self-reflexive relations that have no other purpose than the relation itself. We increasingly see them, in other words, as noninstitution institutions.

Marriage, for instance, has been transformed into a friendship, a more equitable institution, determined ideally by both partners, rather than by fathers and husbands. Women have been the leading force in this democratizing process, converting matrimony into a companionate relation, one that promised both sexual and emotional fulfillment.[33] Pursuing emotional bonds as a motivation for and justification of matrimony, and freeing marriage from reproduction, they unburdened it of its instrumentalist purpose.[34]

Recent developments have pushed marriage to take on more aspects of friendship: the isolation of the husband-wife pair from external ties; the physical withdrawal from neighbors, friends, and peer groups; and the disassociation of sex from reproduction.[35] Beyond this, the nuclear family itself has come into question in modernity, with marriage increasingly treated as an individual achievement and a symbol of successful self-development rather than as an opportunity to raise children.[36] Although marriage still carries legal and religious ramifications, which endow it with a social materiality, for greater numbers of people in the developed world it exists as a sui generis relationship.

For lack of a better word I characterize this conversion of instrumentalist relations into self-justifying ties as an aestheticization, even though this word conjures declarations of late nineteenth-century art-for-art's sake. By aestheticization I mean not that we understand social life as an artistic ideal but that we designate individuals themselves, in contrast to codified obligations and rituals, as the source and the justification for their relationships. On the one hand, this type of connection between people may lead to self-indulgence. But it also results in relations that are self-conscious. Self-institution, of an individual or group, posits the self as the font and master of her own destiny. A person (or a nation) has to think consciously about the rules of engagement that she tacitly accepted before: the nature of the bond, the possibility of intimacy, and her capacity for love.

Again, this development traces the source of a relationship within people themselves rather than in duty to kinship or religious rules. It also represents an exercise in hopefulness since it regards people as creatures who think critically about their relationships. Charlotte must examine why she aids Wilbur. She desires a relationship that is earned rather than assumed. Gilgamesh, in Derrek Hines's modern reworking of the epic, senses that he has begun "living for the first time for someone else" (2002, 15). To enter into a friendship is to gain experience of links with people who are not biologically related. "No human life," Hannah Arendt writes, "is possible without a world which directly or indirectly testifies to the presence of other human beings."[37]

People are, after all, social creatures, born to nurture. Parents expect children to become good and caring adults rather than selfish and cruel. Individuals crave a dialogue between themselves and others.[38] According to Mikhail Bakhtin, the very essence of a human being is the "*deepest communion. To be* means *to communicate*." Or, as Friedrich Hölderlin put it in "Friedensfeier": "we are discourse and hear from one another" (seit ein Gespräch wir sind und hören voneinander).[39] In this interchange with the other, people seek both to ground and exceed their own individuality. In Carmen Laforet's *Nada* ([1945] 2007) the protagonist Andrea finds meaning in her comrades at the university, in being able to form attachments outside of her bizarre family. Friendship offers a kind, welcoming refuge from the hostility and creepiness of home.

Friendship: A User's Guide

Before I move on, I wish to emphasize two points. First, while I investigate friendship through literary writing, I engage in historical and sociological examinations, placing these works on the wider stage of human development. I probe, in other words, the horizontal and longitudinal dimensions of the link between friendship and literature. Wishing to investigate how the history of friendship connects with the history of literature, or more specifically our understanding of literature, I will look at specific works, from the *Epic of Gilgamesh* and the *Iliad* to lyrics from the late twentieth century. In so doing, I would like to trace changing conceptions of friendship and link this to changing views of literature.

For instance, the friendships described in ancient and medieval texts are bound in protocols of obligation that the modern self can hardly endure. The lives of Homeric heroes had a public dimension foreign to our sensibilities. At the same time, the current expectation of self-disclosure would have been incomprehensible to Aristotle. I do not wish to claim a progressive curve toward greater friendship or toward a withering of friendship. On the contrary, I hope to show that intimacy, the contemporary cement of friendship, has been made possible by modern, anonymous society.

Although I try to be as accurate as possible in my historical overview, I recognize that nuance and some detail may be lost in the panorama. Inevitably, specialists in the fields might feel that depth has been trumped by breadth. I acknowledge these dangers, but feel the advantages outweigh them.

Second, my readings obviously circumscribe my perspective. Through the ages the epic, lyric poetry, drama, novels, and short stories have tended to focus on male-male relationships. The prejudice of history has celebrated masculine friendship as heroic and noble while consigning female attachments to the private and, until recently, invisible domain of the home. This tradition has used the metaphor of the journey and conflict to understand male friendship, the *Odyssey* and the *Iliad*, respectively. In other words, it has celebrated male friendship as Odyssean or Achillean, while assigning female companionship to the Penelopean parlor, the garden, or the school. In short, until the twentieth century the great literary friendships have tended to be between men rather than between women.

My book is to a certain extent demarcated by these traditions. It serves as an investigation of friendship that poses general questions: What does it mean to be close to someone unrelated to us by blood? What are our obligations to that person? How do we behave toward him or her? How does friendship relate to family? What is the place of friendship in the wider social community? How is friendship expressed in the fluid world of the Web? I approach these questions from poems, novels, dramas, and short stories that often, though not always, treat male friendship.

Of course, other permutations of friendship arise beyond male-male and female-female pairings. There are friendships between men and women, as for instance that between Mrs. Moore and Dr. Aziz in E. M.

Forster's *A Passage to India*. There are also the bonds between adults and children, like that between Jim and Huck in Mark Twain's *The Adventures of Huckleberry Finn*. Members of one family may form links that approximate friendship. And people may hold their pets as intimate companions, with Odysseus's dog, Argos, constituting an early literary example. Finally, the gender of the writer obviously does not determine the nature of the friendship: the author of "Brokeback Mountain," Annie Proulx, has written a story about the homoerotic love between two young men. Although I take these variations into account, I can't analyze them in detail without expanding my book beyond reason.

Finally, a word on form. Each chapter focuses on key literary texts taken from various traditions. Although I set these works in their historical backgrounds, I also have them converse with one another across chapters. So discussion of a novel or a particular poem will echo in another chapter. I hope to effect in this way a more symphonic approach to the topic. This strategy will permit me to reflect on a trilogy of major themes: the ethics, politics, and aesthetics of friendship. That is to say, I will investigate the love, social location, and beauty of this relationship.

I begin by probing the place of friendship in society, specifically looking at *A Passage to India* and *The Adventures of Huckleberry Finn*. I analyze not only the possibility of friendship as a social building block in fifth-century Athens but also the use of friendship as a metaphor for political coexistence in revolutionary America. In a sense, I explore the private and public expressions of friendship, seeing the literary impulse as the capacity to imagine the world with the eyes of the other.

From politics I move on to death and mourning, for literature, from the *Epic of Gilgamesh* to the twentieth-century Greek poet Constantine P. Cavafy, has often elegized friendship. In the imagination the male friend almost always dies. Why is this so? Is the friend killed because society distrusts two men bound in an unproductive relationship? I raise further questions: Do men wage war in order to make friends? Does armed conflict create the opportunity for men to befriend each other away from society's prying and distrustful eyes? Why do we speak of friendship almost always in memoriam? Does this in itself express the fragility and finite nature of this relation?

In the third chapter I analyze the reasons for this fragility, by looking at the paradoxes of friendship. Specifically, I analyze friendship as a noninstitutional relationship by considering how the tensions between duty and autonomy, compulsion and self-institution shape friends. Focusing on Nikos Kazantzakis's *Zorba the Greek* and Sándor Márai's *Embers*, I look at the emergence of friendship as a largely intimate affiliation no longer bound by rules of gift exchange, hospitality, and kinship. On the one hand, friends, like lovers, have to secede from society to develop their bond. Yet, unlike lovers, they feel guilty that they have escaped from the toils of life to create a nonproductive relationship.

Another anxiety runs through many treatments of friendship, both in literature and popular culture—the specter of desire between the two comrades. This forms the topic of the final chapter. From the ancient preoccupation over whether Achilles and Patroclus were lovers to the modern putdown "that's so gay," we seem to be disturbed by the possibility that the two male friends may be drawn to each other by erotic attraction. In raising the possibility that a father, son, or husband is sensually drawn to his friend, writers destabilize the distinction between heterosexuality and homosexuality.

I conclude by looking at what social networking has to say about friendship and what friendship has to say about social networking. The Internet is opening new associations, while also undermining the possibility of old-fashioned, Montaignean intimacy. At the same time, friendship, which inaugurated humanity's literary odyssey, has become the emblem for digital relations, turning our time into the age of *homo amicus*. We are all bound by an electronically enabled but humanly generated need for empathy—which means that the more we are connected the more literary we are becoming.

1

The Politics of Friendship

Only I will establish in the Mannahatta and in every city of
these States inland and seaboard,
And in the fields and woods, and above every keel little or large
that dents the water,
Without edifices or rules or trustees or any argument,
The institution of the dear love of comrades.
— Walt Whitman, "I hear it was charged against me"

Since we divide social life into formal and informal realms, we think of
friendship as a refuge from politics. Suspicious of cynicism, we are aroused
by the introduction of personal relations in the public arena. Conversely,
we think that politics restricts and taints private life. Although most of
us would rather not like to choose between friend and country, if pushed
many would agree with E. M. Forster's declaration that "if I had to choose
between betraying my country and betraying my friend, I hope I should
have the guts to betray my country."[1]

This celebrated articulation of liberalism and individualism captures
the modern preference for personal fulfillment over the mutual good. But
it would make no sense to Aristotle, Cicero, or even Augustine. For what
type of friendship could this be in the absence of the community? For the
Greeks, friendship was expressed through discourse, an interchange of talk
that united citizens of the polis. It was less a personal quality than a function

of politics that made public demands on people and preserved references to the world. They called this discourse of friendship *philanthropia*, the love of humanity, a readiness to share the world with other citizens. For the world became human only to the extent that it became subject to this conversation.[2]

In modernity, however, friendship constitutes a communal withdrawal, flourishing in spaces free from social strife and obligation. It is a manifestation of intimacy. Sentimental rather than temperate, confessional rather than cool, friendship is a haven from economic motives and political disputes. Herein lies a paradox: on the one hand, modern individuals don't regard friendship as the mortar of society, preferring to conceive friends as social outlaws. But, insofar as they see friendship as a voluntary association, free from the chains of kinship and professional life, they make it the exemplary democratic relationship.

Thus, even though friendship no longer serves as a metaphor for community, it still provides a template in the discussion of many collective concerns. In friendship we pose questions central to modern life: How do we relate to one another? How do we cohere? Can one love people outside of the family? What value do these voluntary relationships have for us? Although friendship may no longer function as a model for politics, it accomplishes something more profound today—it enables us to comprehend our social and political links.

And it is literature itself that allows us to grasp the politics of friendship. Literature succeeds where political philosophy and many other disciplines have failed[3]—to demonstrate the social permutations of this marginalized relation. Even though literature has not embraced friendship as a theme to the extent it has courtship and marriage, when it reflects on friendship it portrays it as a social tool, essential to our representation of governance, of interface among citizens, and of coexistence.

And how does literature accomplish this? It exploits two key characteristics of narrative: (a) the space occupied by stories between illusion and reality, possibility and impossibility; (b) the capacity of stories to enable readers to imagine something that has not taken place, something that might be. In their basic form stories make vivid what might have happened, what might have happened but did not, and what we hope or fear might happen.[4] They give us alternatives to reality or unusual ways of looking at alternatives.

As such, literary narratives portray friendship as a problematic relationship that yokes what is familiar with what is strange.[5] Because of the challenges involved in bringing opposites together, literary friendships almost always fall short of ideal compatibility. But this "failure" proves a social boon because it compels readers to reflect on questions of self-governance and sociability. In this respect nothing succeeds like failure because the latter brings to consciousness questions that might otherwise be ignored: how we live together, whether we can love selflessly those not attached to us by law or blood, how we negotiate the distinction between bonds of intimacy and those of utility and pleasure, and how we deal with the rejection of proffered friendship.

Friend as Other Self

Literature captures the ambiguity of friendship by portraying the friend as "another self." This phrase comes from Aristotle, perhaps his most renowned formulation on the topic. Aristotle writes in the *Nicomachean Ethics* that a person is "related to his friend as to himself (for his friend is another self)" (1984, 1166a, 31). Aristotle's expression, so crucial to our understanding of friendship, is obstinately ambivalent. It suggests that friendship develops as an (imperfect) interaction between self and other. At the very least, it means that a person has the same attitude toward his friends as to himself. But, more likely, in speaking of the friend as another self, Aristotle implies that a person loves the friend "as both other and the same." Aristotle writes that the friend is both an extension of the self and a separate being. In loving the friend one loves him as both the other and as the same.[6] Friendship, then, comprises both similar and dissimilar elements, which is why it is so unstable.

Aristotle understands friendship as an associative but not quite completely sealed bond. His conception is unlike G. W. F. Hegel's definition of love as "the consciousness of my unity with another, so that I am not isolated on my own, but gain my self-consciousness only through the renunciation of my independent existence and through knowing myself as the unity of myself with another and of the other with me" (1991, 199). To love, in this sense, requires the burial of the self in the desire to envelop and be enveloped with the other. Love functions more like a metaphor, where one person is subsumed into the other, merging with him. Aristotle, however, speaks of friendship as a metonymy, the linkage of one with the other.

As such, friendship operates as a combining that does not require the loss of the self in the other, but preserves the self in its embrace of the other. In short, friends are bound in a federation without having to abandon their individualities to a larger identity.

The essential question in any alliance is political coexistence and self-institution: how we postulate ourselves as a group and how we cohere. These are questions that ground us in the here and now.[7] This issue of cohabitation brings attention to the necessity of imaging the other. The philosopher Emmanuel Lévinas, citing the Hebrew Bible, puts this into perspective. The other is the "weak and the poor, 'the widow and the orphan,' whereas I am the rich or the powerful" (1987, 83). Lévinas argues that it is essential for the prosperous and the influential to be able to understand what it would be like to be poor, a widow, or an orphan. And I would add that it is just as important for the marginalized to envision themselves in positions of power. The question of otherness, in other words, necessarily brings to the fore the human capacity for empathy so essential to social relations and social change.[8] For by empathy we try to envision what someone feels, to project ourselves into her situation or predicament.

This is where literature is crucial: insofar as it allows the friend to put on the glasses of the other, it lets her envision both a connection with him while also acknowledging the distance between them. Political life necessitates that people deal with social, economic, racial, and national difference. They have to ask ultimately what constitutes them as a people who occupy a particular space. And these questions come down to how they understand the friend in relation to the other.

The Aporia of Friendship

We find ourselves in a conundrum here. In striving for the fair and good society now, in longing for harmony with the other, we may end up smothering him. When we love, Aristophanes says in Plato's *Symposium*, we desire our other half: "Love is born into every human being; it calls back the halves of our original nature together; it tries to make one out of two and heal the wound of human nature" (Plato 1989, 191d). In *Lysis* Socrates says that the friend needs what is deficient: "That desire is a cause of friendship" (Plato 1979, 221d–e). This yearning for the other brings about the union. If friends love each other, they belong to each other. They are "by nature in some way akin to each other" (221e).[9]

Is there a danger here that love may kill, choking the other half, by appropriating him, turning the friend into an extension of himself?[10] The specter of possession hovers over all matters of love and friendship. But here again literature is helpful. It reveals that my attempt to meld with the friend almost always fails because of the divisions between us, differences in age, social rank, race, commitment, and the imbalances of self-acknowledgment.

The literary evidence shows that the potential for *Habsucht* (force of love) is frustrated by the challenges of bringing together the similar with the dissimilar. The union of two friends is almost always insufficient and never complete. And the friendship usually dies, slain perhaps by the recognition of failure or by the force of the loving drive. The friendship implodes and the survivor is left with the memory of an imperfect merger.

This failure, at the same time, suggests that love must be mutual. If friendship as a possibility arises when someone recognizes his need of the other, then a friendship develops when both parties recognize this need. Desire presupposes not only a lack but also a consciousness of that lack.[11] In making friends a person acknowledges tacitly or explicitly the need of the other person. The desire to own is checked by the call for exchange. Friendship is essentially dialogic, voluntary, and reciprocal because both parties abandon themselves to the other. It does not demand the unity of the self with the world. On the contrary, it recognizes the existence of another, autonomous being with whom it seeks an alliance. Love then constitutes the recognition of the distance between the two human beings and the need to bridge it. The essence of love is the "giving and receiving of freedom."[12]

But because an individual has to reconcile his love of freedom with the necessity of the friend's autonomy, she enters into a collective and political process. Even though we regard friendship as an expression of our most private selves, it actually points to ways in which we can bring together the private and official aspects of our lives. For any time we wonder whether we could be intimate with someone outside our group, we throw friendship open to the winds of public consideration. We stand before a vessel of moral, ethical, and emotional issues, which is larger than our own wish for privacy, as the characters in E. M. Forster's *A Passage to India* discover.

And Forster himself knew this connection between public art and personal friendship. His novel came out of a friendship with an Indian man whom Forster met at Oxford and later visited in India in 1912: "But for him I might never have gone to his country, or written about it" (1983, 296). *A Passage to India* is dedicated to this friend, Masood.

A Passage from Self to Other

Is it possible for an Indian to be friends with an Englishman? This is the opening question in Forster's novel, posed by Dr. Aziz and his two dinner companions, and echoing Lessing two hundred years earlier. They are engaged in a symposium of sorts and the topic introduces the two themes of the novel, friendship and nationalism. In so doing, the novel tries to demonstrate the relationship between our intimate relations and the conflicts in the street. Once the three characters begin to probe into the possibility of friendship between the British and the Indians, they cannot help but touch on the social dimension of friendship. In their country, the three Indian men agree, an intimate relationship between an Englishman and an Indian could not take place because of the iniquitous hold of the colonizer on the colonized. Although they do not refer to Aristotle's argument about the necessity of equality, they tacitly accept its truth, namely, to share a meal, people must be peers. Like Aristotle, but for different reasons, they see friendship as a matter of racial and ethnic rather than personal expression.

The novel offers the ideal forum to consider interior and exterior tensions in the formation of friendship. The play between realism and fiction, so central to the text, allows this work to represent the conflicts of a relationship. Third-person description, with some editorializing from the unnamed narrator about India, the English, and Muslims, allows the reader to form emotional links with Indians as well as Britons. By giving access to the minds of these characters, it allows them to enter that domain between reality and illusion, nationalism and friendship that is an imperative of literature. Thus the work challenges readers to imagine a friendship between a Muslim and a Christian, an Indian and an Englishman, decades before an independent India.

A Passage to India does not just promote an early version of liberal multiculturalism. With its cosmopolitanism the novel impugns British imperialism, astonishing for 1925. But its sympathetic treatment of the other, however noble, is not really original. From Aeschylus's and Euripides's portrayal of Persian and Trojan suffering, respectively, in *The Persians* and *The Trojan Women*, to Harriet Beecher Stowe's humanizing of slaves in *Uncle Tom's Cabin*, to George Eliot's philosemitic representation of Jews in *Daniel Deronda*, art has historically been at the vanguard in its dealing with the other, the enemy, or the different. Forster's achievement lies in the parallel he draws between our aesthetic and affective views of the world.

A Passage to India points to a tantalizing link between the empathy[13] entailed in reading fiction and the empathy essential in friendship, creating an overlap, therefore, between form and content, ethics and aesthetics. Indeed, the most sympathetic characters in the novel, those we are more likely to connect ourselves with, are those who try to fashion friendship across racial, national, and religious boundaries, who try to get to know the inner thoughts and feelings of those different from themselves. They are the ones who risk the metonymic bonds with their own communities for the metaphoric jump into the communion with the friend.

This leap then enacts our encounter with a work of fiction. When we watch a play or movie or when we read a novel, we attempt to jump over the crevasse separating us from the work.[14] Even in the most realistic representations we are still aware of the imaginative invention before us. We accept aesthetic conventions to enter an affective reality. Yet, in proposing a parallel between the making of fiction and the making of friends, I am not suggesting that the characters in fiction are our friends.[15] Rather, both processes, the creation of friends and of fiction, are comparable in that they both are projects of improvisation. Both involve the exercise of storytelling, of contriving, of bridging differences, and of striving for understanding.

Fiction and Empathy

It order to comprehend this interaction between reality and fiction, empathy and friendship, let's turn to the idea of character. For character, the fictional representation of human agency,[16] is one of the primary ways we gain access to literary art. Traditionally we have understood our attachment to characters as identification, the psychological links we form with them. And the emotion that triggers these links is empathy, our desire to put ourselves in the place of another person, the very same mechanism operant in friendship.

Recent research, however, suggests that, rather than strict identification, we engage in a complex interaction with fictional characters, a process during which we align ourselves with them, try to grasp their motivations, and assess their moral worth.[17] This involvement is both emotional and cognitive insofar as emotions have also a cerebral component. They constitute forms of judgments in which we recognize things and events we don't control.[18] Through compassion, for instance—either for real people or fictional characters—we acknowledge our own vulnerability.

But this empathetic engagement does not necessarily let us stroll through the brick and mortar world of their lives.[19] By connecting ourselves with people in a story, we don't become them, nor do we necessarily engage with them politically and morally. It's quite possible that we don't tie ourselves with their fate.

This was the position of Bertolt Brecht, who believed that when we attach ourselves to the actors on the stage, we escape into the illusion of reality and thus tacitly accept the reigning assumptions of society. He strove, therefore, to interrupt this emotional connection because he wanted spectators to engage critically with social issues. To achieve this objective Brecht had to disorient the theatrical experience, to undermine the expectations of the audience.[20] The point of this alienation effect was to turn "the object of which one is to be made aware ... from something ordinary, familiar, immediately accessible, into something peculiar, striking, and unexpected" (Brecht 1957, 143). The ultimate aim was to prevent the audience from taking the play for granted, from assuming it to be a representation of reality. Specifically, this meant actors had to frustrate the audience's wish to identify with the people they portrayed (193). In "epic" theater, according to Brecht, there must be "no illusion that the player is identical with the character and the performance with the play" (195).[21]

Empathy, then, may not be the only goal of literature. We often distance ourselves from what we see or read as we do when watching a comedy by Aristophanes. In the part of the play called the *parabasis*, the action stops and members of the chorus, removing their masks, address the audience directly as citizens rather than as spectators. The momentary "work stoppage" of the show, while actually a part of the play, forces the audience to see the show for what it is, a work of art. What takes place is a defamiliar-ization of the aesthetic experience and its relationship to life.[22]

In short, there may be many factors blocking a reader's identification with the characters on the page or on the stage, which means we can't treat novels as stepping-stones into life.[23] Reading them does not *necessarily* lead to moral action. Even though readers may feel empathy for fictional characters, their identification does not always ignite civic virtue in them.[24]

Although empathy alone cannot inspire altruistic action, it manifests the basic position underlying altruism, namely the acknowledgement of the self as one person among others and of the existence of multiple per-spectives. The recognition of others as human beings with their own points of view allows us to take into account their needs and desires.[25] In this respect, empathy helps dissipate the naïve illusion that one's own immedi-ate environment constitutes the world.[26] Our capacity to feel for someone else does not mean that we are all the same. Rather it reveals the opposite, namely, that we are all different human beings sharing one social space. This discovery help us overcome egotism, self-love, and narcissism. It also offers us some consolation in our suffering: Our pain is alleviated in part by the thought that other human beings are undergoing or have experienced similar hardship.[27]

In this respect we can say that readers *do* extend themselves into the experiences, motives, and emotions of fictional characters. They make con-nections between real and aesthetic emotions. But these psychological links don't necessarily demand that they undertake real-world action or that they become better human beings. But readers' engagement with char-acters is neither straightforward identification nor alienation but rather a nuanced response, cognizant of the tension between reality and represen-tation. They experience both a resemblance of empathy (their attachment to the character) and the transference of art (the distancing created by the tropes of literature). Or, to put it another way, the power of metaphor to represent something as something else displaces the metonymy of emo-tional attachment (our need to form human connections). Readers get to know a person all the while knowing that she is a fiction, seeing her as a product of their love and their (aesthetic) judgment.

Readers' ability to project themselves into another situation or into the mind of another person is what links their engagement with fiction with their capacity for friendship. Both practices involve conjecture and analogical thinking—the search for resemblances. And imagination is central to both the capacity to feel for a character and to connect with the friend.

Gregory Currie and Ian Ravenscroft define imagination as the ability to possess states that are not perceptions, beliefs, decisions, or experiences but that are similar to them (2002, 11). Not simply a recreational faculty, affording us the pleasure of make-believe, the imagination is a guide to reality. By picturing ourselves in other people's positions, we are able to "get a grip on those troublesome bits of reality" (132). Or rather, the imagination opens the door to other minds and other worlds. We simulate other people and engage in acts of mind reading. And mind reading, what philosophers call theory of mind, is something that human beings do all the time, trying to explain behavior in terms of thoughts, feelings, desires, or intentions. We attribute states of mind to others constantly, evaluating body language, facial expressions, tone of voice, and so on.[28] And we take pleasure in mind-reading because it lets us try on different mental states and provides us access to the internal worlds of other people.[29]

Philosophers have known for centuries that people enjoy simulating and learn by patterning themselves on others. Imitation, Aristotle argued in his *Poetics*, "is natural to man from childhood; one of his advantages over the lower animals being this, that he is the most imitative creature in the world, and learns by imitation. And it is also natural for all to delight in works of imitation" (Aristotle 1984, 1448b5).[30] This observation has been confirmed by research into mammals and early childhood development. "Enhancement of behavior modification by watching others" occurs in primates and in children.[31]

Play, of course, takes place among the smartest mammals.[32] Although many animals have developed mimetic capacities and use them for simulation and amusement, only humans produce and consume fictional representations.[33] People, in other words, can move from play to art, from physical recreation to symbolic re-creation. But they engage in more than modeling, for through the imagination they engender images of the possible, trying a scenario out without having to act on it empirically. They imagine experiences they have not yet encountered,[34] anticipating and preparing themselves for such a situation.

What distinguishes humans from the great apes is not the talent to use tools or symbols; great apes can do both. Rather, it is the aptitude to invent and transmit the use of cultural objects. Central to this process is the expansion not only of the frontal lobe in the human brain but also of theory of mind—the gift to see other people as intentional agents like ourselves and the desire to join with them in "attentional interaction."[35] Human beings then are both structurally prepared to recombine ideas and have the motivation to share emotions and activities with other human beings. This capacity to imagine both the minds of others and other states is what makes us into a cultural species: "*Homo sapiens* has an imagination unparalleled in the animal world" (Dehaene 2009, 317).[36]

The faculty of the imagination, so central to the aesthetic process, is also used as a mechanism in assessing risk. Cognitive theorists believe that this adaptive mechanism enabled our human ancestors to evaluate particular situations and to envision alternatives. Natural selection favored those individuals who could read the motivations and feelings of others. This capacity is also necessary today. We consider the options available to us by projecting ourselves into possible scenarios.[37] Mind reading then becomes a way of predicting behavior.[38] If confronted by a threatening person, what should we do? Flee, try to reason with him, explain ourselves, or listen? In short, the ability to connect through simulation enables us also to engage with the lives of others.[39]

Mind reading and mind projection are central to both literature and friendship. The imagination links these two seemingly different activities through the emotions. Indeed, emotions are the only states capable of crossing the line between fiction and nonfiction. In essence, empathy helps the observer envision the distress of others.[40] At the same time, the observer is aware that she herself is not in anguish. She thus feels a simultaneous distance and closeness to the suffering person. An imaginative dramatization of agony is accompanied by a realization of disparity between self and other. A person can feel this for real people as well as literary characters. She comes to identify with individuals in a novel, all the time knowing that they are fictional, engaging the same capacity for simulation and strategy testing that she uses in ordinary life.[41]

We have no immediate experience, Adam Smith argued, of what other people feel, but we can imagine how we would react in similar circumstances. When our brother is on the rack we could try to picture ourselves in his place. A passion "arises in our breast from the imagination" ([1776] 1976, 12). "By the imagination we place ourselves in his situation, we conceive ourselves enduring all the same torments" (9).[42] Smith referred to "changing places in *fancy* with the sufferer" by which we "come either to conceive or to be affected by what he feels" (10, my emphasis).[43]

Standing in the Shoes of Others

Dr. Aziz and Mrs. Moore, among many literary characters, try to access their own feelings. Not only do they permit the reader's engagement with their lives, but more important they engage with each other, taking a *literary perspective* on the other. I define the *literary perspective* as the ability to think our way into the life of another person. This is how Elizabeth Costello, the protagonist in J. M Coetzee's eponymous novel describes the art of fiction. She claims that she rewrote Joyce's *Ulysses* in her novel *The House on Eccles Street* from the point of view of Molly Bloom: "If I can think my way into the existence of a being who has never existed, then I can think my way into the existence of a bat or a chimpanzee" (2003, 80). A fictional character, Costello talks about her ability to re-create another fictional character, Bloom. "Isn't that what is most important about fiction: that it takes us out of ourselves, into other lives" (23)?[44]

Elizabeth Costello says that the ability to fashion a literary character is not much different from our talent for musing. If the capacity for fiction exists in our ability to imagine, she asks her listeners to envisage themselves as suffering victims, human or animal. Fiction then for her becomes a form of communal communication, a way of narrating our private inventions to others, of transmitting imaginings into the public realm.[45] Although people may make imaginative stories for themselves, unless they relate these creations to others, as she does in her novels or to her listeners, their stories remain personal fantasies.

What enables torture and massacres, she suggests, is a lack of fictionality, our unwillingness to consider the perspective of the victim. The horror of the Holocaust is that people said, "it is *they* in those cattle cars rattling." They did not say, "How would it be if it were I in that cattle car" (79)?[46] For Costello a metaphoric energy exchanges one thing for another and, in this case, one person's humanity for another. The capacity enabling her to re-create Molly Bloom is the same as that allowing her readers to befriend the stranger and to embrace the animal.[47]

What I am calling here the *literary perspective* is neither solitary nor aestheticist, that is to say, artistic for the sake of art. It always directs itself to the other, and thus must be seen in the push and pull of social interdependence, the self's negotiation with another self. Perhaps we can get a sense of its function by looking at what happens when it is absent.

Paul, the protagonist of Willa Cather's story "Paul's Case," is a high-school student, a dreamy and isolated boy. He is unsatisfied by the drabness around him on Pittsburgh's Cordelia Street. It is at the theater and Carnegie Hall that Paul "really lived; the rest was but a sleep and a forgetting." The moment he inhaled the odor behind the scenes, he seemed capable of "splendid and brilliant things" (Cather 1996, 42). Although given entirely to "artificiality" and to "beauty," Paul does not share this with anyone, being entirely alone, a teenaged aesthete. So it is not surprising that one day, with money stolen from his boss, he attains a splendid moment in New York—like a Homeric antihero—finely attired at the Waldorf, ordering champagne for dinner. Being among the fantastically wealthy, he observes them only, having no desire "to meet or know any of these people" (47). He is living his dream, "the plot of all dramas, the text of all romances" (46). At the end of the week, with his money exhausted and his father after him, he jumps, like Anna Karenina, in front of a train, falling "back into the immense design of things" (26). Paul has no friends and his literary disposition has led to no empathic connections.

Unlike Paul, both Mrs. Moore and Dr. Aziz are capable of this type of understanding, linking sympathy and fiction, stories and friendship. Mrs. Moore's attempts to get to know Indians, like Dr. Aziz's openness to her, involve the same faculty by which readers get to know Dr. Aziz. At first, Dr. Aziz is very ready to dismiss the strange Englishwoman he encounters sauntering through the mosque, holding her as the racist representative of Anglo India:[48] "Madam, this is a mosque, you have no right here at all; you should have taken off your shoes; this is a holy place for Moslems" (1924, 18). But the flustered Mrs. Moore, newly arrived in his country, has in fact removed her shoes. This act of reverence on her part momentarily erases the political distinction between black and white, colonizer and colonized, Muslim and Christian, man and woman. Both sense the coolness of the tiled floor with bare feet, an experience that allows them an intimate conversation, and that prompts Dr. Aziz to name his interlocutor an "Oriental" (21). Mrs. Moore's genuine wish to know Indians, in contrast to Adela

Quested's search for India as an abstraction (she saw "India always as a frieze, never as a spirit," 48), enables an unlikely friendship.[49]

It is no accident that the racist and boorish members of the British Club in Chandrapore, with whom readers are not meant to identify, have little time for aesthetic pursuits. "They left literature behind" and "their ignorance of the Arts was notable" (40). The most fully imagined characters, Dr. Aziz, Mrs. Moore, and Mr. Fielding, are the most literary in Costello's sense, hence the most likely to entertain doubt about the self and risk making friends with someone different from themselves. Together, they achieve a companionship that is unexpected given their differences in age, gender, religion, nationality, and social standing.

This nuanced distinctions between empathy of *poeisis*, on the one hand, and empathy of *philia*, on the other, play out stunningly in the relationship between Dr. Aziz and Mr. Fielding, the most developed friendship in the novel. Although they have heard of each other, they actually meet through the two English ladies. Wishing to become acquainted with them, Fielding invites Aziz to tea, along with Mrs. Moore and Miss Quested. Like Mrs. Moore, Fielding is unconventional, at an angle to society, as Forster said of the poet C. P. Cavafy. More important, he has no "racial feeling." So when Aziz arrives early, finding his host in the last stages of dressing, they develop a warmth rather quickly, much to the surprise of Aziz who does not expect familiarity with Englishmen. This quick "intimacy" does not astonish Fielding because they are both "emotional" men, and one would add, sensual and idiosyncratic, more easily open to others.

But "the rapidity of their intimacy" is sealed by an act of kindness and generosity unbeknownst to Fielding. Speaking to Aziz from the bedroom, Fielding complains that he can't find his last collar stud. Aziz assures him that he has a spare, moves out of sight, wrenches off his own collar, and pulls out the gold stud to offer to Fielding. What takes place is an ancient ritual of a gift swap to cement friendship, as that between Diomedes and Glaucus in the *Iliad*.[50] Aziz offers Fielding his own stud and in exchange Fielding invites him into the privacy of the bedroom—"if you don't mind the unconventionality" (68). The generosity of spirit each displays, the stud for the bedroom, enables them to enter a near fictional realm of possibilities unavailable to most men outside. Fielding invites Aziz to watch him dress and Aziz willingly accepts, reinforcing here the homoeroticism of the relationship. Aziz feels so strongly toward Fielding that he resents the arrival of the two English ladies, preferring "to be alone with his new friend" (69).

The two men reach out over the fences of race, caste, and sexual identity. And they do so in a fictional space they create for themselves, acting as characters in their own mininarrative of *philia*. If friendship is, as C. S. Lewis reminds us, a form of secession from society, they withdraw from Chandrapore to an invented realm where their relationship can flourish. "No Englishman understands us except Mr. Fielding," Aziz says to himself (108). He then repeats this sentiment to Fielding when the latter visits Aziz at his own home. Astonishingly, he shows Fielding pictures of his dead wife, the first Englishman to see her. "I don't know why you pay me this great compliment, Aziz, but I do appreciate it," Fielding says. He has been shown the photographs because he has become Aziz's "brother" (125). Fiction, as both deception and imaginative creation, allows the two men to partake in their inventive enterprise of *philia*, in the exercise of shortening distance through empathy.[51]

What takes place in these conversations is the self-disclosure necessary in modern relations. Not reliant on the public support of friendship in either the classical polis or Christian brotherhood, the two characters have to devise their own rules for becoming comrades. Since the violence of imperialism and class works against them, they have to ask themselves what keeps them together. Their friendship then becomes a project in self-fashioning, both private and public at the same time. In the absence of the social practices and structures that supported friendship in earlier eras, mutual self-disclosure becomes a mechanism to cement comradeship. At his own house, Aziz matches Fielding's generous hospitality by showing him pictures of his departed wife. But Aziz goes further, saying, "Mr. Fielding, no one can ever realize how much kindness we Indians need" (126). Not just Indians, the novel suggests, however quietly; friends need kindness. But Fielding, as we learn from the narrator, can't seem to repay this trust, feeling inadequate to it. What has he done to deserve this outburst of confidence, Fielding asks himself, and what could he give in return? "I shall not really be intimate with this fellow," he adds, "nor with anyone" (127). Whereas Fielding draws back, Aziz feels they have become "friends, brothers."

But could they remain friends for long? Could their desire for the symmetry of love withstand the asymmetry of power? Their relationship, though not political in the Aristotelian sense, certainly poses civic questions: Is it possible for an Indian to befriend an Englishman? Is friendship an exercise in equality?[52] Can the yearning for love overcome the divisions of colonial occupation? In short, must social justice precede friendship?

There are early hints that, despite their wishes, their friendship may not work. Aziz can't help but challenge Fielding's own privileged place in colonial India. How is England "justified in holding India," he asks? And when he presses Fielding on the fairness of holding a position in the college at the expense of qualified Indians, Aziz gives voice to his quandary. "Personally," he is delighted with Fielding's presence, but he objects to it politically (120).

These issues are brought to the fore and their friendship tested when Aziz, at considerable personal expense, organizes a picnic for the two English ladies, Fielding, and Prof. Godbole to the Marabar Caves.[53] Because Fielding and Godbole have missed the train, Aziz has to entertain the English ladies alone. At one point he takes Adela Quested on a tour of a cave along with a guide but unfortunately loses sight of her. What happens in the cave as Miss Quested wanders off alone remains a mystery.[54] Hearing a piercing and disconcerting echo, she stumbles out. In her bewilderment, she comes to believe that Dr. Aziz has assaulted her. Aziz, for his part, is baffled by Miss Quested's behavior. When he gets off the train in Chandrapore, he is arrested.

Until his detention, Aziz has striven for greater intimacy with Fielding, wanting, as Mrs. Moore says, them to become Muslims together (144). This Nietzschean *Habsucht*, this force of love, this drive for fusion and identification, ends with his detention on rape charges. It is futile, Aziz now concludes, to seek the sanctuary of friendship with a white man. It is impossible, in other words, to attain social secession with a friend while ignoring the uneven relations outside. Colonial occupation intrudes on and blinds the literary perspective that is so necessary to friendship.

But it is the Englishman who, although until this point incapable of intimacy, steps up at great personal risk to rescue an injured friend. And in so doing, he too acknowledges the chasm between inner desires and political skirmishes. Rather than simply offering solace to Aziz, Fielding openly declares his bond with him, vouching for his character, and severing his links with Anglo India. As a consequence, he throws into the communal arena what was previously private. He attains what Costello strives for her characters, a convergence of public and private fictionality.

Both men then come to a mutual insight, namely, that the melding of two souls is impossible, not because they don't want it but because they are kept apart by racial partitions. But this failure leads to a discovery that friendship entails mutual recognition. If a friend is another self, then this negotiation between self and other produces knowledge about both self and other. We come to know our self and the world around us through our interaction with our friend.[55]

The death of the comrade, I shall show in the next chapter, forces the survivor to confront his own transience. Achilles realizes that the slaughter of Patroclus foretells his own demise. Gilgamesh discovers his own mortality after Enkidu's passing. In the same way, the failure of friendship leads to an examination of our desire for this union itself. Why do we require a comrade? This is the question the friend asks.

Aristotle locates this need in the innate sociability of humans. Friendship depends on community, he believes (1984, 1159a32), which suggests that our longing for friendship has its roots in our native instincts for social coexistence. Friendship, therefore, can't grow outside of the polis. But what was a given in Aristotle's time holds no longer. In modernity friendship is a self-invention, neither religiously ordained nor socially inevitable. The friends must agree on the reasons for their friendship without many signposts, determining for themselves the rules and the goal of the quest.

Since Dr. Aziz and Mr. Fielding have willingly entered into a relationship that others around them abhor, they have to think about its meaning in a way not necessary for their critics—the rioters in the street and the gin-soaked members of the Club. Their literary perspective, which enabled the companionship in the first place, forces them to think about friendship, justice, power, and the capacity of love to transcend politics. Their struggle for an ideal union comes to stand for modern, voluntary relationships, those not prescribed by courtship, marriage, or profession. And their relationship, although personal, has greater social import than they imagine because it tries to reconcile politics and ethics. Friendship surges out of the private house, like an illegitimate son that people have to acknowledge.

This leap from the private into the public forces people to think about the relationship itself: What brings us together? How can we stay true to one another when hostile forces work against us? How do we form bonds of comradeship outside of the family and workplace? What is the point of these bonds when they are not really productive? These questions make friendship not a microcosm of the polis (a "micros cosmos," literally a small world), as Aristotle assumed, but rather a mirror, cracked perhaps, of our overall desire to merge similarity with dissimilarity.

The second part of *A Passage to India* forcefully dramatizes the consequences of the political divisions threatening friendship; it puts a lie to Aziz's belief that the picnic, solely "an expedition of friends," has "nothing to do with English and Indians" (178). Friendship here is not just a matter of personal ethics—love, virtue, and commitment—because it has to answer to the hysteria of politics.

With Aziz in jail the focus falls on Fielding's struggle to exonerate his friend. From the first moment he hears of the charges, he protests. He accuses Miss Quested of madness in front of Mr. Turton, the chief administrator of Chandrapore. To Mr. McBride, the superintendent of the police, he argues for Aziz's innocence, as he does later to the entire British community. When this community rallies around Miss Quested, it isolates Mr. Fielding. Even Hamidullah, Aziz's friend, picks this up, saying, "You are actually on our side against your own people" (193). Although Fielding originally wanted to "slink" through India without any labels, he realizes that he would be henceforth called "seditious" and "anti-British" (193). This ostracism is graphically portrayed in the Club when Fielding refuses to stand up when Ronny Heaslop, Adela Quested's fiancé, enters the room. "It was an ungracious, a caddish thing to do," we are told. Fielding knows this. The subaltern screams at him, "Stand up, you swine" (209). Mr. Turton orders him to leave and, as Fielding does, he also resigns from the Club. He renounces his own people for the justice of friendship.

This is the tensest moment in the novel, after the drama of the courtroom where Miss Quested, becoming aware of her delusion, withdraws all the charges. She says she made a mistake. The novel here changes pace, becoming almost anticlimactic.[56] Fielding leaves for the United Kingdom and Aziz abandons Chandrapore, a bitter man. He suspects that Fielding has married Miss Quested for her money and does not respond to his letters. Two years later, on a tour of the Hindu state of Mau, Fielding and his wife, Stella (Mrs. Moore's daughter), stop near Aziz's new residence but Aziz refuses to see them: "I wish no Englishman or Englishwoman to be my friend (339)." This sentence is a dark rebuke of the novel's opening theme, undermining its thesis statement, so to speak. Both friends seem to have pulled back to their own communities. The wall of nationalism blocks the dance of friendship.

Yet Aziz can't really abandon the chaos of intimacy for the tidiness of national identity, fictionality for prosaic understanding, and neither does the novel. So the final chapter touches again on the capacity of empathy to link literature and friendship. As Aziz beholds the English visitors rowing on the water, he says that he finally understands that the "pose of 'seeing India' which had seduced him to Miss Quested at Chandrapore" was really a form of "ruling India; no sympathy lay behind it" (343). This judgment, of course, applies neither to Fielding nor to Mrs. Moore. Their capacity to step out of England and into India facilitates their relationship with Aziz. And Dr. Aziz's willingness to believe that Mrs. Moore and Mr. Fielding were capable of kindness in turn makes this possible. But nationalism intervenes, transforming friendship into an object of anti-imperial struggle, forcing both characters to reconcile the uncertainty of love with the necessity of literal meaning. The only solution is to highlight their racial and national identities at the expense of simulative empathy. In so doing, they unknowingly give credence to Mr. Turton's declaration to Fielding, namely that there could never be any friendship between the English and the Indians: "Courtesy, by all means. Intimacy—never, never" (182).

But the malleability of Aziz's character, its very literariness, means that he will never abide by Turton's denotative certitudes. His need for that figurative leap of friendship suggests he won't be imprisoned by ethnic certainties. In a touching moment with Ralph Moore, Mrs. Moore's son and Ronnie Heaslop's half brother, Aziz confesses that Mrs. Moore was his best friend, acknowledging the possibility of communication with the other. Having delivered this as an act of "homage" to the man's mother, Aziz feels the "cycle beginning again" (350). Must he accept the boundaries of ideology? Can they be friends despite the barriers separating them? Yet just moments before he says to himself, "never be friends with the English" (349).

His inner struggle plays out in the final meeting between Fielding and Aziz as they trot on their horses side by side, like Castor and Pollux, the

famous horsemen of classical mythology. What takes place is a complex ex-
position on friendship, each man on his own animal. From his own horse
Aziz asserts that India shall be a nation: "No foreigners of any sort." India
a nation, Fielding mocks, just like Belgium. " 'We shall drive every blasted
Englishman from the sea and then,'" Aziz responds, "half-kissing him,
and then 'you and I shall be friends'" (362). So Aziz repeats the Aristotelian contention that friendship requires equality. It cannot predate the
polis. " 'Why can't we be friends now?' said the other, holding him affectionately. 'It's what you want. It's what I want.'" Although this scene is difficult to visualize (two men embracing while trotting on their own horses),
it is aesthetically necessary. For, like Homeric gods bedeviling the lives of
mortals, the two horses swerve apart and natural elements conspire "in
their hundred voices, 'No not yet,' and the sky said, 'No not there'" (362).

Friendship, then, as Aristotle says, "depends on community" (1984,
1159a32). The novel makes this position very clear. But Aristotle seems to
contradict himself when he writes that "when men are friends they have
no need for justice" (1155a26). This implies that friends must overcome social divisions or reside in an ideal community with little social strife. If this
is indeed Aristotle's view, then the novel parts ways with him. The seemingly pessimistic finale suggests not an end to friendship but to the conceit
that friendship is possible without parity, which in itself is an Aristotelian
position. Aziz, as the colonized man, can't conceive of intimacy without
equality. Yet, Aziz, the friend, wants to believe otherwise, that Fielding
can imagine what it's like to be an Indian. Neither he nor the novel offers a
release from this tension: Can there be friendship before justice? Does nationalism precede friendship? Or is love capable of resolving the conflicts
caused by race and power?

But the horses tear the friends apart. Violence darkens the literary perspective. And what we are left with is aesthetic empathy, of literature trying to reconcile the ethical and the political. The novel's thunderous ending
suggests that friendship can work as a fiction, as an elastic stretch between
our desire for love and the social denial of that love. It also makes clear
that the mechanisms of friendship frustrate the emergence of homology.
This is so because there is no inner logic to friendship, no essential truth to
discover. It exists in the in-between spaces of imagination and longing, an
ambivalent bond that is fashioned anew each time and often against social
opposition. Nothing perhaps contradicts the contention of male friendship

as a homological, proprietary, and homophilic relation[57] more than the finale to Forster's work where both natural and social forces conspire against the two friends.

Indeed, we can compare this discordant finish with the harmonious conclusion to Forster's posthumous *Maurice*, a work of homosexual love. The protagonist, Maurice Hall, searches for truth with another man, to "embrace" and "mingle his being" with him, as he says (1971, 62). When he falls in love and sleeps with him, he feels finally human, having drunk from an inner well that had been until then blocked. The novel ends with Maurice abandoning his Cambridge friend, Clive Durham, his class, and his family for Clive's gamekeeper, Alec Scudder, who is waiting for Maurice in the boathouse. A text that begins with an adolescent friendship (Clive caressing his hair) ends with an open declaration of homosexuality—"rest your head on me more, the way you like more" (228), so daring for its time that Forster felt he could not publish it. "I have shared with Alec," Maurice insists to Clive, "all I have. Which includes the body" (243).

The essence of identity distinguishes the ending of *Maurice* from that of *A Passage to India*: Maurice's confident strides into Alec's open arms versus the parting horses. The sexual drive promises a fulfillment that is largely unattainable in friendship. The "happy ending [in *Maurice*] was imperative," Forster says in a posthumous note (1971, 250). "I was determined that in fiction anyway two men should fall in love and remain in it for the ever and ever that fiction allows, and in this sense Maurice and Alec still roam the greenwood." And the novel itself is "dedicated to a happier year."[58] This erotic union, it seems, does not rely as much on the literary perspective.

The difference is that there is no ontology to friendship, no secret truth, no outright possession, and no identification of opposites. Maurice and Alec discover an inner key; they find the Aristophanic completion of physically locking into the other half. Aziz has uncovered a similar truth within his national and racial self, the part of him that was shaken by his encounter with Mrs. Moore.

But unlike sexuality or national and religious union, friendship recovers no such code. Maurice himself wonders if friendship—"someone to last your whole life" (197)—can happen outside of dreams. That type of friendship, say with Clive, fails. But the sexual togetherness with Alec lasts into eternity as they both renounce their class[59] and withdraw into what

Forster calls the greenwood, England's last remaining space of natural seclusion. In this way, they mimic the real-life union Forster himself witnessed in the relationship between the upper-class and former academic Edward Carpenter and his much younger and working-class companion, George Merrill. In Carpenter's country house, Millthorpe near Sheffield, Forster discovered that homosexual love was possible in seclusion, unlike, for instance, his experience in Alexandria and later in India.[60]

The bond that *philia* seeks is short lived and brittle because, unlike the discourses of *eros* and *ethnos*, it does not rest on an inner logic. The aim of friendship is to bridge ethics and politics rather than to unearth truth. Yet the parting of the Aziz's and Fielding's horses does not really end their friendship. Both men acknowledge that colonialism rather than love separates them. In this distinction the novel does nothing less than affirms the power of friendship. It recognizes the courage of Dr. Aziz, Mrs. Moore, and Mr. Fielding to form bonds of love despite the firing squads taking aim at them.

The Paradoxes of Friendship

The attempt to form friendship at one's own peril has a long history in literature. Although Georgios Vizyenos (1849–96), one of the founders of the Greek short story, tries in "Moscóv-Selím" to bring together the *philos* and the *ethnos*, the results are as bleak as Forster's. He too begins with the question of whether the private and the public can be reconciled, whether a Greek can be friends with a Turk. But the story answers in the negative. The narrator says, "I wish I'd never met you on my path; I wish I'd never known you in my life" (Vizyenos 1988, 186). In a preamble, addressed in the second person to the protagonist/friend, Moscóv-Selím, the narrator gives voice to the challenges of forming a relationship between a Christian and a Moslem, the narrator and the character, the author and protagonist, the "you" and the "I."

At the same time, he suggests that this friendship can flourish only in the in-between realm of fiction, the place where real life is transmuted into an aesthetic representation. The two-paragraph overture is typographically separated from the rest of the text by a row of asterisks and delivered in the second person, as if composed in a different key. The narrator, as implied author, addresses himself to the dead friend, telling him that he had decided to write his story as epitaph. It is a discordant introduction, a translation from the grammar of the second person to the first person of the main text.

In a way, Vizyenos uses a trope we will consider in the next chapter—literature as a memorial. The friend dies and the survivor tells his tale. But this section implies that friendship is as illusory as in *A Passage to India*: making friends is like an exercise in storytelling, bridging differences, and of contriving. The subterfuge is necessary because of the unfriendly world, which seeks to separate Aziz from Fielding, the narrator from Selím. Friendship, thus, has to struggle against *philophobia*, society's panic at the bonding of two men. Vizyenos writes:

> I don't doubt that the fanatics of your race will curse the memory of a "believer" because he opened the sanctuary of his heart to the unholy eyes of an infidel. I fear that the fanatics of my own race will reproach a Greek author because he did not conceal your virtue, or did not substitute a Christian hero in his account. . . . I shall write your story. (Vizyenos 1988, 187)

The horses once more swerve apart. No, not yet, shout the fanatics. But the friends don't give up and neither does their literary disposition. The two men, in other words, seek aesthetic allusion as a sanctuary for love. Moscóv-Selím, his name incorporating doubleness of identity, the Russian and the Turkish, is predisposed to befriending a Greek, his mortal enemy. In fact, Moscóv-Selím has been prepared for this strange undertaking by his earlier embrace of the hated Russian foe. Having been abused by his father and the Ottoman state, Moscóv-Selím finds refuge with a Russian family. When he returns to the Ottoman lands, he creates a simulacrum of this Russian oasis by building a dacha and living like a Russian. This is how the Greek narrator meets him, as an oddity in the Ottoman Empire.

But Moscóv-Selím was also equipped to befriend a Greek by his upbringing. Unwilling to part with him, his mother dressed her son as a girl and kept him in the harem past his adolescence. His "lively imagination," acquired in the years spent living as a "manly" man among women, enabled him to become a friend and an inspiration for literature, which, as the story suggests, is the same thing. Moscóv-Selím in this way resembles Aziz, a soft, open character, a Muslim willing to befriend Christians; and of course he also resembles Nathan, a Jew willing to form bonds with Christians and Muslims. He has the impulse toward fictionality. Even though Moscóv-Selím dies, he lives on in the preamble before the main story, the space where the stranger turns to a friend. And the narrator/ implied author regrets not the friendship but that he has to apologize for it to the fundamentalists. He pushes against their desire to convert the narration of *philia* into the literalism of the *genos* (race).

No Ontology

"Strange friend," says the speaker in Wilfred Owen's haunting World War I poem "Strange Meeting," which captures the same ambivalence as the previous story. An English soldier dreams of an encounter with the German he had killed a day earlier in the trenches, a ghoulish reunion mirrored in the half rhymes: "bestirred/stared, "hair/ hour," "wild/world." "I am the enemy you killed, my friend," responds the German at the end of the text, having just sung his own elegy: there is "no cause to mourn . . . save the undone years, / The hopelessness. Whatever hope is yours, / Was my life also." As the Englishman listens to this lament, he realizes that in killing his foe he has destroyed part of himself. Indeed, the German voice seems to fade into the speaker's own, becoming almost indistinguishable. Who killed whom? This confusion of selves is echoed in the half rhymes and the half repetition of entire lines: "And by his smile, I knew that sullen hall; / By his dead smile I knew we stood in Hell." Who is actually intoning the lament? And is it a lament? The somber rhythm of the words resembles more a weary march than the wailing of an Andromache. In the dreamy setting of the tunnel, the intermediary space of metaphor, both men realize they are comrades. Is there a mutual recognition here, an exchange of empathy, made possible by the imperfect assonances of Hades? If the friend is another self, then the killing of the other leads to the death of the self. The friend dies when, severed from the other self, he discovers himself separate and deserted. But more likely, the friend dies because of friendship's inability to bridge the differences.

Moscóv-Selím can't bear the possibility of an imminent Russian assault on his native land, an act that would force him to choose sides, to end the (dis)simulation of friendship: to live like a Russian in Ottoman territory and to tell his tale to a Greek. Moscóv-Selím discovers that the goal of friendship is not to be Muslim, or Russian, or Greek. That would be easy. It is rather to silence the feud between love and internecine enmity. What Moscóv-Selím learns is the world outside his invented dacha won't allow a Muslim and a Christian to accept the contradictions of their friendship. It is not paradoxes that kill but rather society's fear of them.

If so, we have to revise the declaration, attributed to Aristotle, changing "Friends, there is no friend" to "Friends, there is no truth to friendship."[61] Does Vizyenos's narrator regret having met Moscóv-Selím because he loved him or because he hated him? And does he despise him because Moscóv-Selím forced the narrator to confront the inconsistencies of love? Are Aziz and Fielding comrades or adversaries? Who takes whose life in the trenches? Is the friend another self, an independent person or a fabrication?

Racial Confusions

Perhaps we are unsure of limits because, as William Faulkner implies in *Absalom, Absalom*, we are immersed in a sublime ambiguity. Narrated from different perspectives that supply more and more detail, the novel relates the unhappy history of a Mississippi family sired by Thomas Sutpen that is as cursed as the House of Atreus. Henry Sutpen, Thomas's son, brings home from Oxford (Mississippi) his mate, the older Charles Bon. A young man of considerable charisma, Bon "seduced the country brother and sister without any effort or particular desire to do so" (Faulkner 1951, 93).[62] Henry promotes the match between his sister and Bon as a means of entangling himself more fully with the cosmopolitan, self-assured young man from New Orleans.[63] It was "as though it actually were the brother who had put the spell on the sister, seduced her to his own vicarious image" (107). The father, realizing that Bon is his son from his previous marriage with Eulalia Bon, an octoroon woman from Haiti, tries to prevent this union. He tells Henry that Charles is his half brother without letting him know of Charles's black heritage. Henry abandons the plantation in despair: Because Henry loved Bon, he "repudiated blood birthright and material security for his sake" (89). He turned his back on all he knew "to cast his lot with the single friend" (91), comradeship trumping kin.

He returns four years later with Charles, his friend/his brother, after the Civil War, having served in the same regiment together. But Henry now knows the truth. During the war Thomas Sutpen reveals to Henry the tale of miscegenation: "He must not marry her, Henry. His mother's father told me that her mother had been a Spanish woman. I believed him; it was not until after he was born that I found out that his mother was part negro" (355). So galloping together toward the gates of the plantation, like Aziz and Fielding, toward a marriage that Henry no longer desires, he tries to stop Charles, having had to confront the horrors of "blood birthright" and of blood mixing. "So it's the miscegenation, not the incest, which you can't bear," Charles says. "You are my brother," Henry responds. "No I'm not. I'm the nigger that's going to sleep with your sister. Unless you stop me, Henry" (356–58). So Henry shoots him at the entrance to the plantation, enacting the fratricidal struggle between Eteocles and Polynices at the gates of Thebes—the two sons of Oedipus and his mother, Jocasta—as dramatized by Aeschylus in *Seven Against Thebes*. Henry disappears again only to return in 1910, when he dies in a conflagration lit by Clytie, the daughter of Thomas Sutpen and a slave woman.

Faulkner's fragmented, unsyntactical narration and the multiple perspectives shroud the reasons for the murder. Did Henry kill Charles because the latter is no longer a companion but a brother, thereby violating the distinction between friendship and kinship? Or did he kill him because he discovered that Charles was black?[64] The friend here is another self in the most hideous way, a party to an incestuous union—between Charles and Henry's sister, Judith, and again between Charles and Henry. In other words, he merges with the other in an unseemly bond, transforming Montaigne's dream into the most literal marriage. The friend suddenly becomes the brother with the promise/threat of becoming a brother-in-law. Yet the friend also discovers that his comrade-in-arms is bound not by likeness but by a biological and racial difference. As Charles reminds Henry, "We even made the laws which declare that one eighth of a specified kind of blood shall outweigh seven eighths of another kind" (115).

Did Henry murder Charles because of resemblance or dissimilarity? Because of the enforced dissimulation? Or was it because their relationship could not handle the contradictions that friendships always have to bear and which his own comes to represent in the most exaggerated form? You are my friend, my brother, my enemy; you are white like me but black unlike me. I love you and I hate you at the same time, as Catullus says in "*Odi et amo*."

How impossible it is for Henry and Charles to tread on orderly paths? Their decisions involve them in wider struggles despite their desires for certainty and serenity. Although they both yearn for intimacy, the divisions of the American South convert their wishes into tinder for racial bonfires. The novel affirms the power of friendship, while at the same time showing how implicated our inner desires are with civil wars.

We impose on friendships both our ideals and fears. One the one hand, we see in friendship an analogy for social cohesion, a representative relationship outside of the family, a democratic, noncoercive form of association that is liberating. Friendship is the basis for sociability. But this community also distrusts friendship. It fears that friends, preoccupied with each other, will neglect the polis. Achilles, obsessed first with his own wrath and then with avenging Patroclus's death, cares little for the Achaeans. "Ardent for some desperate glory," he fights for personal love rather than national goals, a dimension also underscored in Wolfgang Petersen's 2004 film, *Troy*. In contrast, Hector, friendless that he is, a son, brother, and father, breathes for Troy. "Fight for your country—that is the best, the only omen," he exhorts his comrades in one of the most celebrated lines of the *Iliad* (1990, 2.282). Achilles could never have shouted these words, devoted as he is exclusively to Patroclus. He would more likely embrace Forster's declaration—if he could grasp its liberal impulse—and betray his country for his friend.

We are left with the muddles of friendship and thus have to revise the famous line from Owen's World War I poem "Dulce et Decorum Est," changing "Dulce et decorum est pro patria mori" (It is sweet and right to die for your native land) to "Dulce et decorum est *pro amico* mori" (It is sweet and right to die *for your friend*). Despite the attempts of the friends to be alone, political gyrations around them turn personal longing into a violence that kills them. Friends are punished for the hubris of thinking they could live outside the community.

Amicitia and Patria

This punishment becomes the theme of Friedrich Schiller's historical play *Don Carlos* (1787), which is loosely based on the life of Carlos, prince of Asturias (1545–68) of Spain and which dramatizes the conflict between progressive and conservative forces. Key to the drama is the relationship that

Schiller develops between Prince Carlos and the Marquis of Posa, his mentor and mate. Imbuing both protagonists with the revolutionary zeal of the late eighteenth century, Schiller makes them into intimate friends and rebels against Carlos's despotic father, King Philip II of Spain (1527–98).

Schiller portrays both men as ideal companions. Early in the play the young Carlos declares the Marquis his "only friend," having "no one in the world." With their similar appearance they meld into one another as one body: "The hand of nature / Made Carlos and Roderigo like one person." Of course, they must recognize the disparities in their friendship as Carlos declares to Roderigo that "I will love you wholly since I could not be you" (Schiller 1996, act 1, ll. 184–85, 199).

Having established this greater-than-life love, Schiller has Carlos and the Marquis engage in the struggle to liberate Flanders from Phillip's control. It is here that he creates the dilemma for the Marquis. On the one hand, as servant to the king, he has to remain loyal to him; on the other hand, as Carlos says of his friend, "I am dearer than his fatherland" (act 1, l. 593). And the Marquis himself recognizes the pricelessness of their friendship: "I made his soul a paradise for millions! / The beauty of my dreams could rival heaven" (act 4, ll. 157–58). In the end he decides to sacrifice himself for his friend and their greater cause, the end of despotic rule. One of the great moments of the drama comes at their final conversation when the Marquis openly declares his love and the reason for his sacrifice. "Everything I love / I have exchanged for this—and Carlos, this moment, / How very great it is—I am content" (act 5, ll. 100–101). He dies for "eternal friendship" (act 5, l. 144). He sacrifices himself for both Carlos, the friend, and their cause, as Carlos confesses to his father: "A higher god than nature made us brothers, / Sir, we were brothers, love was his vocation, / And love of me his glorifying death" (act 5, ll. 275–76). The friend dies to save the son, as he also betrays the father. And the father despises them for both for their mutinous and exclusive love. We encounter again circular reasoning: friendship is sedition is love is sedition is friendship.

Friendship forms one of the scaffolds of political society. Yet, political authority suspects the isolation that friendship needs, considering it tantamount to rebellion. The king senses a double exclusion. If only the Marquis had died for him, he laments, "I loved him." He feels shut out of their relationship and he does not believe that such self-sacrifice is possible.

Who was he saving with his sacrifice?
The Boy, my son? Never. A man like that
Would hardly give his life to save a boy.
I do not think the slender flame of friendship
Is strong enough to fill a heart like that.
————Schiller, *Don Carlos*, act 5, ll. 502–6

But friendship is not that "slender." For what could be more transcendent than the courage to betray your king and die for your friend? The king's disquiet, however, suggests that the social good may be incompatible with the love of the friend. Is this why friendship has to remain scheming and guileful?

Friendship as Social Block?

Schiller's play shows society's ambivalent relationship to friendship. On the one hand, it sees the social, even military, benefits of comradeship but, on the other, it distrusts its secessionist, subversive, and homoerotic tendencies. It is a tension that we have seen in antiquity, from the early epics to Cicero. But it becomes particularly acute in the modern period with the rise of autonomous states and autonomous friendship: self-sufficient societies and self-sufficient friends can coexist only a short while, as experience in eighteenth-and nineteenth-century America shows.

At the birth of the republic Americans espoused an Aristotelian concept of friendship as collective tissue. In the eighteenth century, for instance, people encouraged loving relationships between men because they saw these bonds as tendons for social and national unity. What were in a sense private relations were regarded as "affective bonds" that served as the "emotional sinews of a larger identity."[65]

These "romantic friendships" became a metaphor in revolutionary society for citizenly love. Whereas the colonial bond to Great Britain was seen as either a filial or marital relationship, the colonists' links with one another were conceived as reciprocal comradeship. According to Caleb Crain: "Romantic friendship was egalitarian. It could bind men without curtailing their liberty. . . . Like confederation into civil society, friendship bestowed benefits that were other than financial or sexual."[66] Friendship was considered more suitable for republican ideology than filial or conjugal relationships because it was voluntary and because it could bind men without limiting their freedom.

The founders of the American republic understood friendship as a human mode of social interaction. Although they considered it a virtue, they incorporated it in their enterprise of political sovereignty. They viewed friendship through the prism of federal self-institution as opposed to divine revelation.[67] In their quest for societal cohesion, Americans looked at friendship as one means among many. Persuaded by Scottish philosophy of the adhesive power of feelings and beliefs, American political thinkers came to believe that commitment to sympathetic love would help hold society together and, conversely, that society itself would encourage private well-being.

Thomas Paine in *Common Sense* remarks that society "promotes our happiness *positively* by uniting our affections" ([1776] 1976, 65). The authors of the Federalist Papers often invoke the trinity of friendship, love, and virtue.[68] The writer of Federalist Paper No. 49 (James Madison), for instance, speaks of the stability of the legislative branch, held together by the "connections of blood, friendship, and acquaintance" (Madison, Hamilton, and Jay 1987, 315). The authors believe that these connections, shared also by the general American population, endowed the United States with an unparalleled cohesiveness. Letter No. 2 argues that "Providence has been pleased to give this one connected country to one united people—a people descended from the same ancestors, speaking the same language, professing the same religion, attached to the same principles of government, very similar in their manner and customs" (91).

Ordinary Americans came to believe this dictum as well, expressing it in their diaries, letters, journals, and newspaper articles. These artifacts of everyday life reveal the link in the popular mind of sympathetic love first with political revolution and then social coherence. The idealization of sentiment and sympathy helped lay "the foundation for effective collaboration between citizens," and these "affective associations" played a key role in shaping the political upheavals and transformations of the eighteenth century. Although this language of sentimental friendship may seem an idiosyncratic discourse today, it had profound public effects, having become a crucial component of republican discourse. Its ultimate aim was the enlightened collaboration among citizens who could work together in freedom and mutual trust. In short, sentimental friendship was a subject of intense national interest. Numerous articles appeared in the nineteenth-century American press extolling the virtues of friendship and drawing a connection between male comradeship and social harmony. These friendships, broad in conception and practice, allowed men broad emotional and physical scope for the expression of intimacy.[69]

We observe similar developments in late eighteenth-century England where friendship was appropriated by patriotic discourses. These decades witnessed the rapid rise of a radical conception of friendship as seen by the growth of Friendly Societies. The Friends of Liberty, for instance, became an umbrella for more than one hundred radical organizations established in England between 1790 and 1797. Members met in taverns and swore oaths of inviolable friendship to one another while committing themselves to their political projects.[70] Friendship denoted more than sympathy: it signified political solidarity based on egalitarian principles. To think of someone as your friend meant you accepted him as your equal. Friendship emerged as central in conceptions of British liberty at the time. In the case of Samuel Taylor Coleridge, the idea fused politics, sentimentality, and eroticism.[71]

Both the American and British examples demonstrate how friendship can serve as a voluntary relationship outside the walls of marriage, family, and business and as a metaphor for social attachments. In other words, friendship presents a social bond beyond the traditional pairing offered by kinship and the division of labor: husband/wife, father/son, employer/employee, teacher/student, buyer/seller, client/patron. It is not that friendship alone leads to social concord; rather, it allows people to think of others, to be concerned about their welfare, and to wish them to flourish.[72]

This mutual concern suggests that reciprocity is more important in friendship than in kinship relations, say, of parent and child.[73] In the absence of law or blood linking the two people together, reciprocity, either of gifts or of mutual acknowledgement, serves as a binding agent. You cannot force someone into a friendship in the way you can arrange a marriage. But you may point out to that person that it is in his interest to consider the welfare of friends while expecting him to reciprocate. We show our concern for our friends and desire that they do the same.

Of course, the gift of altruistic regard is not free, in the same way that the material gift, according to Marcel Mauss, does not come gratis. For it places the receiver in the position of obligation ([1923–24] 1990, 5, 33). The gift as both disinterested and obligatory captures the paradox in friendship, being public and private simultaneously, free yet socially determined, expecting affection from others while asserting its autonomy. That gift giving may be reciprocal does not mean that it is always symmetrical. Indeed, as I will show in my discussion of the gift exchange between Glaucus and Diomedes in chapter 3, rarely is this a one-to-one exchange. The receipt of a gift embarrasses and makes us search for a countergift. We are not sure whether we have behaved properly. Equally, when receiving and acknowledging affection or confronted with another's problems, we can feel anxious, concerned that we have not done enough, or exactly the right thing. If friendships fail it is often because of an imbalance, actual or perceived, of this mutuality. When a person, for instance, says that he is in pain, the listener must sympathize by at least acknowledging the pain. But this acknowledgment, Stanley Cavell has shown, is characterized by as many failures as successes (1969, 263). And the failure results in confusion and suspicions of indifference or callousness. These disappointments in personal relations have their origins in the disparity between the friends' commitment to each other and their individual capacities for expressing their commitment.

They also point to a gap in our understanding of friendship, that is, between a theory and its application. That we expect friendship to work through reciprocity does not mean that we always succeed. Furthermore, that philosophers or ordinary people believe that friendship holds a community together does not prove that it can. But fifth-century Athens, like eighteenth-and early nineteenth-century America, considered friendship as a cornerstone of their respective cultures. Whether or not it could carry such a load is beside the point. The interaction in American society between the personal and official spheres provides a historical illustration of the ancient idea of reciprocity and of the link between ethics and politics. It demonstrates that for Athenians and Americans friendship was implicated in the discussion of what makes a society adhere—an inherently political issue.

Of Slavery and Freedom

The idealization of friendship in American society came into doubt toward the end of the nineteenth century, having been associated with sentimentality, female sensibility, and eventually homosexuality. Male friendships, which had played such a crucial role in sustaining republican ideology, came to be seen as "dangerous and subversive."[74] By the 1880s the model of masculinity hardened and men's emotions were increasingly directed toward family and spouse. Opportunities for male nonsexual intimacy shrank considerably. Of course, friendship still incorporated within itself the tension between privacy and social affect but the relation now became one of suspicion rather than of idealization. *Philophobia*, always lurking in the shadows, now allied itself with the specter of homophobia. As a result, people came go hold friendship in lower esteem and even with a certain suspicion.

This transformation had a literary manifestation, expressed in the life and work of Samuel Clemens or Mark Twain (1835–1919). Twain's youth was marked by the homosociality of sentimental friendships characteristic of antebellum American society—physically intimate and emotionally intense. But in the latter part of his life Twain himself retreated from these attachments and avoided the representation in his work of male friendship that strayed from the new heterosexual restrictions.[75] Although his novels supported the new conventions of masculinity, they questioned the national discourse so centered on the ideals of whiteness and sameness. The most obvious example is *The Adventures of Huckleberry Finn* (1884).[76]

In dramatizing the friendship between Huck, an uneducated youth, and Jim, a much older slave, Twain shows the asymmetrical relations existing between white and black people. Like Forster, he asks whether justice precedes friendship. Can a white boy be friends with a slave? Moreover, he too suggests that this unorthodox friendship can take place in the empathetic milieu of literature. Literature, Twain implies, with its perennial smudging of the lines of illusion and reality, can bring about a mutual understanding between two racially and socially antithetical figures. As in *A Passage to India*, the power of the novel lies not only in its unremitting critique of racism but also in the link it draws between literary imagining and sympathetic perception. The capacity to befriend someone so different from the self requires an imaginative leap, the ability to jump back and forth between acting and being.

This simulative capacity reinforces the public, American dimension of both the friendship and the novel. For Twain's work heats up Aristotle's formulation of the friend as another self by converting the friend (as in *Absalom, Absalom*) into a "nigger" and thereby undercutting the self's racial and political certainty. Neither Aristotle nor American republican theorists could ever have imagined such an association between a free boy and a slave.[77] Twain achieves exactly this, a shocking and forbidden bond. At the same time, he affirms the power and hold of friendship. By pulling such a relationship through the cataracts of racist society and having it survive, Twain shows that loyalty can rise above injustice. What makes this possible is fiction's aptitude for make-believe, the capacity it fosters in the protagonist (and reader) to place himself or herself in the situation of another. Literature forces the white self to share a bunk with society's outcasts.

Huck is a boy who lies, tells stories, and dresses like a girl in order to survive. He fits very much the description of Odysseus etched by Athena in the *Odyssey*: a "chameleon," a "bottomless bag of tricks," a "contriver," and "guileful" (1961, 13.373, 374, 379). Huck, like Odysseus, improvises continuously, deceiving and telling stories as he tries to gain autonomy for himself and Jim. But Huck is conscious of his own fictitious nature, as he informs us in the novel's introductory sentences, an overture reminiscent of "Moscóv-Selím": "You don't know about me, without you have read a book by the name of 'The Adventures of Tom Sawyer,' but that ain't no matter. That book was made by Mr. Mark Twain, and he told the truth mainly" (2000, 70). Twain's winking preamble presents a paradoxical Huck, the unschooled boy who is aware of fiction's possibilities: "I never seen anybody but lied, one time or another." People tell fibs in real life and so has Mr. Twain who has "stretched" but mainly "told the truth."[78] Huck's readiness to bend reality makes him both an appealing literary character and a likely candidate for true friendship. The novel, a first-person narrative, charts Huck's efforts and travails to accept Jim as an equal. Huck's coming of age involves the development of his empathetic understanding.

Jim himself also undertakes a personal journey, though less one of self-discovery than the pursuit of freedom. Obviously his main intention is to gain political autonomy, to own himself (110). He too has the literary capacity for an attachment with another person, a white boy. But this capacity is presented as something given, not acquired. It is as if it is natural for a black man to befriend a white boy while the reverse requires considerable imagination. Jim's ability to identify himself with others is never an issue as it is for Huck. The novel, after all, is about Huck's education and the large role that Jim plays in that process. He already seems to have the empathic talent that Huck must discover in himself.

The work shows how the constant give-and-take between make-believe and reality leads to appreciation of other perspectives. What allows Huck to transcend the limitations of racism is his proclivity for stories, his capacity to create and live in fictions. For Huck has the freedom to go between reality and acting: he is capable of figurative thinking. As a consummate liar, thief, and actor, he engages in the creation of narratives; he also observes and appreciates masterful plots as when he becomes entangled with the Duke and the King, two Shakespearean actors and swindlers. So this young pretender from St. Petersburg, Missouri, who lives life like fiction, uncovers the reality of slavery while also bursting through society's stage set.

Huck's first narrative adventure is his escape from Miss Watson, the sister of Huck's main guardian, the Widow. Unable to bear any longer her mission to "sivilize" him (91), he flees, only to come upon Tom Sawyer, the supreme reader of picaresque fiction like *Don Quixote*, who suggests that they start a gang of robbers, calling it Tom Sawyer's Gang (76). Unfortunately, Huck's father, Pap, disrupts this scheme by dragging Huck away and locking him up in a cabin. Wanting neither to stay with his father nor to return to Miss Watson, Huck breaks out of the shed and then fakes his death.

This is the first of Huck's assault on reality and, as is often the case, Jim pays for it. When Huck happens upon Jim, now a runaway slave on Jackson Island, he overhears people talking about his own drowning. Wanting to get more information on how people were perceiving his fictitious death, he dresses up as a girl and goes into town, where he learns from a woman that Jim had been accused of his murder. Huck's imaginings, so crucial to his transformation as a bildungsroman character and to his discovery of Jim's humanity, come always at Jim's expense. In a sense, he comes to love Jim by first hurting him. His willingness to stand in the shoes of a slave is directly related to his capacity for fiction, which often harms the slave because, as a slave, he is not granted the same capacity for magical, analogical thinking.

Both white boy and black slave are now escapees, having established for practical reasons a bond of equality between them. They load up a raft and push off, heading for freedom in Ohio. They become, like Gilgamesh and

Enkidu, two heroes in exile, cementing their relationship through shared adventures: nearly drowning in the surge of a ferry, coming upon a slain man in a boathouse, getting caught between the feuding Grangerfords and Shepherdons, being betrayed by two swindlers (the King and the Duke), the King's selling of Jim, and Jim's final escape from slavery. They witness murder, death, deception, and the "staging" of Shakespeare. The story then turns out to be a buddy narrative, albeit a very unorthodox one, separated as the two are by age and race. But more important, this odyssey down the Mississippi transforms them both. It allows Jim to gain his freedom and enables Huck to envisage Jim as a real human being, someone of Huck's own stature. This is indeed an act of imagining at first for, although both are fugitives—Jim in a real and Huck in a figurative sense—Huck has complete autonomy of movement. He can effortlessly venture into town to buy supplies or to "borrow watermelons." This lawful freedom mimics the metaphorical freedom to contrive narrative, to enter into and out of real and simulated situations.

His assessment of Jim begins with prejudice. He says a number of times that Jim "had an uncommon level head, for a nigger" (134). Eventually, however, he places himself on the same plane as Jim, going so far as to offer an apology for playing tricks on him: "It was fifteen minutes before I could work myself up to go and humble myself to a nigger—but I done it, and I warn't ever sorry for it afterwards neither. I didn't do him no more mean tricks, and I wouldn't done that one if I'd a knowed it would make him feel that way" (142). Here Huck gains agency through sympathetic understanding to acknowledge Jim as his counterpart. He equivocates, at one point wondering whether he should turn Jim in: "It would be a thousand times better for Jim to be a slave at home where his family was, as long as he'd got to be a slave, and so I'd better write a letter to Tom Sawyer and tell him to tell Miss Watson where he was" (255). But he knows he could never do it, as it would mean betraying his friend.

It is Huck's proclivity for storytelling, illusion, and deception that paradoxically allows him to reach out to a slave. Jim, of course, has his own capacity for fiction as he too can embellish and he has his own way of reading nature and interpreting events. When we are introduced to Jim in chapter 2, Huck tells us how Tom had slipped off Jim's hat and hung it on a tree while Jim slept. "Afterwards Jim said the witches bewitched him and put him in a trance, and rode him all over the State, and then set him under the trees again and his hat on a limb to show who done it" (75). No doubt Jim has to dissimulate in order to survive in a slave society.[79]

But it is Huck's storytelling and his sense of fiction that are the focus of the novel. One sees this in how differently they both conceive liberty. For, incredibly, they miss the turn for the Ohio River and continue floating down south on the Mississippi, into greater danger for Jim. Freedom then becomes an aesthetic exercise for Huck to turn into a more humane person: "You feel mighty free and easy and comfortable on a raft" (177). These are his words. Freedom represents relief from civilization, their trip an odyssey in his self-discovery, another version of the travel narrative. Yet Jim can only imagine his freedom as a most literal condition. Not all narratives are literature, he seems to say, as his own have life and death consequences. For him freedom can only mean acquiring the means to own himself, a very distant possibility as they float deeper into peril. To be sure, he is captured, becoming doubly a slave, after the King sells him. Again he becomes a victim of play, as the actor/swindler makes money out of him.

By coincidence he is purchased by Mr. and Mrs. Phelps, Tom Sawyer's aunt and uncle. Tom himself arrives and devises another elaborate plan to "steal the nigger out of slavery" (272). Influenced as he has been by European literature ("hain't you ever read any books at all; Baron Trenck, nor Casanova, . . . nor Henri IV"), Tom can only deliver Jim through a literary plot. When Tom suggests to an incredulous Huck that they would have to saw Jim's leg off in order to remove the chain, Huck protests. Tom replies that "some of the best authorities has done it." And in any case, "Jim's a nigger and wouldn't understand the reasons for it, and how it's the custom in Europe" (278). Tom denies Jim a literary sensibility and thus excludes him as a protagonist in this fiction. Both white boys reserve metaphor for themselves, abandoning Jim to the shackles of metonymy. Indeed, Tom says that this "was the best fun he ever had in his life"; so much has he enjoyed the adventure of "freeing" Jim that he would love to keep it up for another eighty years and thus win literary fame. As Huck remarks about Tom, "And he said it would make us all celebrated that had a hand in it" (285).

Although up to now literary imagining has enabled compassion for another person, in Tom's case it becomes a dangerous aestheticism. Tom's elaborate stories come at Jim's expense, prolonging his enslavement and humiliation. By living life as literature, Tom and Huck celebrate their freedom for creativity while Jim remains locked up in the shed. The symmetry achieved by Huck and Jim on the raft is undone—or perhaps it was only a momentary fiction. It was possible as a brief social secession on a vessel heading down the Mississippi.

Tom's games are exposed only when Aunt Polly arrives as a deus ex machina and forces Tom to confess that Miss Watson had died two months earlier, after setting Jim free: "She was ashamed she ever was going to sell him down the river, and *said* so; and she set him free in her will." So when Huck asks him why he devised this elaborate scheme to liberate an already freed Jim, Tom responds that he did if for the sake of fiction: "Why I wanted the *adventure* of it" (316). Literary sensitivity, so crucial in establishing channels of communication between friends, is here transformed into a cruel aesthetic ideology—art for art's sake rather than for the friend's sake.

Tom lies in order to elaborate a narrative. He prolongs Jim's enslavement to tell a story of imprisonment and escape. Huck himself realizes the dilemma of the literary exercise: at the end of the novel he declares that "if I'd a knowed what a trouble it was to make a book I wouldn't a tackled it and ain't agoing to no more" (320). So rather than return with Aunt Polly, who wants to adopt and "sivilize" him, he flees west, inevitably to tell more stories and collect material for another book.

Fiction then can both sharpen sensitivity and desensitize us. Fictionality, so central to the development of an empathic understanding, as Elizabeth Costello notes, can take on its own momentum, often at the cost of human affections. This double tendency of narrative, to free and to hurt, goes back to the Homeric poems. In a brief exchange with Hector in the *Iliad*, Helen, blaming herself as the cause of the conflict and calling herself a "bitch," adds an astonishing insight about poetry and suffering: "Zeus," she says, "planted a killing doom within us both, / so even for generations still unborn / we will live in song" (1990, 6.423–26).[80] She suggests here that the gods incited Paris to elope with Helen, causing the great suffering that ensued from this act, in order to create the pleasure of the story for humans and immortals alike. And this sentiment is repeated in book 8 of the *Odyssey*, where Odysseus, as a guest of the peaceful and hypercivilized Phaeacians, listens to the blind minstrel, Demodocus, recount the tale of Troy's sacking. Moved to tears by hearing his own story converted to art, Odysseus says, "That was all gods' work, weaving ruin there / so it should make a song for men to come" (8.618–20)! And coming millennia later, are we not grateful to read the *Iliad* and the *Odyssey*, though indifferent to the human anguish that inspired them? Don't we, too, in identifying with Huck, come to appreciate our own humanity and liberalism by witnessing Jim's degradation?

The historian Herodotus recognized that the human propensity for narrative could be unsympathetic to the subjects of that narrative because there was an element of deception to all stories. While traveling through Egypt he discovered that Helen had never gone to Troy. The vessel carrying her and Paris to Troy was blown off course and moored in Egypt. Helen herself remained there while a phantom (*eidolon*), fashioned by the gods, made the journey to Troy with Paris. So the Greeks and Trojans slaughtered each other over a ghost: "The Trojans did not *have* Helen to give back and, when they spoke the truth, the Greeks did not believe." But all of this was part of the "plan" laid out by the "Divine" to make manifest the destruction of the Trojans for their wrongdoings (Herodotus 1987, 2.120).

Herodotus was referring to an alternative, but marginalized, version of the Helen story. Given voice originally by the archaic poet Stesichorus (640–555 BCE), it created a double Helen, one real, the other a simulacrum. Herodotus was the first major writer since Stesichorus to give credence to this tradition by locating the actual Helen in Egypt (for until then her whereabouts had not been made clear). Interestingly, he claims that Homer, the author of the popular and authorized version of the Trojan War, was familiar with this history of doubleness. He explains: "I think Homer knew the tale: but inasmuch as it was not so suitable for epic poetry as the other, he used the latter and consciously abandoned the one here told" (Herodotus 1987, 2.116). In other words, Homer remained silent over this deception because it would have undermined the grand sweep of his story: men slaughtering each other over the most beautiful woman in the world is the stuff of epic. The alternative version—human butchery over a phantom—does not sell books. So people suffer to make the tale possible. And we are mesmerized by these accounts even while we sympathize with the suffering souls.

Our capacity to empathize with another person may be based on the human adaptation for fiction, the ability to substitute one tale for another. But this metaphorical faculty, which allows us to stand with the friend, can—because of the distancing effect of fiction—force us to pull away from her so as to tell her story. The fiction-making process is twofold: first, the imagination allows us access to another's soul, and then the fabrication of a narrative demands that we take a step back. In Hesiod's *Theogony* (written between 750 and 650 BCE) the Muses say that they know "how to tell lies that pass for truth" (1983, l. 27). We embellish while we empathize. Storytelling, in short, necessitates faith and fabrication.

So does friendship. But this dialogue between fact and feint intersects with the dialectic between sameness and difference. Aristotle says the friend is another self, which suggests that in seeking out a friend we accept part of what is different. Aziz becomes an extension of Fielding, Charles of Henry, the British soldier of the German infantryman, Moscóv-Selím of the Greek narrator, Jim of Huck—all striving for comradeship against the flames billowing around them.

2

MOURNING BECOMES FRIENDSHIP

> Yet perhaps it is the dead, not forgetfulness,
> who return to collect pictures we hold of them,
> as if, like damp photos pressed face to face,
> we pull random images from each other
> when we separate, carrying them till we die.
> —DERREK HINES, *GILGAMESH*

Literature has welcomed friendship. Yet paradoxically authors often kill the friend. Ever since the *Epic of Gilgamesh*, written between 2000 BCE and 1700 BCE, the friend inevitably dies, a pattern that gives the literature on friendship an elegiac tone.[1] Why is this so? Why do poems, novels, and short stories end on the battlefield, the grave, the pyre, or at the memorial service?

From the perspective of narrative death is more fascinating to write and read about than life. The writer kills off the friend to tell a story, particularly a tale of failure. All happy friendships are the same but an unhappy friendship is worthy of poetry and novels. The passing of a life allows the author, narrator, and reader to engage in a diagnosis of and resurrection of that life. But this act of remembering and reconstituting exposes the very vulnerable position of friendship in society. It is the one affiliation that cannot be. Being neither marriage, nor kinship, nor profession, it straddles a world of identities (gender, religion), utilitarian values (work), and productive relationships (marriage).

The death of the friend then serves a double duty in literature. It occasions a sustained reflection on the vicissitudes of relationships as well as testifying to these vicissitudes themselves. In other words, it acts as a tool for looking into the fragility of a social institution as well as illustrating this fragility. Mourning becomes friendship because the survivor laments the loss of a bond and also acknowledges that bond's original evanescence. This is what makes the friendship elegy much more poignant and bitter than other elegies. It mourns something that is short lived, often a product of youth.

But it is not all about the end of life. At the most basic level the friendship elegy opens up a channel of communication with the dead. The mourner goes to the underworld and, in the confines of the text, returns to talk about that world's secrets. In antiquity only a few heroes were able to come back alive from Hades: Gilgamesh, Odysseus, Orpheus, Theseus, Heracles, and Aeneas.[2] The elegy, both ancient and modern, turns the dead friend into a sojourner into Hades who then initiates the survivor into the mysteries of life and death. The friendship elegy sings of a *nekuia*, a descent into the underworld. It is a lament, of course. But it is also as much about the living as the dead, allowing a dialogue between those who still walk the earth and those who have departed. The elegy gives voice to the necromantic character of human society. Whereas all other creatures obey the laws of vitality and a cycle of recurrence—ignorant of their mortality—we follow in the footsteps of the dead, giving them authority over our lives.[3]

Love and Death in the Ancient World

The lament intoned by Gilgamesh for Enkidu illustrates that the elegy for the friend is as old as poetic composition. Perhaps it points to the genesis of poetry itself—a paradox of sorts—that life begins with death. Indeed, it can be said that the origins of certain arts, such as architecture, dance, song, are funerary.[4] So it is not an accident that this ancient poetry should sing about mortality and friendship and not, say, about commerce or marriage. That the earliest surviving epic should deal with comradeship indicates how crucial cooperative actions and thinking were for the foundations of communal life.[5]

But the epic also touches on the ambiguity of close association. Gilgamesh is troubled by strange dreams during which he falls in love with a human form and embraces it as though it were a woman. His mother, listening to his complaints, foresees that he will find a "partner," a true companion:

> Your falling in love with it, your caressing it like a woman,
> Means there will come to you a strong one,
> A companion who rescues a friend.
> He will be mighty in the land, strength will be his,
> Like the force of heaven so mighty will be his strength.
> You will fall in love with him and caress him like a woman.
> He will be mighty and rescue you time and time again.
> —*Gilgamesh*, I, ll. 268–74

Eventually Gilgamesh meets Enkidu, who has in fact been civilized from a wild state by a harlot, after a week of copulation. Interestingly, the two young men engage in a wrestling match outside a bridal chamber that Gilgamesh wins—introducing here the familiar trope of the fight in friendship that continues through the Annie Proulx's story, "Brokeback Mountain." To seal their companionship "they kissed each other and made friends" (II, l. 115).[6]

What does it mean that they kiss or that Gilgamesh falls in love with Enkidu and caresses him like a woman? Were they lovers, fellow combatants, adventurers, kindred spirits, or blood brothers? It is difficult to tell because the cuneiform texts bear little information about male-male love.[7] On the one hand, both heroes are manly men, possessing great courage, physical strength, and sexual prowess. Yet they derive their emotional and erotic satisfaction exclusively from each other. Enkidu shows no interest in the harlot, Shamhat, and Gilgamesh spurns the voluptuous Ishtar after he meets Enkidu.

Shamhat herself describes Gilgamesh to Enkidu in seductive language, as if she expected him to be attracted to Gilgamesh: "Look at him, gaze upon his face. / He is radiant with virility, manly vigor is his, / The whole of his body is seductively gorgeous" (I, ll. 235–238). Gilgamesh and Enkidu desire each other. Yet, rather than being brutes, as Shamhat assumes, they show tenderness to one another.[8] As Shamhat describes it to Enkidu, Gilgamesh recognizes that "he was yearning for one to know his heart, a friend" (I, l. 214). Gilgamesh, in turn, dreams of caressing Enkidu, holding him like a bride. Their bond might strike modern readers as unorthodox.

But it should be remembered that in stratified societies, where women are segregated from public life, the most meaningful and emotional relationships often take place between men. So it is with these two heroes.

Scholars have noted that the original text suggests a highly erotic relationship. The wrestling contest, for instance, that clinches their friendship is sexually suggestive. Gilgamesh and Enkidu, much like David and Jonathan, Patroclus and Achilles, assume spouse-like roles.[9] When Enkidu dies, Gilgamesh covers the face of his friend "like a bride."

His lament borrows from the feminine discourse of mourning. First Gilgamesh calls on the natural world to weep for his friend, then on those people around him: "Here me, O young men, listen to me, / Hear me, o elders of [Uruk], listen to me! / I mourn my friend, Enkidu" (VIII, ll. 41–43). Then in a manner typical of lament, both ancient and modern, he addresses Enkidu directly using metaphors from the natural world:

> O Enkidu my friend, swift wild donkey, mountain onager,
> panther of the steppe,
> You who stood by me when we climbed the mountain
>
> .   .   .   .
>
> What now is this sleep that has seized you?
> Come back to me! You hear me not.
> —*Gilgamesh*, VIII, ll. 49–55

He begins to tear at his hair and rip off his fine clothes, gestures of mourning we see also in Homer and the Hebrew Bible. He also promises to erect a statue of Enkidu, an aesthetic memorial to the departed mate.

But this monument does not suffice. The death of his friend causes Gilgamesh, the fearless hero, to dread death itself. So he goes on a long quest for immortality, wanting especially to find Utanapishtim, the survivor of the flood. The friend's passing inspires Gilgamesh to contemplate human transience.[10] This should not surprise us for the self recognizes itself when reflecting on the other, friendship becoming a process of mutual acknowledgment.

In his search for Utanapishtim Gilgamesh comes across many wise people, until he arrives at a tavern on the edge of the earth. When the tavern keeper asks him why such a renowned figure should be wandering the earth, looking so wan and weathered, he answers that he would not be roaming the wilds were it not for Enkidu's death:

> Enkidu, whom I so loved, who went with me through every hardship,
> The fate of mankind has overtaken him.
> Six days and seven nights I wept for him,
> I would not give him up for burial
>
> . . . .
>
> Enkidu, my friend, whom I loved, is turned into clay!
> —*Gilgamesh*, X, ll. 56–69

After hearing Gilgamesh's woeful tale, the tavern keeper delivers her wise advice, one of the most celebrated sections of the epic:

> Gilgamesh, wherefore do you wander?
> The eternal life you are seeking you shall not find.
> When the gods created mankind,
> They established death for mankind,
> And withheld eternal life for themselves.
> —*Gilgamesh*, X, ll. 77–81

She introduces here one of the most familiar themes in ancient literature, and, certainly, of Greek writing—the impassable line between the human and the divine. Since we will all die, she tells him, our only choice is pleasure in life itself: food, dance, children, and spouse. "This, then, is the work of mankind" (X, l. 75). This injunction of carpe diem, she suggests, is the sole response to the slumber of death. But Gilgamesh is inconsolable. "What are you saying, tavern keeper?" he asks desperately. "I am heartsick for my friend. . . . I am heartsick for Enkidu" (X, ll. 92–96).

It is significant that Gilgamesh finds the truth about death from a human being rather than from an immortal. Yet, death is the only area where mortals have more expertise than the gods,[11] a fact that hardly causes rejoicing. After discovering the secret of life in death, Gilgamesh comes to another insight, namely that friendship is a dialectic between self and the other; and from this dialogue comes (self-)knowledge.

Does the friend have to die for us to solve the mystery of life itself? This is a fascinating tension that the *Epic of Gilgamesh* proposes. Indeed, the epic describes many of the emotional and ideological conflicts that render friendship an ambiguous relationship. On the one hand, the two friends are equal partners. In fact, when Gilgamesh's mother adopts Enkidu, they become brothers, an act suggesting either that they are incorporated into the kinship network or that friendship is understood as kinship. But this is socially troublesome for it smudges the lines between family and non-family that subsequent texts, such as Faulkner's *Absalom, Absalom*, try unsuccessfully to redefine: you are my brother, you are my friend, I want to marry you, and I hate you.

Yet the heroes come from two different cultural realms. Gilgamesh, as a founder and ruler of Uruk, is half divine, while Enkidu is a wild man. In early versions of the poem, Enkidu is presented as Gilgamesh's servant. Their friendship is thus sealed by emotional symmetry yet torn apart by social asymmetry. This conflict between egalitarianism and stratification is played out in their attraction for one another. On the face of it, both heroes display stereotypical masculine traits—aggression, competitiveness, and bulging sexuality. Yet, after they meet, they lose interest in women. Their spouse-like union, however, puts them into direct conflict with the normative gender roles of Mesopotamian society, which conceived of sexuality as a hierarchy of the active male and passive female.[12] By endowing the heroes with women-like characteristics, the poem renders them unsteady, casting them as both male and female simultaneously.

The instability of their friendship is worth further notice as it alludes to the special relationship between literature and friendship that the *Epic of Gilgamesh* established. First, it illustrates the vanguard tendency of poetry, even in antiquity, to penetrate forbidden areas. Second, it points to the same tendency of friendship itself. Both poetry and friendship stand inside and outside of communal standards. They are, in fact, companions in their own right, partners in taboo. And this is why, perhaps, poetry ends up killing the friend. The epic shows that friendship is an enterprise of bringing two unlike people together. Yet, by having the friend die, it also reveals the unsustainability of friendship. We spend the rest of our lives, like Gilgamesh, looking for that lost half. Gilgamesh knows that in losing Enkidu he loses a part of himself. "Shall I too not lie down like him, / And never get up forever and ever?" (X, ll. 70–71). In undertaking his quest for immortality, he wants perhaps less to live forever than to recover the self that has been severed from him.

The epic does not state, as modern literature does, that the friend dies because friendship itself is an ambiguous relationship. But it strings together ambivalence, friendship, and death into a bracelet of cause and effect. The resigned words of the tavern keeper don't really soothe Gilgamesh, his only response being that he is "heartsick for Enkidu." Is he heartbroken because he has discovered the finality of death, that Enkidu will turn to dust? Or is it because he realizes that their comradeship didn't fit into reigning social roles? Is he lamenting in essence that he wanted Enkidu as a "lover" but could only have him as a brother?

David in the book of Samuel finds himself in a similar predicament. When he learns that his friend Jonathan has been killed in battle along with his father, Saul, he is heartbroken because he had sworn a bond of ritual friendship with him: "Then Jonathan and David made a covenant, because he loved him as his own soul. And Jonathan stripped himself of the robe that was upon him, and gave it to David, and his garments, even his sword, and to this bow, and to this girdle" (1 Samuel 18:1–4). The covenant between the prince, Jonathan, and his vassal, David, who was once a shepherd boy, establishes a bond of equality between them. The superior and the subordinate become one when Jonathan announces that "he loved David as his own soul."

Scholars who have investigated the original Hebrew find the language of these passages eroticized. Susan Ackerman, for instance, interprets the section to mean that Jonathan loved David in a way a woman would love a man and that David returned that love (2005, 192). The intensity of their relationship comes out particularly in David's lament over the death of Jonathan. David "took hold on his clothes, and rent them; and likewise all the men that were with him" (2 Samuel 1:11). He then uttered that notorious cry: "I am distressed for thee my brother Jonathan: very pleasant hast thou been unto me: thy love to me was wonderful, passing the love of women" (2 Samuel 1:26). He freely returned Jonathan's love and found it marvelous. Indeed, David sees this bond as superior to the one with his wife, Michal, his association with Jonathan superseding his conjugal tie.[13] If this is the case, then we have a violation of Semitic gender laws.[14] At the very least, the David-Jonathan relationship does not conform to assumptions about love, affection, and gender. The friend's demise spells the end not just of the friendship but also of the self because friendship represents an attempt to overcome life's social, ideological, and sexual divisions.

Tragically, the hero learns the meaning of life and of friendship only with death. So the only answer seems for the hero to concentrate on a resplendent life on earth.

When Achilles learns of Patroclus's death, he is overcome by a "black cloud of grief." Like Gilgamesh, he engages in public displays of anguish. Falling to the ground, he claws at dirt and soot to foul his "handsome face" and war shirt. He tears at his hair, "defiling it with his own hands" (1990, 18.23–29). Finally he lets out a cry so wrenching that his mother, Thetis, a sea nymph, hears it in the depths of the ocean. When she arrives to console him, Achilles weeps, "My dear comrade's dead— / Patroclus—the man I loved beyond all other comrades, / loved as my own life" (1990, 18.93–96).

Exhausted from grief, Achilles falls asleep only to see Patroclus in a dream, complaining that he cannot pass the gates of Hades unburied. Patroclus also reminds him that godlike though he is, Achilles is still a mortal. But he has one request of Achilles, that their bones be buried in one pot: "So now let a single urn, the gold two-handled urn / your noble mother gave you, hold our bones—together" (1990, 23.109–111).[15] In this very stirring scene, the urn, bearing the bones of two fallen comrades, symbolizes their inseparability. Mortal life, like happiness itself, is fleeting. But friendship, the human attempt to bridge social contradictions, seems to continue after the last breath.

So, with the friend's parting, Achilles, like Gilgamesh, senses the irrevocability of his own end. As he tries to embrace his friend one last time, "to take joy in the tears that numb the heart," his hands seize air and the ghost disappears like a "wisp of smoke," much like the shade of Odysseus's mother as he tries to embrace her in Hades. With the shadow of death closing in upon him, Achilles lets out a lament that in its language and imagery is as touching as the one Andromache intones for Hector:

> So even in Death's strong house there is something left,
> a ghost, a phantom—true, but no real breath of life.
> All night long the ghost of stricken Patroclus
> hovered over me, grieving, sharing warm tears,
> telling me, point by point, what I must do.
> Marvelous—like the man to the life.
> —1990, 23.122–27

Achilles then lays the body on the pyre, cuts off one of his own red locks, places it in Patroclus's hand, and lights the fire, stumbling around the flames, "choked with sobs." The funeral itself is followed by games in honor of Patroclus, which, like Enkidu's statue, commemorate the fallen hero. But they also lead to a bitter discovery, as was the case for Gilgamesh, that the deceased has entered a world with which there is no (nonliterary) communication. The disappearance of Patroclus's ghost into a tendril of smoke visually reinforces this. But it also exposes another truth—the imminent defeat of Achilles. Thetis has foretold that her son would die shortly after slaying Hector. "Even for me, I tell you, / death and the strong force of fate are waiting" (1990, 21.123–24). Being the first tragic hero, Achilles has a choice: "If I hold out here and I lay siege to Troy, / my journey home is gone, but my glory never dies" (1990, 9.500–501). But if he returns, his glory perishes, but he will die of old age. He chooses a short, magnificent life.

The killing of Patroclus, of course, becomes an opportunity for Achilles to display his unmatched prowess on the battlefield, creating a "total war" (1990, 21.437). In book 11, he rushes headlong against the Trojans, a human tank, obliterating all in his path, even picking a fight with the River Scamander, becoming, as Ahab would millennia later, "madness maddened" (Melville 1956, 142). He is obsessed here with his role as killing machine, as if he were just one function, one cell. And he fulfills this mission with unsparing savagery.

Yet, after returning from the battlefield, and coming upon the body of his comrade, he reverts to his tenderness. Patroclus is the only nonkin person that Achilles cherishes. He has no other intimates. The light of their bond shines only on the two of them, its brightness eclipsing the rest of the world.[16] Not even the captured Briseis, who was taken from him by Agamemnon and who was the cause of Achilles's wrath, commands the same affection. Indeed, when Patroclus had come earlier to him in distress over losses the Argives were sustaining, Achilles embraced him fondly "like a baby girl, a baby running after her mother / begging to be picked up, and she tugs her skirts" (1990, 16.7–9).

That this tenderness is eroticized is beyond doubt, captured also by the Sosias Painter on the interior of a red-figure cup (510–500 BCE). Patroclus, with his legs spread out and genitals exposed, turns away from his wound, as Achilles, crouched between his friend's legs, wraps bandages around his left arm. This eroticism goes beyond the power nexus of the Hellenic pederastic love by which one member is dominant while the other is passive.[17]

Of course, as in *Gilgamesh*, the two friends are socially asymmetrical. Patroclus, the older of the two, is Achilles's attendant, cooking and taking care of the horses. Even though Achilles is superior in status and military prowess, upon Patroclus's death he becomes his friend's servant, adopting a woman's role. The language of his lament, paralleling Andromache's dirge, assumes a feminine voice. Achilles turns into Patroclus's Andromache. Indeed, Homer represents their friendship as having the emotional and physical intensity of husband and wife.

The nature of their bond was debated even in antiquity. In Aeschylus's play *The Myrmidons*, for instance, which survives only in fragments, the friends are portrayed as lovers, "speaking of the devout union of the thighs." This view is further developed in Plato's *Symposium*, in which the various guests discourse on love. Phaedrus, for instance, says that the gods sent Achilles to the Isles of the Blest because "he dared to stand by his lover Patroclus and avenge him, even after he had learned from his mother that he would die if he killed Hector" (Plato 1989, 180a).[18] In other words, Achilles sought to avenge the death of his lover though he was the *eromenos* (the object of love) as opposed to the *erastes* (the dominant pursuer of love). The gods were delighted, according to Phaedrus, that an *eromenos* would seek to die for an *erastes*. According to the fourth-century Athenian politician Aeschines (389–314 BCE), the relationship was pederastic, though, he claimed, Homer refrained from naming it as such. Xenophon, on the other hand, believed that Achilles and Patroclus were devoted but virtuous friends. In the *Symposium*, Xenophon writes that Homer "pictures us Achilles looking upon Patroclus not as the object of his passion but as a comrade, and in this spirit signally avenging his death" (1922, 8.31).

Ultimately, it does not really matter whether they were pederastic lovers, reciprocal sexual partners, or chaste friends. What is relevant is how their relationship overlapped these categories. In this Patroclus and Achilles turned into paradigmatic friends: trying to bridge the demands of a world that did not, and still does not, understand their love. The bond of friendship is socially suspect because it can't be restrained by law (as marriage) or by blood (as kinship). Perhaps this is the reason why the friend dies. And poetry tries to exceed the perimeters of the community by imagining a relationship that is untypical but marvelous. Friendship, as such, incorporates the ancient tension between our need for limits and our desire to break out of them. It is this tension perhaps that renders friendship so evanescent.

Death Is for Mortals

We all die, the tavern keeper says to Gilgamesh. This sentiment, *et moriemur*, is the oldest concept people have devised to deal with the end of life.[19] It unites all humans in one fate—the one "advantage" they have over the immortals. But heroes confront this fate very early in life: the end of friendship marks the end of life. Or we could put it in another way: the nearness of death makes friendship intense and the intensity of friendship brings death near.[20]

Both the *Epic of Gilgamesh* and the *Iliad* describe martial societies, which celebrate war as a forum for men to demonstrate their military prowess. They use conflict as a trope to reflect on the brittleness of friendship. We see this device in the course of history repeatedly, not least in the medieval French romance *The Song of Roland*. Written anonymously at the end of the eleventh century about a battle between the Saracens and Charlemagne's army in 778, the poem also focuses on the friendship between Roland and Oliver. In the male world of combat it is this relationship that is emphasized rather than, say, that between Roland and Aude, his fiancée and Oliver's sister. Bound by an exclusivity that characterizes the love between ancient fighters, this friendship becomes the center of their affection. Linked like these heroes by the social inequality of the lord (Roland) to this vassal (Oliver), their friendship is intense and self-absorbed. The two men express the ennobling love that characterized the Carolingian court, a love that was deployed as a social and political gesture.[21]

The death of Oliver halfway through the poem gives Roland the opportunity to display grief grandly. He affirms his status as noble by lamenting and fainting, as does Charlemagne himself when he learns of Roland's death. Mourning here takes place on an epic scale. Seeing his friend wounded on the ground, Roland dismounts and rushes to him: "Sir, my companion, did you mean it that way; / Look, I am Roland, that loved you all my days" (Anon. 1957, ll. 2000–2001). Oliver, however, barely recognizes him. But he manages a prayer, asking God to bless France and Roland "above all men" before he dies. At the sight of Oliver's head sinking toward the ground, Roland weeps for him. "No man on earth felt ever such distress" (l. 2023). He faints.

> The County Roland, seeing his peers lie dead,
> And Oliver, who was his dearest friend,
> Begins to weep for ruth and tenderness;
> Out of his cheeks the color all has fled,
> He cannot stand, he is so deep distressed,
> He swoops to earth, he cannot help himself.
> —*Song of Roland*, ll. 2016–21

But, like the other two epic adventurers, Roland also senses his own mortality in the death of his comrade-in-arms. "Now Roland feels he is at death's door" (l. 2059), a phrase repeated two other times. Oliver's death presses on him in a figurative and real way. It announces his own demise; at the same time, the loss of his dearest friend makes life unlivable. Roland, like Achilles, mourns his own death in advance, with Oliver (like Patroclus) serving as a surrogate of his own anxiety. When Roland himself dies, the French emperor drops upon his nephew's body in great distress: "Barons and knights all weep and make their moan, / Full twenty thousand swoon to the ground for woe" (ll. 2415–16). Charlemagne stays up all night, lamenting the deaths of the two warriors.

These emotions and gestures, denoting passionate friendship, are part of the rhetorical tradition of the chanson de geste rather than simply manifestations of inner feeling.[22] They are meant to emphasize the ennobling love of aristocrats in the absence of women. There is no Isolde to steal the knight's attention.[23] The glorification of male-male bonding here is part of a greater medieval poetic paradigm that relegated male-female bonds to the margins of rhetorical concern in contrast to the tradition of *fin'amor* that idealized them as the supreme form of social relations. Sexual desire has little place in medieval friendship poetry. This tradition takes pain to place male bonding on the opposite pole of erotic love, seeing it almost as the alternative.[24]

We Make War So as to Make Friends

The Song of Roland celebrates a soldier society where armed conflict and the military life forge tight links among men. Wage war to win friends, seems to be the message. Although we tend to think that war destroys friendship,[25] actually the opposite is true. The horror of warfare, the untold privations, and the absence of women give rise to tenderness and devotion, eroticism and self-sacrifice, and, above all, to the recognition of the frailty of the male body and its physical and emotional links with others. War binds men together in a logical circle.

When confronting the barbarity of an arsenal, the delicate soldier seeks a mate. In Stratis Myrivilis's best-selling novel *Life in the Tomb*, based on the author's journal as soldier in the Balkan conflict during World War I, the narrator, who will be incinerated in the trenches, refers to the merciless "mechanisms that warfare opposes to the soldier's body." As he prepares for the battle's final campaign he observes that it is not thirty thousand Greeks fighting thirty thousand Germans and Bulgarians but sixty thousand "human bodies fighting countless mechanisms of steel" (Myrivilis [1923–24] 2003, 326). Confronting death in the trenches by the thousands, the young men discover strange bonds between themselves, which perhaps would not have emerged outside the conflict zone.

The recurring sentiment of World War I diaries, letters, and memoirs is that comradeship made life in the dugouts bearable. Men nursed and fed injured soldiers; they bathed together in ponds and rivers, and clasped each other in the wintry nights under one blanket. They were haunted by the sensation of dying buddies in their arms and the lingering final kiss.[26] These episodes may not be unique in themselves, as the scene of Achilles tending to the wounds of Patroclus in the Sosias Cup demonstrates. Many World War I poems featured men bandaging their mates, juxtaposing male beauty with war's awful mangling.[27] Yet, soldiers themselves considered these experiences so profound that they wrote about them en masse. Here are two examples, the first by Raymond Heywood and the second by Robert Nichols:

> I bend above him and his tired smile
> Will linger in my heart until the end . . .
> *O God! 'tis only they who loved a friend*
> *Can understand*
>
> O my comrade,
> My comrade, that you could rest
> Your tired body on mine! That your head might be laid—
> Fallen and heavy—upon this my breast!
>
> —Taylor 1989, 95, 99

What is significant about these poems is less the emotions they convey than the morality they are written against, that is, the inflexible masculinity of the early twentieth century.[28] Under the ever-present threat of destruction, eroticism, even sexual intimacy, become conceivable. In times of war, Paul Fussell writes, drawing on lines from W. H. Auden, even "the crudest kind of positive affections between persons seems extraordinarily beautiful." The gender of the person one loves does not matter much (1975, 271).

War here acts like art, waving a magic wand over men, making ordinary experiences seem extraordinary and vice versa. It breaks down the barriers between soldiers, intensifying their emotional and physical consciousness. Same-sex contact becomes something to be imagined and realized because the threat of mortality normalizes male intimacy. At the same time, however, outside the combat zone the lines between the acceptable and unacceptable remain rigid. This is why the love among soldiers seems more disturbing than male homosexuality.[29] Intimacy among fighters, who are thought to be heterosexual, can't be labeled, contained, and silenced as sexual deviance. Although the friend goes to war as father, husband, or brother, he adopts new roles in the field. The husband becomes a tender "wife" to a dying mate, much like Achilles, blurring the line between the conventional and unconventional. But, because he is a father, the friend can't be dismissed as queer.

Not only erotic but also social walls come crumbling down in war. The texts from World War I show that men unsurprisingly formed unions across class lines. "It is in war," the Third Earl of Shaftesbury writes, "that the knot of fellowship is closest drawn" (Shaftesbury 1999, 52). Superiors and subordinates often linked hands, in defiance of the stiff social stratification back home. On September 15, 1916, an officer, Anthony French, cradled his dying friend, Bert, a recruit, in his arms. Left alone in Wimbledon on Armistice Day, French writes Bert a poem, idealizing his dead comrade's beauty and youth: "One happy hour to be / With you alone, friend of my own, / That would be heaven to me."[30] These lines, expressing affection that vaults over the trenches of class, are indicative of the crossover nature of the attachment.

It is telling that these relationships, formed under the whistling threat of the artillery, rarely continue outside of the barracks. It is as if war, acting itself like a literary trope, enabled men to imagine something that was impossible in real life. Looking into the friendships among men in the Israeli army, Danny Kaplan discovers that affinities formed by soldiers exceeded the emotional and physical connections among civilians. This type of combat fraternity was heroic and brittle at the same time. Men found themselves crying, hugging, and kissing each other in ways that they would not have done outside of the military unit.[31] One of his informants captures the situation succinctly with words reminiscent from the book of Samuel: "At this stage you become very close together in the unit. You have more time to sit and chat. You get to know them better and you love them more. This is the famous love among soldiers, which is as much a mystery as the love of women" (Kaplan 2006, x).

But why do these relationships inevitably stop at the camp's gate? Is it because the outside world is uneasy with friendships that approximate the love of men for women? Or is it because these unions, inspired by the imminence of death, normalize same-sex intimacy? War becomes hospitable to friendship in the way that literature does—simultaneously destructive and creative. War, of course, is an extraordinary occurrence, forcing men in their prime to witness the perishing of boyish beauty. It is not unexpected that virility in an all-male enclave should manifest itself toward other men.

In another powerful scene from Myrivilis's *Life in the Tomb*, a few soldiers from the island of Lesbos go on an outing in a forest near the encampment, located in Macedonia. With no experience of a northern forest, the men have nothing to compare it with other than with a dive into the ocean. Through hyperbolic writing, Myrivilis defamiliarizes their "swim" in the woods: "The instant we entered it we were painfully crushed—by its bulk more than anything else" (86). Amazed and confused by the forbidding canopy, the perfumes of wild resin, and the "insane" sounds maddening with their power, the soldiers try to melt into the forest's mystery. Indeed, it is spring and everywhere they pick up the signs and scents of "arboreal concupiscence." The luxuriant soul of the woods "drips upon them like semen ejaculated from the tree-trunks"; the "erotically entwined branches" are covered with mating birds and animals, all responding to some "endurably gratifying sensuality" (91). Aroused by this fecundity, the soldiers act like satyrs, indulging in dirty stories and obscene gestures. Their "inhibited instincts" given free rein, they wrestle with one another, knocking one of their mates onto the ground, removing his trousers and "festooning" his testicles with nettles. Suddenly he jumps up, kicks off his shorts, spreads his legs, gyrates his belly and buttocks, and "clasps his erect penis in his fist and begins to dance in a climax of sexual excitement" (92).

This vivid scene captures the impossibility of their situation. While the woods hum with the sounds of copulation, they return to the dreary and damp dugouts. Whereas nature carries on the process of reproduction, indifferent to the men's plight, their task is to kill or die. Being seems to burst forward but death thrusts downward to the grave. Inevitably life's procreative energy, which propels the men, is released in an orgy of gratification. Same-sex intimacy here becomes natural, so to speak, responding to a mysterious urge to survive in the trenches of industrialized destruction. Men ejaculate semen because they will perish. Even though this fluid is wasted on the ground, its secretion represents both a protest against death, say, of the narrator, and an act of male camaraderie.[32]

The external world is understandably made uneasy by this intimacy. Or perhaps it can accept it only under the guise of combat. War provides the stimulus to friendship only to destroy it. The survivor feels intimations of his own mortality in the urn that contains his mate's bones. But who has died and who is about to die is not really clear. For the friend's demise marks the end of not only the other but also of the self, that is, of the self in union with the other. If a person relates to his friend as to himself, as Aristotle claims, then the death of the friend and the discovery of this separation ushers a whole life of commemoration and recollection. He remembers a time before the divide by erecting statues, holding games, or composing poetry. Friendship sings an elegy for the "utopia" of war.

Perhaps the texts about war show that our thinking about friendship is often in memoriam. These poems and novels normalize this situation beyond the battlefield. By turning war into a metaphor, they show that death and friendship are unexpectedly intimate companions. When we reflect on friendship we remember what has been severed.[33] We recognize the friendship, in other words, once it is over. We become conscious of it when we think of ourselves no longer as one but actually as one half in search of the other part.

In Search of the Other Half

No text exemplifies this insight better than Montaigne's essay on friendship. Written in 1563 after the death of his friend Etienne de La Boétie, it tries to make sense of the loss, combining personal experience and philosophical introspection. Montaigne was thirty at the time, and trapped in a cold marriage. Without meaningful love, he spent much of his life trying to commemorate his friend. "Since the day I lost him, I only drag on a weary life. And the very pleasures that come my way, instead of consoling me, redouble my grief for his loss" (Montaigne 1958, 197). He cites a line from Horace: "Why should I be ashamed or exercise control, mourning so dear a soul," and claims that there "is no action or thought in which I do not miss him, as indeed he would have missed me" (198). La Boétie is his other self: "We went halves in everything" (197).

Montaigne understands friendship as one indivisible unit where the two souls "mingle and blend with each other so completely that they efface the seam that joined them" (192).[34] In this he echoes Cicero, who wrote that in friendship a man searches for a companion "whose heart's blood he may so mingle with his own that they become virtually one person instead of two" (Cicero 1971, xxi, 81). Aristotle conceived of the friend's relationship to the other as complementary. But for Montaigne the two friends meld their personalities. Critics have believed that this condition has characterized more accurately the dynamics of female rather than male friendship. Women, they contend, strive to merge with, not merely to know, the friend.[35] But Cicero and Montaigne suggest that the pursuit of seamless union is a feature of all friendship, indeed, of all human relationships, as Plato argues in the *Symposium*.

In the most celebrated section of the *Symposium*, the comedian Aristophanes lays out a theory of love as a quest for "wholeness." According to this fanciful cosmogony, human beings were completely round with two faces, one head, four hands, and two sets of sexual organs. Because these creatures threatened the authority of the gods, Zeus had them cut into two separate halves, one male and one female, to increase their number and to sap them of their strength. "Now, since their natural form had been cut in two, each one longed for its own other half, and so they would throw their arms about each other, weaving themselves together, wanting to grow together" (Plato 1989, 191b). The source of love, according to Aristophanes, lies in the human need to call back the "halves of our original nature together." Love then is that "wonderful" quality that propels humans to belong to one another and not be separated again. It conveys the state when a person mingles and melts "together with the one he loves, so that one person emerged from two" (192e).

Montaigne's understanding of friendship bridges ancient and modern forms. On the one hand, he has in mind the Platonic ideal of wholeness, when he writes of a "perfect friendship," when each person "gives himself so wholly to his friend that he has nothing left to distribute." Indeed, Montaigne adds, the friend is only sorry that he is not composed of double, triple, or quadruple selves to give to his friend (195). If his readers still don't understand, Montaigne reaches back for a biographical detail with a disarmingly simple line: "Because it was he, because it was I" (192). Yet, Aristotle could never have understood this sentence. Friendship was a product of mutual devotion to decency and virtue rather than to one's personal desires and needs. Although Montaigne believes in the connection between friendship and virtue, he can no longer presume the Aristotelian polis of interconnected citizens. Therefore he posits a modern notion of friendship as a self-validating project: "Our friendship had no other model than itself and can be compared only with itself" (193).

Such a statement would have shocked Aristotle because for him friendship was an institution enmeshed in the politics of the city. Yet Montaigne lived in a time when this no longer applied. In a sense his essay is an elegy for both his friend and for Aristotelian friendship. It is a moving portrait of a dead companion and of an institution that can no longer rely on wider social connections. In Montaigne's essay friendship begins its modern odyssey to become a noninstitutional institution. It is frail and constitutes its own self-sufficient universe, no longer an extension of a wider social cosmos. This is why perhaps the imminence of death permeates Montaigne's understanding of friendship in a way not seen in Plato, Aristotle, or Cicero.[36] Montaigne's elegiac tone suggests that he longs for a form no longer possible. And the literary tradition that follows Montaigne gives voice to this situation, namely, that friendship cannot count on social and political connections.

The death of Montaigne's friend is really the death of the self. And this death marks the start of a different friendship—as an imaginary act, a process of reconstituting and remembering. Indeed, in his essay the dual principles of literature and love, fiction and empathy come into play most strongly. If the elegy form reconstitutes the dead friend in an invented realm, we can say that Montaigne inaugurates the modern version of this elegy. His essay has as many literary as philosophical references. Montaigne does not simply mourn La Boétie, he also commemorates him through art.

To be sure, Montaigne begins his memorial with a reference to La Boé-tie's essay "On Voluntary Servitude," which, he says, had become a very influential work.[37] "Nothing of his remained except this treatise," he writes of La Boétie's text, adding that he knows no one "who can be compared with him" (188). For this reason Montaigne wishes to glorify this work, and thereby grant its writer immortality. Yet, critics doubt that La Boétie was the author, believing that Montaigne had penned it himself and as-cribed it to his mate.[38] If indeed this is true, we can say that Montaigne had physically assimilated the Aristophanic ideal friend as an indivisible entity, a communion of two people, his essay becoming a sarcophagus (the word literarily meaning flesh-eating). He was one and the same with La Boétie, the single writer of the same text, much as Achilles and Patroclus, wear-ing the same armor. By composing the essay himself and attributing it to La Boétie, Montaigne attenuates inadvertently that tension between *figura* and *amicitia*, fiction and friendship. He falsifies its authorship because he knows that friendship involves as much lying (imagining) as it does loving, writing as it does living. And from this point onward that love, reconsti-tuted in elegy form, remains in the realm of invention.

Was Montaigne's forgery an attempt to elude the division of death, al-lowing the departed friend to live in the writing of the survivor? More-over, was this deliberate misidentification his version of Gilgamesh's statue to Enkidu or Achilles's memorial games to Patroclus, a desire to elevate his friend to the realm of immortals? This is really friendship in memoriam, a union that takes its meaning through death, in which the friends are intermingled in each other's composition, like ashes held by the same urn.

We also have to ask whether self-aggrandizement fueled Montaigne's guilt. A pervasiveness of culpability differentiates his essay from previous treatments of friendship. The demise of the friend yields less intimations of mortality, as in the case of epic, than feelings of remorse at survival. The friend mourns the passing of unrealized youth, "a youth to Fortune and to Fame unknown," as Thomas Gray would say (1973, l. 18). La Boétie, like Fulke Greville's Sidney, Shelley's Keats, Gray's Christian West, and Tennyson's Arthur Hallam, becomes a modern-day Marcellus figure,[39] all examples of promise unfulfilled. Indeed, John Dryden (1631–1700) calls his friend, the poet John Oldham, who died in 1683 at the age of thirty-one, "Marcellus of our tongue" (1972, 175). Written in heroic couplets, the poem, "To the Memory of Mr. Oldham," begins by addressing the deceased himself: "Farewell, too little and too lately known, / Whom I began to think and call my own." And W. B. Yeats, enumerating the exceptional qualities ("soldier, scholar, horseman") of Major Robert Gregory, who died in Italy in World War I, ends the poem simply by asking, "What made us dream that he could comb gray hair?" ("In Memory of Major Robert Gregory"). The eroticism sparked by the imminence of death on the battlefield is normalized, becoming an everyday attraction. War turns into a literary trope for the travails of ordinary life.

The omnipresence of guilt in the survivor guarantees a different type of memorial, a commemoration not as a single act, a statue, an oration, or games, but as a continuous remembering. What informed the ancient notion of friendship was the sense of collective resignation—*et moriemur*.[40] In other words, my friend's death means that I too will die. But Montaigne puts the emphasis on the surviving self as a truncated whole, combining "la mort de soi" (death of the self) with "la mort de toi" (death of the other).[41] My friend's death means I am half dead. And I devote my life to remembering my severed half.

And this self is now seen as an autonomous being rather than as an extension of social networks or obligations. Ancient heroes experienced their friendship through protocols of behavior, rituals of exchange, and codes of mourning. Montaigne and La Boétie, on the other hand, lived to love one another. This is the meaning of their self-conscious friendship. Rather than fighting together or engaging in shared adventures, they relinquish social compulsions to be alone with each other. Upon La Boétie's death, Montaigne does not perform prescribed rituals but simply talks about his feelings. For this reason, the modern elegy is both commemoration and self-disclosure. It reveals the self as much as it extols the deceased.

Montaigne's essay manifests the emergence of a new mode of friendship, what C. S. Lewis calls a secession. According to Lewis, "Friendship . . . is enjoyed according as it is desired; it is bred, nourished, and increased only in enjoyment" (Lewis 1988, 190). Of course, there is an element of withdrawal in all friendships. Enkidu and Gilgamesh turn their backs on civilization in search of great exploits. They affirm their friendship by engaging in mutual quests. Achilles and Patroclus are comrades in arms in pursuit of glory. Their bond is also strengthened by their physical closeness. But whereas heroes may have abandoned society to perform great deeds and thereby win fame, in modern times friends remove themselves because, like Montaigne and La Boétie, they have fallen in love. They perform an affective secession. They seek, in short, emotional intimacy, a connection that is self-revelatory and inward. Of course, not all friendships have to have the emotional intensity here described by Lewis or Montaigne. There exist gradations of closeness. But both authors pose an important question: How can this intimacy be understood outside the extraordinary limits of war? Is it only through death? Is this why, in the controlled setting of civilian life, that death is indispensable to friendship? We discover love when it is gone.

Montaigne reveals himself only after his friend's passing; death gives him words. What does he say? That pithy line, "because it was he, because it was I,"[42] which has such a self-evident ring to the contemporary ear. Yet it would have struck Aristotle or Cicero, let alone Achilles and David, differently. The modern self, having become aware of its own solitude, longs for the confidence of friendship. And in this negotiation of closeness, the self opens up and seeks disclosure in return. Friendship begins to equal knowledge and vice versa.

But the dead friend cannot answer back directly. He comes, like Patroclus, in dreams, in the tales the survivor creates. Death then spells a double loss. If the modern self seeks to know the other by revelation, then who can listen to this story when the friend dies? Does death render friendship into a soliloquy, a reminiscence of a once fulfilling dialogue? This is the conundrum of modern friendship and it inspired Alfred Tennyson's "In Memoriam."

Friendship in Memoriam

Tennyson shows how transcendent male intimacy had become:

> And what delights can equal those
> That stir the spirit's inner deeps,
> When one that loves but knows not, reaps
> A Truth from one that loves and knows?
> —Tennyson, "In Memoriam,"
> XLII, 9–120

No poem captures this revelatory and epistemological approach to friendship better than "In Memoriam." Written in 1850, it commemorates the life and death of the poet's true love, Arthur Hallam, whom he met in 1829 at Cambridge but who died in Vienna in 1833. Tennyson worked on the poem for seventeen years and when it was published, it attained astonishing popular success.[43] Tennyson, like Montaigne, devoted a long period of time to mourning. Both his experience of bereavement and the seventeen years of the poem's gestation suggest that friendship was a continuous remembering. The survivor is preoccupied with death. Writing exaggerates the period of mourning, to bring attention to the lost object of affection. But does this mean that it converts mourning into a pathology?

In his comparison between melancholia and mourning, Sigmund Freud characterizes the latter as a "reaction to the loss of a loved person, or to the loss of some abstraction which has taken the place of one, such as one's country, liberty, an ideal, and so on" (1957, 243). We expect to overcome it after a period of time. But during bereavement, we may suspend many activities of life because the ego is absorbed "by the work of mourning" (245). But in some people, he explains, the loss of the loved one produces the psychotic condition of melancholia, "a grave departure from the normal attitude to life" (243). Freud calls it a "pathological mourning," a condition that brings about "self-torment" and "self-punishment." Although the melancholic cries out for the lost object, Freud says that melancholia is brought about by the ego's self-love (252). Paradoxically, this narcissism creates "a diminution of self-regard." Thus, while in mourning the world becomes empty, in melancholia the ego itself seems poorer (247).

The protracted bereavement of Tennyson and Montaigne suggests that writing extends grief, much as Freud described, transforming it into a case of extreme melancholia. But looked at more closely, the act of recording sorrow, and then the rereading of that sorrow, creates less a Freudian disorder than a lament in the anthropological sense. Instead of an aberration from life, and an "impoverishment of [the] ego on a grand scale" (246), it represents an interpenetration of the realms of living and of the dead.

Ethnographies of the ritual lament show that women willingly induce the conditions of mourning for many years after the death, during memorials, in their visits to the gravesites, at home, or while working in the fields. In contrast to Freud's definition of normal mourning, which "impels the ego to give up the object by declaring the object to be dead" (257), lament performers continue to grieve yet without his "obsessional self-reproaches" (258). Women can "recall effortlessly almost the original intensity of their grief over the loss of a beloved person who has been dead for a considerable length of time." Any activity, from household tasks to another funeral, can become an occasion "for the continuation of the dialogue between the living and the dead." One woman from a Cretan village visited her son's grave once a week, changed the oil in the lamp, and brought new flowers all the time, performing "metrically flawless" laments.[44] That is to say, she conveyed the lament with the same force as at the time of the funeral.

With some justification anthropologists characterize these practices as performances because they are in a sense poetry of/in pain, combining aesthetics with heightened emotional content. The women themselves see the laments as a song for the dead "inspired" by pain. A folk expression, separate from the Orthodox religious tradition, the lament uses melodic conventions, stylized interjections, lyrical images, manipulation of shared metaphors, and metrical delivery.[45] It follows prescribed formal rules: an antiphonal structure (contrasts between past and present, for instance), repetition of emotive words, alliteration, assonance, and metaphor (light, spring, harvest, journey), and allusion (communication of pain through symbols).[46] In short, the laments are "artistic narratives" prized by the community. The women, depending on their own talent, appropriate these structural features along with nonverbal elements such as voice quality, rhythm, gesture, and melody.[47] Rather then being the uncontrolled ranting of the bereaved, the lament is a song that facilitates the transition from the ordinary to the extraordinary and back. It marks the entry into the realm of the spirits, a place as real for the practitioners as that of the living.

Like folk laments, the elegy promotes a dialogue between the domains of the dead and the living. As literature, the elegy provides access to this zone of in-betweenness, a space that I have called elsewhere the *parabasis*, a connection between actuality and simulation.[48] The poetry of mourning thus converses with those who have departed, protests against their loss, while also affirming death's place in life. The performer and listener, the writer and reader, become like Gilgamesh and Odysseus, figures who enter the underworld and return to tell about their extraordinary experiences.

We should, therefore, read texts like "In Memoriam" with an understanding of both the specific literary tradition of elegy and the wider anthropological paradigm of ritual dirge. It is poetry about/in agony that makes pain more tolerable by using a high literary convention.[49] Tennyson's poem, in form and content, shows a modern conception of friendship and death. The meter and language take on a confessional tone. The recognition, for instance, that "loss is common to the race," is less a resignation than self-revelation. Indeed, ostensibly a memorial to Hallam, the poem is as much about Tennyson's own self-doubts, religious questioning, and scientific concerns. The poet asks if it is right to speak about himself in a requiem. The "la mort de soi" merges with "la mort de toi."

The elegy, as a work of art, has to follow the inner logic of its genre. And Tennyson's certainly does, being conscious of its own artfulness. Of course, all elegies, ancient and modern, are performances. Elegies and laments are recitals, converting personal bereavement into public utterance.[50] But they are not all aware of themselves as works of art. Whereas all elegists are performers, not all mourners are elegists.[51] In Tennyson we have both: the creation of art and a reflection on the creative process. The poem is scattered with references to the role poetry plays in mourning.

> For I am but an earthly Muse,
> And owning but a little art
> To lull with song an aching heart,
> And render human love his dues
> —XXXVII, 13–16

But the poet has doubts about his craft. "What hope is here for modern rhyme," Tennyson asks, to compose verses that "leave thy praises unexpress'd?" (LXXVII, 1; LXXV, 1). Although "these mortal lullabies of pain" bring relief to the writer, they hardly do justice, he believes, to the one who is gone. Can poetry really commemorate an extraordinary life, one cut off so short? What is worse, he wonders, is that the elegist profits by converting inner ache into public performance: "He loves to make parade of pain / That with his piping he may gain" (XXI, 10–11). Art's inadequacy in expressing sorrow leads to the ethical question of turning sorrow into art. Is the poet talented enough to create a fitting epitaph for a worthy friend? And by doing so, is he exploiting Hallam's death for personal gain? Who wins lasting fame from poetic apotheosis, the poet or the deceased? Tennyson's doubts touch on the relationship between literature and love: Does death make a lasting friendship possible? Do Tennyson and Hallam seal an eternal bond because of death? Does the grave transform an evanescent relationship into a prolonged imaginary process of reconstruction?

These questions also reveal an uncertainty about the friendship as well, which will become a hallmark of literary approaches to the topic in the twentieth century. Increasingly, the elegy asks: Was the relationship real? Were the emotions genuine? Is intimacy possible? Are the feelings proper for one man to have for another? Gilgamesh, Achilles, and David had no reservations in describing their friends affectionately, embracing them as if they had been women. Modern writers, by contrast, express disquiet about their love, desiring yet made uneasy by it. Montaigne, for instance, writes tenderly about his devotion to La Boétie, presenting it as purely spiritual. Although he makes clear in one misogynistic statement that women are incapable of such affection, he also condemns the "licentious Greek love," squelching any hint that such a bond existed between them (Montaigne 1958, 191).[52] He touches on the erotic ambiguity evident in the heroic friendships without confronting it. Even if friendship is revealed truth, this particular truth cannot be revealed.

Grief here becomes a substitute for the friend and offers a shield against the insinuation of sexual dissidence. "Each line reveals as much as it conceals," as the allusive language of Tennyson's poem becomes a vehicle for longing.[53] On the one hand, Tennyson takes pains to treat the love of friends as being as natural as that of the love of women.[54] But his language is often erotic, the poetic voice turning feminine and masculine in turn. Grief becomes a mistress and a wife, as in the following verses: "Tears of a widower" (XIII, 1); "O Sorrow, wilt thou live with me / No casual mistress, but a wife . . . O Sorrow wilt though rule my blood, / Be sometimes lovely like a bride" (LIX, 1–2, 5–6). Then we have these lines of unrestrained erotic, if not, sexual craving: "Dear friend, far off, by lost desire, / . . . Mine, mine, for ever, ever mine" (CXXIX, 1, 8); the repetition of the possessive pronoun emphasizes the physical custody possible only in death: "My love involves the love before; / My love is vaster passion now" (CXXX, 9–10); "Descend, and touch, and enter; hear / The wish too strong for words to name" (XCIII, 13–14). The four insistent imperatives almost harangue the dead Hallam to return, to answer a yearning that in life could not be given conscious intention. This very longing is then transmuted into the touch of the dying kiss, a traditional sign of parting:[55] "I, falling on his faithful heart / Would breathing thro' his lips impart / The life that almost dies in me" (XVIII, 14–16). But do we have here the ancient ritual of the dead or veiled sensual passion?

Both probably. Death offers in the imagination what can't occur in life. It makes friendship possible, friendship, that is to say, as commemoration. But it would be simplistic to see in these lines only a latent homosexuality, to look at the poem exclusively from the perspective of sexual orientation. The contradictory last verse should warn against reductive readings. Indeed, the entire text tries to contain as it also suffers from paradox—as in the famous line "Let love clasp Grief lest both be drown'd" (I, 9). What do these words mean? That love can or cannot grasp grief? And how can both drown? Does the speaker want love to be victorious or is he willing to have grief as his constant companion? What the poem does, however, is further complicate the conflict between death and friendship, turning *thanatos* and *philia* into mates and enemies, exhorting them to grasp hold of each other in a manner ungraspable to us.

The poem nevertheless attempts at times to disentangle itself from these tensions, to step out of the unending cycle of mourning and remembering. It finds its answer in consolation itself: "That God, which ever lives and loves, / One God, one law, one element" (CXXXI, 142–42). In his search for transcendence in his friend's death, Tennyson manifests a central feature of premodernist English elegy—its quest for relief. Writing becomes a form of compensatory mourning.[56] Here Tennyson follows a direction first modeled by Milton. In "Lycidas," published in 1638, Milton bewails the drowning of his friend, Edward King, a year earlier, using the tropes of classical elegies.[57] From Milton onward, the shepherd grieves for his departed friend, describing their life together, while looking for answers to his untimely death.

Indeed, the modern elegy shows signs of continuity with its classical precursors. Although Greek elegies themselves do not offer the conciliatory promise of Christianity, they presume the natural rhythms of return and rebirth. In the first Idyll of Theocritus, for instance, Daphnis's death is understood in the context of the "pastoral song," in which all the natural elements weep for his death. Aphrodite in Bion's "The Lament for Adonis" sheds tears for the dead Adonis who turns into spring flowers. Like Persephone, Adonis returns every year. "Give over thy wailing for to-day, Cytherea [Aphrodite], . . . thou needs wilt wail again and weep again, come another year" (Bion 1912, ll. 96–98). In these verses death is part of a recurring cycle of events. Finally, the speaker of the "Lament for Bion," attributed to Moschus, wishes he had the talent of an Orpheus to bring back Bion just as he rescued Eurydice from Hades:[58] "Even as once she granted Orpheus his Eurydice's return because he harped so sweetly, so likewise she shall give my Bion back unto the hills" (Moschus 1912, ll. 123–26).

Milton returns to this bucolic tradition. The line "Lycidas is dead, dead ere his prime" alludes to Moschus's "Bion is dead" and to Bion's "The beauteous Adonis is dead."[59] But Milton also appropriates this pastoral sense of eternal recurrence. The ambiguous verse, "For Lycidas, your sorrow, is not dead," seems to indicate that Lycidas lives on, even as heartache lingers without end, much like Tennyson's love and grief. Lycidas's resurrection is symbolic since he has become part of the natural world.[60] He has turned into the rising sun, the guardian spirit of the shores: "In thy large recompense, and shalt be good / To all that wonder in that perilous flood" (Milton 1983, ll. 184–85). The shepherd too rises to "fresh woods, and pastures new" (l. 193). Life persists somehow despite the interruptions of death and bereavement. It is in this way that sorrow and Lycidas both are paradoxically alive.

Shelley's "Adonais" (1821) similarly lays the dead poet John Keats into the ever-changing but ever-constant natural universe. He too hearkens back formally to this bucolic tradition with the first verse, "I weep for Adonais, he is dead?" (1, 1).[61] This story of recurrence is, of course, contained in the myth of Adonis himself, of winter giving way to spring, with Urania grieving for Adonais, just like Aphrodite for Adonis. "The soul of Adonais, like a star, / Beacons from the abode where the Eternal are" (55, 494–95). These final two verses, referring back to lines Shelley quotes from Plato in the Preface to *Adonais*, are compensatory in two ways. They not only refer to the ancient myths of resurrection but they also immortalize Keats, and by implication Shelley, by elevating him into the pantheon of "Eternal" English poets. The dead poet, whose "genius" was cut off so early, resides in the Platonic realm of unchanging aesthetic forms. Thus, despite the disappointing reception of Keats's "Endymion" (1818) and the "wasted promise of his genius," he still achieved immortality.[62] The line "Death is a low mist which cannot blot/ The brightness it may veil" (44, 391–92) shows that human ingenuity, both of the dead poet and of the mourning artist, shakes off the pall of physical corruption.

A. E. Housman returns to the tradition of seasonal change in his translation and recasting of Horace's Ode VII, "Diffugere Nives." In the first stanza, the "snows are fled away" and the "grasses in the mead renew their birth." But although nature thrives in this cycle, Horace reminds us that we humans can't win immortality: "Thou wast not born for aye" (Housman 1965, 163). While we partake in the dynamic fluctuation of death and birth, we lose our individuality in the universality of death.[63] Not even divine intervention (Diana) or the force of love (Theseus) could lift us out of Hades:

> Night holds Hippolytus the pure of stain.
> Diana steads him nothing, he must stay;
> And Theseus leaves Perithöus in the chain
> The love of comrades cannot take away.
> —Housman 1965, 164

Tennyson avoids this myth of eternal recurrence that we have seen in Milton, Shelley, and in Housman. At the end he finds solace in the afterlife. "In Memoriam" passes from stultifying sorrow to consolation.[64] His Arthur Hallam lives on "in God," rather than as an organism in nature's cycle of recurrence. This relief is only temporary, however, as the poem vacillates in its uncertainty.[65] It does not ultimately believe in its central insight, namely that death gives voice and shape to friendship. Nor does it address the uncertainties it raises about intimacy or the ethics of a genre that grieves while exploiting the departed. Finally, it does not confront the unresolved erotic impulses that streak through the text. If friendship is a union of two selves, it is not clear whether the bond is real or a funerary reconstruction. If the poem becomes compensatory we're unsure whether the recompense arises from the reunion in the afterlife or from the recognition that death allows things to be said that social pressure silences. With death comes a release, the revelation of long-held feelings and longings.

"In Memoriam" raises these disturbing questions: Is friendship possible outside the battle zone? Or does the friend, the other self, have to die in order for the friend left behind to love him? Finally, does a lasting friendship, expressed in elegy, depend on death? Yet, the friend does not die to be converted into literary form. Rather he dies because friendship is caught in a dialectic between fiction and empathy. And the survivor demonstrates his love by imagining it continuously through literary language.

Writing as Reconstruction

When the narrator of *Zorba the Greek* learns that his old friend, Zorba, has died, he reaches for his pen:

> I was filled with an irresistible desire to reconstitute the life we had lived to-
> gether on the coast of Crete, to drive my memory to work and gather to-
> gether all the sayings, cries, gestures, tears, and dances which Zorba had
> scattered in my mind—to save them. (Kazantzakis 1952, 309)

On the face of it, there is nothing exceptional in these lines: he is in effect saying that with his friend in the grave, he has to try to immortalize him through literature. But the act of commemoration turns out to celebrate both intense friendship and its frustrations. Ostensibly the novel is about "the life and times of Alexis Zorbas," its Greek title, but it also records the collapse of their comradeship. Hence the narrator's desire "to bring the past back to life, trying to recall Zorba and resuscitate him" is prompted by the self-reproach of the survivor. Guilt, we should remind ourselves, is the most painful companion of death.[66] But the narrator's remorse is prompted less by the passing of Zorba, who is in his seventies and about thirty years older than the narrator, than by the dissolution of their bond.

This is why the novel seems to be written as an afterthought, a remembrance of a brief but magnificent relationship, an attempt to resurrect aesthetically the departed companion. Built over a series of conceptual oppositions—memory vs. time, freedom vs. obligation, enlightenment vs. tradition, art vs. life, thought vs. action—the novel asks whether the hero must die because he cannot be a friend.[67] The intent to commemorate is reflected in the style of the novel; the narrative is transparent, seemingly unaffected by decades of textual experimentation in Greek and Western fiction.[68]

The Greek original, however, begins with an introduction (omitted in the English translation) in which the author talks about the process of artistic creation, how he converted life into literature. For years, he says, he wondered what form he should give the myth of Zorba forming within him—a novel, a song, or short story. Could writing do justice to the greater-than-life figure he spent a year with on the southern coast of Crete (Kazantzakis 1973, 9). Eventually, Kazantzakis chooses the novel, the genre he adopted after his marathon forays into epic, drama, travel writing, philosophy, and translation.

This introduction, described appropriately enough as a "memorial,"[69] ends with a Homeric all-souls-day of sorts. In an obvious allusion to the *nekuia* scene in book 11 of the *Odyssey*, in which Odysseus performs a sacrifice to enter the kingdom of the dead, the narrator offers blood from the heart to the "shade" of Zorba: "Let us thus give him our blood to bring him back to life" (13). Just as Odysseus, after slaughtering an animal, encounters in Hades the ghosts of his dead mother and comrades, the narrator wants to resurrect the friend whom he abandoned in life.

To introduce the novel with the Homeric *nekuia* ties the text with the heroic trope of the descent to the underworld. This identification with the *Odyssey* is significant for not all heroes make the voyage to Hades for the same reasons. Hercules, for instance, sought to retrieve Alcestis, while Orpheus wanted to rescue Eurydice. Both traveled to the realm of the shades to bring back a beloved. Odysseus, on the other hand, made the journey in pursuit of knowledge, particularly about the future. As he tells his companions when they depart from the island of Circe, "We must go / to the cold homes of Death and pale Persephone / to hear Teiresias tell of time to come" (Homer 1961, 10.622–25). Odysseus himself, knowing that "no man has ever sailed to the land of Death" (10.557), asks the sorceress Circe for the secret. She, in turn, explains the rituals he has to perform. When he reaches the spot at the sea's edge, he sacrifices a "black lamb" to assuage with blood "the nations of the dead" and then observes the shades as they arrive (11.40). When the blind prophet, Teiresias, finally appears, he foretells that Odysseus's journey home will be followed by one final voyage to a people that mistake the oar for a winnowing fan. Then he explains how Odysseus will be able to communicate with the phantoms of the underworld: "Any dead man / whom you allow to enter where the blood is / will speak to you, and speak the truth" (11.164–66). The shades come, one after the other, first his mother, whom Odysseus vainly tries to embrace.

Kazantzakis employs this trope as a pretext to open the novel, coaxing the ghost of Zorba to reveal itself. But Zorba does not speak in the way that Odysseus's mother does. He is not appeased by the blood sacrifice. As such, the novel turns out to be an autobiographical revelation of the narrator/author. The writing is motivated by survivor's guilt that stemmed from his decision to end the friendship. The friend destroys the relationship in order to write about it. The modern *nekuia* does not disclose the secrets of the dead as it serves the opportunity for the survivor's self-disclosure. Truth is inner truth. But in the absence of dialogue with the dead person, there is no reciprocity, no communication. Friendship perhaps constitutes our effort to differentiate between the shade and an imaginative resuscitation.

3

Duty and Desire

I'm Nobody! Who are you?
Are you—Nobody—too?
Then there's a pair of us!
Don't tell! They'd banish us—you know!
—Emily Dickinson, "I'm Nobody!
Who are You?"

Friendship today seems like a light relationship. No longer enmeshed in nets of duties and obligations, it is the most unrestricted of all our social connections. But friendship pays for its unconventionality, having become a delicate relationship, held together by the urge for personal fulfillment. This is what makes friendship a paradox, what I have called a noninstitution institution.[1] Although subject to social influences, friendship is like art, a pastime to be pursued after work, marriage, and family. In this chapter, I ask two questions: What are the implications for friendship that it exists without the explicit support of law, religion, education, or the bureaucracy? What does this observation say about modern society's unresponsiveness to friendship?

In order to come to terms with these questions, I will compare the duty-bound friendships of the past with current bonds. I won't ask whether people were happier in the past or whether we have lost an Eden of *philia*. Indeed, I will show the opposite: rather than destroying friendship, modernity has created more opportunities for intimacy. But I will consider the social and personal cost of making friendship unstable and mistrusted, a relationship best left to children and adolescents.

Rules of Exchange

In premodern societies, certain relationships required reciprocal obligations of favors, hospitality, and gift exchange and can thus be termed duty-bound. Such an understanding of obligation emerges in book 6 of the *Iliad*. The Greek warrior, Diomedes, meets Glaucus, the Trojan, in one of these touching dramas of the epic when the light falls on two individuals, bringing the international conflict into sharper focus. Diomedes, unsure if his opponent is an immortal in disguise, asks about his lineage. Glaucus in turn replies with that famous simile that compares human beings to "a generation of leaves" scattered by the wind: "And so with men / as one generation comes to life, another dies away" (Homer 1990, 6.174–75). Unlike leaves, the simile implies, human beings yearn for lasting glory yet are swept away by time.

In the course of their exchange, both heroes discover that their ancestors had shared hospitality, when Glaucus's grandfather had once visited Argos for twenty days, and given each other "handsome gifts of friendship." Though established two generations earlier, both warriors feel the compulsion of *xenia* (guest-friendship). This ritualized personal relationship, manifested in an exchange of goods and services between two unrelated men, imposed obligations on their descendants.[2]

Once Glaucus and Diomedes realize that they are bound by *xenia* they cease their hostilities and swap their armor, just as their grandfathers had exchanged gifts.[3] In this they behave differently from Paris who violated the hospitality offered by Menelaus. In book 3 of the *Iliad* Homer says that Paris was given "friendship" by his host but did evil to him in return. First Hector rebukes his bother for robbing Menelaus of his wife (1990, 3.61). And Menelaus in frustration shouts out that Paris wounded the host who received him with kindness" (1990, 3.412).[4]

In contrast to Paris, once Glaucus and Diomedes discover they are bound by *xenia*, "Both fighters sprang from their chariots, / clasped each other's hands and traded pacts of friendship" (1990, 6.279–80). The heroes are aware of their place in the social order, what they owe and what is owed to them. They trade armor, so that men will know that "we are sworn friends from our fathers' days" (1990, 6.277) and vow to stay clear of each other in battle. Diomedes assures his friend with a disarmingly guileless formulation that Schiller might have had in mind when he characterized Homeric poetry as naïve. There are plenty of Trojans for him to kill, Diomedes says, and likewise many Greeks for Glaucus to fight with and gain glory (Homer 1978, 6.278). The relationship of *xenos-philos* (guest friend) trumps ethnic attachments.

This position brings to mind E. M. Forster's pronouncement I citer earlier: if "I had to choose between betraying my country and betraying my friend, I hope I should have the guts to betray my country" (1951, 68). Forster, arguing against the glorification of abstract causes and institutions at the expense of the individual, knew that his statement would "scandalize" the patriotic ear for putting personal love over national duty. But Forster's declaration could not lie further from Bronze Age Greece. In Homer the exchange of armor highlights the reciprocal nature of relationships. Although Forster's concept of friendship renounces these structural coercions, Homer's can't be imagined outside of them. There is no dilemma in the epic between individual desire and national loyalty, between intimacy and country. Friendship is a public relationship, guided by codes of mutual obligation.

In suggesting that relationships in antiquity are compelled, I am not all saying that Homeric heroes were devoid of human feelings, merely expressing social conventions. As I have shown, ancient friendship, like that between Achilles and Patroclus, could convey tenderness and strong emotions. Indeed, later in the classical city friendship came to represent "in principle . . . a space of personal intimacy and unselfish affection distinct from the forms regulating public and commercial life."[5] In other words, friendship could constitute an association of feelings and devotion beyond the rules of hospitality. But it took its meaning in the collaborative enterprise of the city itself, rather than from the desires of the friends themselves. Aristotle states quite plainly that "friendship depends on community" (1984, 1159b32). Indeed, the tie of friendship symbolized for ancient thinkers and poets the social adhesive of the polis. Life outside of the polis would be unthinkable, a common refrain in Greek tragedy.

In Sophocles's *Philoctetes* the eponymous hero, abandoned by the Greek army on the island of Lemnos and thus prevented from fighting in Troy, protests to the chorus that he has been left "friendless" ("*aphilon*") and lonely (1919, l. 228). In her plea to Creon not to exile her in Euripides's *Medea*, Medea reminds him how she is a refugee from a foreign land, while he enjoys the life and the company of friends in his own city of Corinth (Euripides 1955, ll. 253–57). And who would believe that Helen, long reviled as a self-indulgent woman, mourns her ostracism in Egypt in Euripides's *Helen*. Bewailing her fate, she cries that both Greeks and Trojans hate her, blaming her for the war. Yet, they don't know that "the gods have uprooted me from my home, and planted me among an outlandish race, where I am friendless " (Euripides 1972, p. 143). In all three examples, to be banished from family and friends is a frightful fate—as Oedipus comes to discover in his own self-imposed exile in Colonus. A life without companions, here meaning an extension of bonds outside of kinship, is unthinkable. To paraphrase Aristotle, the community depends on friendship and friendship depends on community.

In a formulation that would influence thinkers for centuries, Aristotle describes three types of friendship, those of utility, pleasure, and of virtue. He leaves no doubt, however, that the most enduring tie is the last: "Perfect friendship is the friendship of men who are good, and alike in excellence, for these wish well alike to each other *qua* good, and they are good in themselves. Now those who wish well to their friends for their sake are most truly friends" (1984, 1156b16–19). Aristotle elevates virtue as the social glue between friends in contrast to the modern values of authenticity and mutual self-disclosure. Although he also emphasizes this mutuality, he has in mind the reciprocity of love rather than the revelation of inner secrets. Aristotle accentuates virtue in a reciprocal exchange of good deeds and good thoughts rather than in the pursuit of emotional satisfaction because he believes society aims for the realization of the common interest.[6] The bond of friendship, based on good will, symbolizes the shared recognition and agreement that for Aristotle constitutes the mortar of the polis.

What this means is that the bond between two friends joins them to the other pairs of friends in the community. When friendships are inspired by virtue, as opposed to utility, they partake in this wider social solidarity. For Aristotle, then, friendship seems to lie "in loving rather than in being loved" (1984, 1159a27). You do what is good for the friend's sake (1166a15), embracing that person for what he is rather than what you yourself can get from him. When you love someone for his sake, you identify his actions as also your own.[7] You become, in other words, one with that person. This is what Aristotle means when he says that the friend is "another self"; the virtuous person relates to the friend exactly as he does to himself. If he is good, he will accept his friend for the goodness of his character.

Cicero largely follows Aristotle in fastening friendship to the ethics of virtue. Friendship, he writes, cannot exist except between "truly good men" (1971, 18.65). That is, only righteous men can attain the ideal friendship, which is based on selfless love rather than on political or economic advantage. Those who form friendships "for the sake of advantage destroy the link in friendship that is most productive of affection (1971, 15.51).[8] People, according to Cicero, seek friendship for the integrity inherent in the relationship rather than for any advantages they may accrue from it.

Even though friendship in antiquity could flourish as a private relationship between two people (and not just as an extension of economic exchange or as a function of political patronage), it was regarded as a vital component of the polis. Thus, when Seneca says that friendship should be sought "for its own sake" rather than for some other utilitarian purpose,[9] he has in mind an ideal, Aristotelian bond, rather than our understanding of friendship as a self-sufficient relationship. For while the modern notion of friendship embraces this noninstrumental view (friendship for its own sake), it rejects the system of ethics and social networks into which ancient thought placed it.

Modern friendship too has its public expressions, as we have seen in *A Passage to India* and *The Adventures of Huckleberry Finn*. What seems like a private relationship touches on contentious communal conflicts over race, nation, or religion. But these social intentions seem invisible and their existence has to be demonstrated. Rather than considering friendship as an object of political interest or a bedrock of civic unity, we value it as an autocephalous relationship, not subject to religious or state control.[10] Furthermore we perceive a conflict between personal authenticity and public life, as the quotation from Forster indicates, presuming that ceremony and social obligation obstruct intimacy. Finally, while we recognize rituals in dating and marriage, we rarely do so for friendship.[11] Friends may engage in ceremonies together—at a birthday party or football game—but these rites rarely guide or restrict their behavior.

Medieval Pairing

Compare this situation with the formal sacraments in the ritual brotherhood of medieval times, an institution sanctified by the church in a ceremony with the legal and economic compulsions of marriage.[12] "By allowing the vows of sworn brothers to be confirmed by the Eucharist," Alan Bray writes, "Latin Christianity gave them a potentially binding force" An example of this friendship is a tombstone of two knights with their two helmets touching as though in a kiss. Perhaps startling to the modern eye, the kissing helmets symbolized the medieval seal of friendship.[13] The men, whose relationship was formalized by the church, wished to be buried together, much like Achilles and Patroclus, and perpetuate their bond in eternity.

When western Europeans (like the Crusaders) traveled to the territories of the Byzantine Empire, they discovered that their coreligionists practiced a similar form of friendship ritual.[14] The Byzantine practice of *adelphopoiesis*—literally, the making of brothers—obtruded into and gained legitimacy in the worlds of religion and politics. A man entered ritual brotherhood with another through a rite performed by a priest. After a series of prayers, chants, blessings, and the kiss, the two men became "brothers." Not a friendship either in the Aristotelian or the modern sense, ritual brotherhood served the purpose of social and political networking. It was, to use the Aristotelian vocabulary, a bond of utility that allowed ambitious young men to gain patronage and form political alliances beyond those offered by kinship and godparenthood. In short, *adelphopoiesis* extended friendly ties beyond the family and bound individuals in a network of duties; exchanges of gifts, favors, promotions, and military assistance; and access to future brides.[15] The emperor Basil (811–66) serves as an example of ritual brotherhood, having climbed the Byzantine hierarchy by seeking and creating political/affective bonds.

The word scholars often use to translate ritual brotherhood into current vocabulary is marriage, the only modern word that can convey the obligations and attachments that *adelphopoiesis* imposed on the two men and their respective families. Some historians interpret *adelphopoiesis* as a prototypical same-sex marriage—gay betrothals before the advent of homosexuality—because of similarities in both rites: the couples held hands in front of the altar, were bound together by a stole, were blessed by a priest, and ended the ceremony with a kiss of peace (as a part of the Eucharist).[16]

However we interpret these religious services—as brotherhood or marriage—we must recognize that they gave friendship a formal and objective character. Participants became members of multiple families, extending, like marriage, the range of kinship groups.[17] Of course, this institution did not preclude the brothers from building ties of affection and love between them. What was true of classical antiquity also held true for ritual brotherhood, namely, intimacy could develop in formalized relationships.

We can see this in the writing of Aelred (1110–67), an abbot (and once Scottish noble) of the Cistercian monastery of Rievaulx in Yorkshire, whose *Spiritual Friendship* constitutes one of the most influential medieval documents on friendship.[18] Heavily indebted to Cicero's *De Amicitia*, indeed adopting the predecessor's dialogic form, Aelred's own treatise translates classical *philia* into Christian theology, endowing friendship with a spiritual dimension.[19] Aelred's text shows the discursive continuity between the classical and medieval period in the treatment of love and friendship as a public, ethical subject, rather than as an expression of private life.[20] Yet Aelred's positive valuation of friendship seems remarkable considering the ambivalence, if not hostility, shown toward friendship by monastic writers, if not by Christianity itself.[21]

Nevertheless, Aelred writes of a fellow monk with sweetness and tenderness that rivals Montaigne's gushing adoration of his friend, Etienne de La Boétie: "There was no pretense between us, no simulation, no dishonorable flattery, no unbecoming harshness, no evasion, no concealment, but everything open and above the board; for I deemed my heart in a fashion his, and his mine, and he felt in like manner towards me" (Aelred 1974, 3:125).

In their correspondence monks like Aelred spoke of ardent passion for their companions, longing to embrace and kiss one another, and grieving about the friend's absence.[22] But these emotions may also be expressions of a particular mode of writing, as their authors did not necessarily distinguish, as we do, between sincerity and rhetoric. We should be cautious, therefore, about reducing human sentiment to signs or seeing signs as human sentiment. The passages in these letters stressing obedience, prayer, and spiritual admonition outnumber those expressing affection.[23] The love of God takes precedence over fellow feeling.

Aelred manifests the medieval (and ultimately classical) belief in love as a virtue, an ennobling bond focused on the future.[24] Sublime friendship seeks to hold the society of monks together while helping them transcend earthly being. Not an end in itself, it takes its cue from life in the monastery as a manifestation of a universal Christian, brotherly friendship. The ultimate purpose of *amicitia Christiana* is to serve God. Earthly friendship is only a foretaste of the blessedness of heavenly love: "from the sweetness of fraternal charity to wing one's flight aloft to that more sublime splendor of divine love, and by the ladder of charity now to mount to the embrace of Christ himself" (Aelred 1974, 3:127). Although Aelred appropriates the Aristotelian and Ciceronian conceptions of friendship as moral excellence, here translated as spiritual goodness, his ideal is a stepping-stone toward a more fulfilling bond: "The foundation of friendship should be laid in the love of God" (Aelred 1974, 3:54). This paints a picture of friendship as a universal ideal, hovering above the vagaries of personal emotion. Rather than a withdrawal from the community, it was a means of reaching a transcendent brotherhood.[25]

In short, friendships developed as webs of obligations, patronage, and exchange of favors and gifts, a pattern that continued into the Renaissance.[26] The "Florentine self as presented even in private letters and diaries was always and necessarily a social one" (Kent 2009, 5–6).[27] Citizens understood their behavior as obligations owed to relatives, neighbors, and friends. They were entwined from birth to death in overlapping circles of kinship and patronage. Men relied on patronage systems for support without necessarily differentiating between friendship and business. But love and trust could grow within these friendships. Once established, an instrumental relationship could offer the space for love to flourish (Kent 2009, 59). Ultimately, however, friendship could not be distinguished from community, nor love from duty.

Self-Revelation and Self-Institution

This is why Montaigne's essay proves so revolutionary, pointing to a modern view of friendship. Montaigne justifies his relationship with Etienne de La Boétie by recourse to the relationship itself rather than, say, a system of patronage or family obligations: "If you press me to tell why I loved him, I feel that this cannot be expressed, except by answering: Because it was he, because it was I" (Montaigne 1958, 139). Try to find this sentiment in Aristotle.

Of course, Aelred expressed similar feelings for his fellow monks. But Montaigne's intense pronominal declaration portrays friendship as a self-sufficient entity. His friendship "has no other model than itself, and can be compared only with itself" (Montaigne 1958, 139). To my knowledge, this marks the first appearance of the view of friendship as a self-validating entity whose goal is nothing other than to maintain itself—much like the autonomous work of art that would appear a couple of centuries later.[28]

Although Montaigne is steeped in the texts of Aristotle and Cicero and although he too presents a "perfect" friendship untarnished with promises of "services and benefits," he is as much removed from classical *philia* as from Aelred's *amicitia Christiana*. To be sure, the deeply personal tone of the writing distinguishes it from Aristotle and Plato. But what is profound is the virtual absence of references to a wider community. Ideal friendship is granted "absolute sovereignty" (Montaigne 1958, 141).

Montaigne follows Aristotle in separating affective from utilitarian friendship. But he goes one step beyond in conceiving of friendship as private, supreme, complete unto itself. Friendship now becomes an exercise in joining with the other in a seamless and indivisible unit. Rather than being another self in pursuit of the good, the friend unites with the other in a cloistered ceremony of mutual revelation. In Montaigne, friendship is about falling in love rather than vowing fraternal fidelity before a priest. Although he takes care to point out that he does not mean the "licentious Greek love"—in what must be one of the earliest manifestations of homosexual panic—his understanding of intimacy is the losing of the self in the other. Montaigne brings us one step closer to the ideal friendship as both nonutilitarian relationship based on emotional fulfillment and a withdrawal from social obligations and traditional loyalties.

Of course his is not the only paradigm for friendship in modernity. Americans before and after the revolution, I have argued, conceived of friendship as a political relationship, one essential to the new republic. But the Montaignean model of a seamless union with another person has taken precedence. Today people hardly think of friendship as a political institution even if in reality it can't be divorced from collective purposes.

What marks the modern from previous modes of friendship is less the presence or absence of affections than the objectification of intimacy. People in modernity view their friendship as stemming outwardly from the self and inwardly toward the self. Social withdrawal, rather than being feared and condemned, is constitutive of friendship. Individuals themselves may be socially and politically engaged but they regard true friendship as private. No longer an archetypal political relationship or a stepping-stone toward grace, friendship has become a self-regulating relation unique unto itself, a noninstitution institution.

Georg Simmel, the sociologist of the early twentieth century, misses this point when he contends that the "absolute psychological intimacy" in friendship that we have inherited from antiquity is impossible in modernity. First of all, it is not clear that the ancients aspired to this type of closeness at all. Simmel must have in mind the Montaignean conception of friendship when he says that "modern man possibly has too much to hide to sustain a friendship in the ancient sense" (Simmel 1950, 326). On the contrary, modern friendship is sustained exactly by its revelatory, confessional impulses. In the absence of institutional support, the loosening of obligations and duties, what remains is mutual self-disclosure. Understanding replaces political virtue and religious ritual as the sinew of friendship. Trust is achieved through the externalization of the internal.

Intimacy, Intimacy, Intimacy

One of the overriding goals for modern individuals is to reach perfect contact with another person through the disclosure of inner feelings. This condition is captured memorably in D. H. Lawrence's *Lady Chatterley's Lover* as "revealing everything concerning yourself to the other person, and his revealing everything concerning himself" (Lawrence 1959, 286). What Lady Chatterley describes is an unobstructed attachment to someone else for which I don't believe we can find classical or medieval antecedents. Indeed, this mutual self-revelation actually converts the ancient exchange of gifts into the exchange of feelings. Rites of friendship give way to rituals of emotion: I reveal myself and expect you to do the same, otherwise our relationship won't hold. You betray my trust and risk losing my affection if you don't open up as I have done.

It is fascinating that intimacy arose under conditions that, according to such pioneering sociologists as Ferdinand Tönnies, Max Weber, and Georg Simmel, had destabilized traditional relationships. Simmel, for instance, believed that the functional differentiation in society, that is, the ever-increasing compartmentalization of social and economic life into specialized activities and professions, undermined friendship by forcing it to become itself specialized. "The modern way of feelings tends more heavily toward differentiated friendships, which cover only one side of the personality, without playing into other aspects of it" (Simmel 1950, 326). Modern friendship itself breaks down into many different relationships, mirroring the overall division of society. The individual fractures into many selves, different modes of identification by class, gender, race, profession, nationality, and so on.

Even though compartmentalization has in fact occurred, the fear of these sociologists has not been borne out. Friendship has not disappeared under conditions of differentiation. On the contrary, the impersonal forces of modernization have created conditions for intimate friendship. This seems counterintuitive to those who believe that the modern age weakens the social body. Yet, rather than causing friendship to wither in the desert of rationalization, modernity has in fact augmented opportunities for more personal and intense relations (while also providing infinitely more occasions for impersonal contact).[29] Greater differentiation, in other words, creates an additional need and place for emotional understanding. Moreover, this closeness presupposes the modern sense of individualism. In a paradoxical way impersonal society and intimacy seem to feed off one another. *By freeing friendship from community, modernity has bred more prospects for friendship.*

Historically, capitalist society "created a democratized arena of private and elective affinities, in which persons might culturally value each other for their 'true,' that is, their unproductive selves" (Silver 1997, 69). In bringing together disparate individuals in the conduct of business, it opened up a realm of privacy in the vastness of bureaucratic administration and economic exchange. And friendship, presenting itself as voluntary in the Aristotelian sense, that is, untouched by economic profit, began to function as the quintessential, the most pure, private relation.

Modernity has flipped Aristotle's understanding on its head by making the goal of life intimacy for the sake of intimacy (rather than for a greater good). At the same time, having liberated people from their dependence on traditional relations for their well-being, such as political alliances with the lord or financial ties with the patron or godfather, it has abandoned them in an anonymous economic and administrative order. Therefore the quest for personal ties, such as friendships, becomes more desperate, people seeing in these relations a refuge from the expanding social network.[30]

Modern society, in short, multiplies exponentially the direct and indirect interactions among strangers. It has created a context in which individuals are engaged in associations of cooperation and competition that blur the distinction Hobbes and ancient theorists made between the friend and the enemy. Most people we meet will be neither. According to Adam Smith, an early theorist of modern society, in this throng the individual "stands at all times in need of cooperation and assistance of great multitudes while his whole life is scarce sufficient to gain the friendship of a few people" (Smith 1991, 12). Since we need the "help" of these strangers, we can prevail only if we can "interest their self-love" in our favor. We expect our dinner not from the benevolence of the butcher or the baker but from "their regard to their self-interest" (13). Under these conditions of tacit competition and cooperation, people who are neither comrades nor foes seek love from a small circle of individuals.[31]

Modern society compelled people to confront the divide between the outer and inner realms of social life, the language of intimacy having emerged in seventeenth-century Europe to help individuals cross this gap. With the rise of the autonomous, free-thinking individual, capable of making decisions about relationships, the conception of love, particularly in marriage, gradually changed from love as duty to love as choice.[32] Matrimony came increasingly to be seen as a loving partnership, based on compatibility and a sharing of interests, rather than as a reproductive arrangement.[33] This rising emphasis on greater emotional commitment was promoted by women who themselves increasingly took control of the decision to marry instead of following the dictates of their fathers.

This discourse of intimacy acquired an emotional as well as a physical connotation, as it began to confine the male body to the marital home. Until the Renaissance, for example, men ate and slept together in the great houses and universities.[34] Starting in the seventeenth century in Europe, however, what men had once done in public with other men, such as the sharing of beds and tables, they now conducted with their wives. And they came to see the body as a gift between themselves and their spouses while growing suspicious of physical attachments with other men.[35]

This privatization of (heterosexual) intimacy grew out of the demands of family members for more equitable relations among them,[36] something that Alexis de Tocqueville understood. Although not referring to friend-ship per se but to the connection between fathers and sons, Tocqueville ar-gues that the democratization of social relations leads to greater familiarity and warmer ties: "As the mores and laws become more democratic, the re-lations between father and sons become more intimate and gentle." When the "experience of an old link loosens," he continues, there is less rule and "authority" and more "confidence and affection" (Tocqueville 1969, 587).

The erosion of male-controlled authority enabled individuals to build less formalized relationships, even among members of the family. Inti-macy then became a way of collaborating on questions of trust, familiar-ity, and communication by individuals who regarded each other as peers. This concept again strangely approximates Aristotle's understanding of the ideal friendship as a bond fashioned by two men (by definition, citizens) devoted to virtue. The relationship, in other words, has to re-spect someone else's autonomy. But modern intimacy seeks not virtue—reciprocal good will—but maintenance of the relationship itself through emotional (and sexual) equality. And the goal of intimacy is to sustain the relationship itself.

This self-justification, however, deprives friendship of the understruc-ture in law, religion, the family, and the workplace that it had previously presumed. In the absence of the traditional formal ties and obligations, what keeps friends together? Is it mutual disclosure, the modern equiva-lent of the ritual kiss? If friendship has been displaced by marriage as the symbol for social cohesion, what shape can it assume today? If friendship once took on meaning in a swap of gifts and favors, now it seems to func-tion as an exchange of inner thoughts and feelings more costly than armor or gold. We are all Aristotelians in seeking noninstrumental friendships but modern in creating self-sustaining affiliations.

Friendship is the *first* interpersonal relationship to confront this para-dox of the desire for ideal attachments with unencumbered autonomy, the first, in other words, to experience the clash of the idiom of personal sovereignty (I want to be free) with the vernacular of affection (I want to be loved). As such, it serves as a template for our affective affiliations—loose, nonbinding, economically and politically inconsequential, freed from the obligations of kinship and increasingly now from those of fam-ily in general. Although marriage has long displaced friendship as the figurative brick of social relations, it is friendship that really expresses the challenges of our age: how to maintain attachments in the absence of formal restrictions, to speak the language of autonomy and empathy at the same time.

Mining for Friendship on a Cretan Shore

Nikos Kazantzakis's *Zorba the Greek* dramatizes this conflict between self-sufficiency and social amplitude, self-institution and social compulsion. In so doing, it presents two different conceptions of friendship, one harking back to the world of obligation and reciprocity and the other pointing forward to a relationship with a tenuous hold. The novel is the record of a "strange meeting," the attempted union of the narrator and Zorba on a deserted Cretan cove, a relationship pulled apart by disparities in age, education, philosophical disposition, and temperament. The narrator is a young man of thirty-five, an idealistic author, who has little experience outside of his books. Zorba, twice his age, has amassed the insights of many centuries. These two come to represent many ideological struggles that ultimately tear their relationship apart, the dominant one being the tension between the expansiveness of freedom and the compulsions of reciprocity. By dramatizing these battles, the novel uses war as a trope for the creation of friendship but normalizes it on the idyllic Cretan coast.

Each character represents antithetical notions of friendship. For Zorba friendship signifies ancient loyalties—blood brotherhood, self-sacrifice, and hospitality. The narrator, on the other hand, considers friendship a matter of intimacy, self-revelation (both of which he is incapable of), and autonomy. Zorba is portrayed as having a primordial mind-set in which comradeship is to be unselfconsciously lived rather than thought about. Friendship means doing things together. But the narrator is a post-Enlightenment man, immobilized by self-reflection and a sense of inadequacy. Whereas he is tortured by the contradictions of his inner world, Zorba seems to have been untouched by them. As the narrator confesses to Zorba, he would prefer to read a book about love than to experience it. Opposite him stands a chthonic sixty-five-year-old womanizer, former guerrilla fighter, current vagabond, and an amoral individual who has killed in war and who in a fit of passion cuts off his index finger for getting in the way of his pottery-making. The tension between the bookworm and the earthmover pushes the plot forward as it also proposes that friendship is about taking risks.

The novel thematically and structurally incorporates this imbalance between the two characters. As the narrator admits, he has been consumed all his life by the desire to find a synthesis in which "the irreducible opposites would fraternize" (Kazantzakis 1952, 52). In staging this confrontation between these two conceptions of friendship, the novel suggests that Zorba's idea of comradeship may be disappearing along with him. But then it also asks how the narrator's own version of friendship could be possible. Is self-revelation enough to lock a friendship in place? And what happens when it's not reciprocated?

These questions are posed on an idyllic Cretan cove, far removed from the world of political struggle, as the narrator himself is aware.[37] The choice of setting is not an accident. "Friendship must exclude," as C. S. Lewis points out; it needs isolation to flourish. The "element of secession, of indifference or deafness . . . to the voices of the outer world, is common to all Friendships." (Lewis 1988, 86, 81). In order to enjoy their company fully the two companions have to flout social rules and regulations. When Zorba returns from work, he cooks and the two, sitting on the beach, converse long into the night. "Talk, Zorba, talk," the narrator commands, sensing that "these months would be the happiest in my life" (Kazantzakis 1952, 49).

Of course, even the ancient heroic friendships entailed some form of physical removal from the community. A shared pursuit, like slaying monsters or simply fishing, is a way of strengthening a bond. In this novel the self-ostracism of the narrator and Zorba is justified because the outside community does not understand their friendship or may suspect it. The novel, therefore, touches on the central contradiction of modern friendship: it needs isolation to thrive but in thriving it is isolated. In the absence of wider protocols, and in the face of suspicion of, if not hostility toward, male intimacy, friendship becomes precarious.

This is why modern friendship needs a commercial subterfuge.[38] As the narrator informs Zorba, their professed reason for coming to Crete is to mine coal. At the start of the novel the narrator feels himself pulled by a stranger's riveting stare at the window of the café. After a brief conversation he realizes that Zorba is the man he has been searching for—a living heart, "voracious mouth, a great brute of a soul"—to help him put his ideas into practice (13). Zorba asks him to take the plunge: "Take me with you." They go off to Crete under the ruse of Aristotelian instrumentalism, needing the ploy of the mine because their relationship is, like art, unproductive.

The narrator, who knows this from the start, only explains it to Zorba halfway through the narrative. The "coal was a pretext, just to stop the locals being too inquisitive, so that they took us for sober contractors," he confesses (69). This justification is not a fluke. Male intimacy requires a double effort to neutralize the tensions within the relationship itself and to thwart the external forces seeking to squelch it. It is compelled to disguise itself as a utilitarian association, exactly the type that Aristotle (and Cicero and Montaigne after him) considered inferior. That the locals would accept such a productive bond, but not one whose goal was affection, demonstrates the precariousness of friendship.

Happiness in modern friendship involves the pursuit of a journey with the other, rather than Homeric glory, Aristotelian goodness, or monastic communion with God. It is an exclusionary act, which simultaneously claims social validation. This, of course, is true of sexual love. Solitude is necessary to an affair and society encourages the amorous exclusivity of lovers as potentially productive. But there is no similar acceptance of like pairing without the pull of the sexual. Indeed, the "secession" of two friends provokes suspicion, with the specter of homosexuality always haunting male friendship from Montaigne on. It must be confronted and denied at every turn.

Interestingly, there is no homosexual panic in *Zorba the Greek* (suggesting perhaps that it is a western European and North American preoccupation). In a letter to his other friend, Stavridakis, whom he hails as a new Prometheus struggling for his people, the narrator recounts his bliss on Crete with Zorba. In the concluding lines, he reveals something that he could not when he and Stavridakis were together: "Now that you are no longer before me and cannot see my face, and now I run no risk of appearing soft or ridiculous, I can tell you I love you very deeply" (93). There is less here of sexual alarm than a terror of closeness. In a sense, friendship fears itself, anxious that it can't fulfill its own ideals. Ironically, the act of writing, which the narrator loathes, allows him to express the affection that he was unable to at Stavridakis's departure. In his response, Stavridakis confesses, though he is also embarrassed, that "I, too, have loved you very dearly" (142).[39]

Thus the anxiety in Kazantzakis stems from the social relevance of friendship rather than from its potential for sexual dissidence. For the novel asks a central question: If modern friendship is self-centered, if it requires privacy, if it entails the exploration of interiority, then how can it be justified in the face of injustice? We should bear in mind that, while the narrator exults in the Cretan coast, Stavridakis struggles in the Caucasus region to rescue Greeks from imminent slaughter. His descriptions of horrific scenes unwittingly bring to the fore the luxury and self-indulgence of friendship.

They also oblige us to ask a number of questions. If friendship cannot be justified by a system of ethical values (Aristotle's politics or Aelred's religion), if it does not arise through a communal effort (war), if its goal is not social reproduction (marriage), then what authority does it have? This question is ethical and political, and also aesthetic: like art, friendship has a problem of legitimation because it offers itself to those who have the time and peace of mind to pursue it.

Unencumbered by formal rules, the two protagonists in the novel are relatively free to create their friendship as they see fit, exactly as Montaigne described. Because they have no model to follow, they improvise, fashioning a noninstitutional institution. But the process of improvisation renders friendship delicate. The narrator and Zorba sense this precariousness toward the end of the novel, when the pulley system that transports lumber down the side of the mountain falls apart. The "pretext" tumbles down and the protagonists face the moment of decision. What will they do now when their enterprise is in ruins?

Rather than despair, Zorba miraculously jumps up to dance: "I've never loved anyone as much before. I've hundreds of things to say, but my tongue just can't manage them. So I'll dance them for you" (290). The narrator joins him, the first time he has been able to fasten hands with Zorba in this Dionysian act. The narrator himself experiences "no ordinary joy," but a "sublime, absurd, and unjustifiable gladness." Although he has lost everything, his money, the trucks, his workers, he feels a "sense of deliverance" (292). It would seem that the narrative logic was heading toward this moment of revelation, when both protagonists come to understand the true nature of their friendship: it's not about mining coal but about mining themselves. Division ends as the self and the other join in Montaigne's seamless union.

Yet at this instant the narrator decides to leave. He receives the last communication from Stavridakis, informing him of the dire situation he is in
and letting him know that "happiness is doing your duty" (292). In contrast, happiness for the narrator means spending a year with Zorba. Is this
why he ultimately abandons his friend, because he has elevated personal
and aesthetic values over social and political problems? Can the "unjustifiable gladness" in being with your friend ever be justified in the face of
larger-than-life altruism? Does the narrator depart because of his guilty
conscience, the shame of finding fulfillment and great *art*, when others
seek their calling and the great *act*?

We are never fully informed about the reasons. The failure of their
shared project seems to remove the ostensible reason for their remaining
together. So the narrator runs away, saying that he still has a lot of writing ahead of him. Their "separation" is devastating to Zorba: "And what's
going to happen to me without your company, boss?" (299). Indeed, he
breaks into the doleful song of the camel driver in the desert, a cry of suffering and isolation. Zorba still belongs to the orality of friendship, when
duty and rules of obligation determine one's behavior. Relationships constitute a part of a perennial exchange of goods, or in this case, of affection.
The narrator's orientation is textual and, thus, more inwardly oriented.
Throughout the novel he is shown reading Dante or working on his Bud-
dha manuscript.

Although the narrator concludes that "love is stronger than death," it is
really writing that is triumphant. He leaves Zorba to become an artist, to
fulfill himself, so as to compose a novel about their friendship. In a sense,
he departs so as to gain the distance to write. He abandons the "ruse" of
friendship to seek the "lies" of literature. Intimacy for the narrator perhaps
involves finding the right tone to relate Zorba's story. Does the narrator's
ultimate duty to his own self as a writer come at a high price?

That the narrator textualizes his friendship is paradoxical, for throughout the novel he disdains the written word. He fears a type of poetry that
(with reference to Mallarmé's work) seems like "hollow words," sterile
verses, "bloodless, odorless, void of any human substance" (133). He hopes
that Zorba can help him overcome this tendency toward pure textuality.
But he ends up with a self-conscious relationship that sees validation in
itself. Although he disparages modernist literary experimentation, he promotes a modern understanding of human affiliation.

Here again we encounter the interplay of fiction and empathy in friendship. In order to write about his love for Zorba, the narrator has to desert him. To conjure up Zorba's words and inner thoughts in realist fiction and to imagine what he feels, he needs the distance of art. The (self)-fulfillment of the aesthetic task, the imaginative reconstruction of their time on Crete, necessitates the abandonment of the friendship. This contradiction reflects wider tensions in the novel, such as action versus art, life versus literature, the deed versus the text. The meaning of friendship is tied to the possibility of imaginative reconstruction.

Many years after his departure, the narrator receives a letter from Zorba's widow in Serbia, where Zorba had settled, informing him of his friend's death. The widow invites him to visit her, stay the night, and to pick up the santuri, Zorba's beloved stringed instrument, which he had played every night on the beach. The widow still operates according to the rules of oral, peasant hospitality. The novel ends and we don't know whether the narrator accepted her invitation. But it is interesting to ask what the narrator could offer the widow in return for hospitality—Zorba's narrative, aestheticized into a novel? These two notions of the gift, a musical instrument and an act of writing, an object played by Zorba and a commemoration of him, highlight two different versions of human relations.

Friendship's freedom, its capacity to be a noninstitution institution, to build a unique model of itself each time, renders it fragile. Does the narrator abandon Zorba because he has discovered that the conditions that make intimacy possible, that push us ineluctably toward closeness beyond the rules of kinship and reciprocity, also undermine our chances of attaining it? Or, was it his discovery that friendship's social secession can only be short lived? "No Man in Civil Society can be exempted from the Laws of it," according to John Locke (1960, 348). Although not referring to friendship specifically, his aphorism helps elucidate the frailty of friendship. The world's millstones grind down personal happiness.

Friendship juxtaposes social limitations with love's limitlessness. Yet, without the ethics of reciprocal benevolence and universal affection, or an anthropology of exchange, friendship seems always partial and egotistical. Is this the lesson the narrator has learned? If so, the novel then dramatizes the possibility and the impossibility of friendship, the finite and the infinite. It tells us that intimacy, the elusive goal, is real but also fleeting, like a wave on the Cretan coast or the strumming of Zorba's santuri.

The novel ends on an elegiac note. Yet it is not friendship that fails. On the contrary, Zorba would have been quite happy to go on living together with the narrator. And obviously during the year on Crete, both men attained a remarkable degree of closeness. But the novel suggests that intimacy, the strange filament of communication, is slender. The conditions that make it possible also render it tenuous. By grasping it, you also lose it.

Friendship at the Edge of Empire

Echoes of this paradox reverberate in Sándor Márai's Hungarian novel *Embers* ([1942] 2002). Set in the twilight of the Austro-Hungarian empire, the novel describes how a retired general (Henrik) prepares his castle to receive a friend (Konrad) who has been absent for over forty years and whom the general loved as much as his now-dead wife. In telling the story of the two old men, *Embers* describes the possibility of friendship as both ideal and real experience. Upon the arrival of the guest, the two friends engage in a verbal struggle over the past, their shared love of the general's wife, and over the meaning of central European aristocracy in the modern world. The conflict between them is expressed in the style of the novel. Written in a languid, plush language of country castles, refined gentry, piano sonatas, and exquisite furniture, the narrative logic is driven by a fast-paced suspense, generated less by the question "Who done it?" than by "Why?" The elegiac tone of a *Brideshead Revisited* is interrupted by the insistent demands of the mystery novel. We turn the pages to determine why someone would try to kill his best friend, who is also his soul mate and metaphorical twin.

But the more penetrating question is how friendship can flourish in a society where friends are no longer bound by moral duties. When the two protagonists, Henrik and Konrad, meet as boys, they realize that this adolescent friendship "would impose upon them lifetime obligations" (39). When Henrik confronts Konrad forty-one years later, he reminds him that "one of them may find a new friend or a new lover, but without the other's tacit consent this doesn't release their bond" (116). But Henrik and Konrad are not Glaucus and Diomedes, who are bound in friendship by their grandfathers' *xenia*. What obligations bear upon the modern protagonists?

The answer, the novel portentously concludes, "eludes the power of language" (213). Friendship, the narrator learns belatedly, is made up of paradoxes. Finally facing Konrad after forty-one years, Henrik comes to terms with the Aristotelian concept of the friend as another self. "We were friends, and the word carries a meaning only men understand," he says. "If we had not been friends, you would not have raised your gun against me that morning on the hunt in the forest." He, Henrik, would not have gone to Konrad's apartment the next day, that sacred space forbidden to him. And had they not been friends, Konrad would not have fled the city the next day only to return four decades later (140). Finally, Henrik adds, "you killed something inside me, you ruined my life, but we are still friends" (141). One contradiction is piled on another.

How is it possible, the novel asks, for the self to kill the self, the twin brother, Castor shooting Pollux? Is it because the union proved unworkable? Or had its intensity crushed the self who had to murder the friend to find relief? Or did the appearance of the other, in this case Krisztina, Henrik's wife, complicate the friendship by introducing sexual competition between the two friends? Can the male friends themselves have an erotic (but not sexual) relationship? Or does such a romantic friendship flourish only in "ancient sagas" (139), the world of blood brotherhood?

We need to know, Henrik says, where the boundary lies between two people. So the story takes us back to the beginning of the friendship, when Konrad and Henrik meet as ten-year-old boys in the military academy. Although they are young, they realize that their relationship exacted from them ongoing duties: "The friendship between Konrad and Henrik had the glow of a quiet and ceremonial oath of loyalty in the Middle Ages" (41). It is not a coincidence that this novel, like *Women in Love*, understands male intimacy in terms of medieval blood brotherhood. Such a close bond has to be transposed anachronistically onto other texts and other eras because romantic friendship today needs a ruse. The two boys envision themselves as medieval knights withdrawing within the imaginary space of *amicitia*.

Here again we encounter the link between the imagination and empathy. The exclusiveness of friendship takes place in the expansiveness of literature. Because this friendship is unattainable in person the boys idealize it as a fiction, as a bond from an era of knights and heroes. It is a form of dissimulation, as in *Zorba the Greek*, but here the "pretext" of narrative is necessary because the erotics of *philia* are threatened by the specter of homosexuality. Medieval legend helps them accept that they have fallen in love with each other.

After four years of friendship, the boys begin to "shut themselves off from other people and to have their own secrets" (40). They become so close that they turn into a duo, the other of the self, a merger of body and soul. The pairing is so intense and obvious that the other boys in the academy give them a "single name," calling them "the Henriks (41)." Innocently, the other classmates see them like a married couple.[40] They own the same clothes, underwear, and books. Together they discover Vienna, the military life, and love. They develop over the years a friendship and brotherly trust that only twins can share.

Their relationship manifests an older version of friendship as reciprocity as well as Montaigne's conception of friendship as a hermetic relationship. Yet, the latter paradoxically depends on the former. The boys justify their withdrawal from society by imbuing their relationship with social and political bonds from the Middle Ages. Yet, unlike the knights who followed codes of duty, these modern companions make their own rules. This is the weakness that causes their relationship to crumble. Many years later Konrad has an affair with Henrik's wife and plots with her to kill him; he abruptly abandons his friend. Despite his sworn promises, he acts with neither a sense of duty nor constraint.

Henrik, however, refuses to see the possibility of conflict in the relationship, understanding their friendship as an imaginary enterprise. "The boy made clear that he wished he could present Konrad to the whole world as his own creation, his masterpiece," jealously guarding this work from others (40–41). Self-referential, self-evident, and self-begetting, their companionship has no purpose outside their bond. It is beautiful but delicate, context-bound but context-less, desired but despised. Friendship has the fragility of an aesthetic object, a body in search of justification.

But in their adult lives rivalry and jealousy intervene, leading to attempted murder and betrayal. The writing pulls the narrative away from nineteenth-century aestheticism toward realist conventions. And Henrik himself strives for the truth behind the mystery, demanding answers from a man who has been away for forty-one years. In their climactic confrontation Henrik speaks grandly about friendship and their specific relationship. Konrad rarely talks and only to interject conjunctions and exclamations, like a character in a Platonic dialogue.

The passion of Henrik's desire for absolute friendship is so self-consuming that it necessitates social withdrawal. It requires the exclusion of others, and eventually even Krisztina, the wife/mistress. This may be why Konrad has to flee. The intensity is magnificent and unbearable at the same time. The two have attained not the friend as another self (Aristotle) but the friend as union with the same (Aristophanes and Montaigne); they have achieved wholeness.[41]

Henrik's dutiful and perspicacious nurse, Nini, understands that the boy's craving for complete identification with Konrad would eventually lead to disaster. "It's too much," she says to his mother; "one day Konrad will leave him, and he will suffer dreadfully" (41). Indeed, the morning after the hunt, when Henrik enters Konrad's apartment, the space he had been excluded from, he discovers an aesthetic retreat. "This apartment . . . was a work of art" and also a "refuge." The furniture, the curtains, the rugs, silver, bronzes, and crystal were all arranged with sensitivity and flair, not for Henrik but for Henrik's wife, Krisztina (118).

Henrik uncovers his exclusion from both the friend's sanctuary and the conjugal bed, a double betrayal by comrade and spouse, by his two other selves. But clearly the infidelity of friendship is the more painful. This is what propels the narrative logic—a double rejection by brother and wife who collude together against him. The loss of both, but particularly of the "twin," leaves Henrik grieving for forty-one years.

Henrik voices his devastation to Konrad when they meet across his dinner table: "I grasped that you had created this masterpiece of a rare and hidden retreat in secret, defiantly, as a great act of will, in order to conceal it from the world, as a place where you could live only for yourself and your art" (119). If Montaignean friendship needs the magic of fiction, if it requires secession, Konrad's creation of another retreat violates these assumptions by constructing a real refuge for another person rather than for the friend. Konrad's asylum breaks, in Henrik's mind, the sacred bonds of friendship. If Henrik once believed that the two friends breathed and acted in unison, then his discovery of this clandestine haven spells for him the collapse of brotherly union and the economy of reciprocity as it also questions the possibility of passion outside sexuality and marriage. Friendship's failure forebodes an endless isolation: Konrad is gone and Krisztina is dead.

As in *Women in Love* and *Brideshead Revisited*, the profound object of the protagonist's love is the friend rather than the wife. The women form a part of the partnership but clearly not its most treasured half. It is worth asking whether this marginalization of the wife causes the friendship to collapse. Is this why Konrad tried to kill Henrik? Is the story of matrimony and its betrayal incompatible with the romance of friendship? The saga of friendship here confronts the tale of broken marriage. But how can Henrik tell the world that the unfaithfulness of friendship is more painful than the betrayal of wedding bonds? Who would understand or care?

The social withdrawal of the conjugal couple is desirable and comprehensible. Is this not a major preoccupation of the nineteenth-century novel—courtship and eventual marriage?[42] But can one write a similar novel about two grown men who are not homosexual? In short, is a novel about a successful friendship possible? If such a story must be told, it seems to lead to death and mourning. For this reason, perhaps, the melancholy of the novel stems less from the loss of Austria-Hungary, as both state and state of mind, than it does from the discovery of the frailty of male friendship, or rather the impossibility of telling a story about ideal friendship. "The magical time of childhood was over, and two grown men stood in their place, enmeshed in a complicated and enigmatic relationship commonly covered by the word 'friendship'" (139). Friendship is "complicated" because it merges the erotic with the nonerotic; it is "enigmatic" because it embraces freedom in the midst of unfreedom. But ultimately it collapses because it has no support other than its own faculties and its will for self-institution. And the community witnesses this fall with the disinterestedness of someone entranced by the beauty of a crumbling edifice. From the perspective of its own selfish reproduction, society needs the relationship with Krisztina, either Konrad's or Henrik's, to succeed. But does it need the friendship between Konrad and Henrik?

In his reunion with Konrad, Henrik reminds him that friendship is "the most powerful bond in life and consequently the rarest." He wonders and rejects the idea that sympathy is the energy behind such a relationship. At the core, he affirms to Konrad, every friendship is bound by an "erotic attraction." Immediately in the next sentence, as in almost all modern novels, he affirms that by eroticism he does not mean men "driven by morbid impulses to satisfy themselves in some fashion with others of the same sex" (108). The "eros of friendship," he adds, needs no body. In long passages that resemble philosophical treatises rather than realistic descriptions, Henrik describes friendship as the most noble of human bonds (109).[43] But he is unsure now if it demands obligations. Deep down he believes that it must, hence the feelings of betrayal he has nursed, Miss Havisham–like, for forty-one years. Yet he realizes that this noble friendship is not possible in a time of crumbling castles and collapsing empires. "What is the value of a friendship in which one person loves the other for his virtue, his loyalty, his steadfastness? What is the value of a love that expects loyalty?" (110). In other words, can friendship exist outside the rules of exchange?

The answer for both men seems negative. Henrik declares: "We have no right to demand unconditional honor and loyalty from a friend" (112). And Konrad agrees: "I owed nobody an accounting" (113). How could this be, given the promises they made as children to blood brotherhood? Don't medieval knights expect allegiance and dedication from the friend? Although both men are in their eighties, they have reluctantly come to a modern understanding of friendship: love-as-feeling trumps love-as-duty. And friendship-as-self-institution defeats friendship-as-reciprocity.

Henrik has spent his life trying to figure this out. He realizes that ideal friendship, the erotic merging of the self and the other, of becoming twins, of blood brotherhood, is as fleeting as youth. Yet he also wants to believe in the permanence of male friendship. "We weren't comrades or companions or fellow-sufferers." Nothing can replace what they had, not even "all-consuming love" (140). His observation confirms the self-absorption of this love, its banishment of women, and then its own consequent exclusion from the reproductive economy. Konrad has to kill Henrik because Konrad has "complicated" the friendship by reintroducing Krisztina as the wife/mistress/sister. Are the friends still twins or are they rivals over the woman? Or both?

But sexuality was not the sole factor leading to the collapse of the friendship. As he mentally creates an inventory of the objects in Konrad's apartment, Henrik traces their life, trying to understand where the division began. He remembers the class disparities between them, he as the son of an aristocrat and emperor's confidant and Konrad as a child of poverty. Then there was Konrad's artistic bent, his love of music, which allied him with Krisztina and Henrik's mother, the softness of his character, his lack of fit with military life. So Henrik begins to suspect that Konrad actually hated him all his life because there was something "in me that you lacked" (138).

It is left open why Konrad flees. Part of the difficulty stems from the structure of the novel, built almost as a dramatic monologue, a poem of

Robert Browning's. Although this gives the narrative an easy flow, there is no dramatic contest of wills. Nor do we have access to Krisztina's diary, which the general has been holding on to all these years. Both decline to read it and Henrik "throws the little book into the embers of the fire, which begins to glow darkly as it receives its sacrifice" (204). The silence from the two possible interlocutors, one alive, the other dead, is coerced narratologically so as to focus the reader's attention on the general's obsession.

We are left to conjecture about the reasons for Konrad's betrayal with only evidence of his friend's speculation. Was it a yearning for the other or suffocation by the same? Or both? According to Henrik, Konrad abandoned the relationship, perhaps never having felt their union with the same intensity. He explains that "there is no feeling sadder or more hopeless that the cooling of a friendship between two men." Men and women, he argues, always manage to negotiate a "web of terms and conditions." But significantly, male friendship rests on a "pact wordlessly made between" them. They expect "no tenderness from each other" (138). The silent, tacit nature of male bonding, in contract to the legal and religious covenant between men and women, underscores the defenselessness of male friendship. At the same time, they can't expect much support from the society outside of the castle, so distrustful as it is of male secession.

At the end, Henrik is left friendless but confronting his contradictions: you tried to kill me because you were my friend. If you had not been my friend, you would not have fled for forty-one years and you would not have returned to face me. And now, despite the deceit and treachery, we are still friends because of the obligations imposed by the law of friendship but also because of your resistance to this law. Friendship, in other words, is broken down by the quarrel between duty and desire.

But are Henrik and Konrad friends in the end? And what does this friendship mean to them? Perhaps it is the weight of the past, the memory of their togetherness that obliges them to describe their relationship as a friendship. For they, particularly Henrik, have experienced adulthood as a life of dispossession. Henrik enumerates for Konrad a series of bereavements: the death of his parents, the loss of his wife, the erosion of a way of life, and, above all, Konrad's disappearance. What confronts him, from the present looking back, is isolation. Not the self-pitying solitude of Willy Loman (who says to his son Biff, "I was lonely. I was very lonely") in Arthur Miller's *Death of a Salesman*, but the bereavement of a man who has lost part of himself.

Friendship for Henrik becomes the existential condition of scarcity, the memory of the self-as-the-other and the current resignation to the self-as-self. But by excluding Konrad from the conversation, he further reinforces his deprivation. Since Konrad does not speak, we are left with an image of the friend not as two-selves-in-one but as a solitary self. If friendship "eludes the power of language," it may be because the novel portrays *philia* as a monologue. But can friendship exist as a soliloquy?

4

Friends and Lovers

It must have been that you were thinking of me.
In my dream, I thought I held your hand
And asked you to tell me what your thoughts were.
And *you* said: "I miss you bitterly."
— Po Chü-I, "The Letter"

Were they or weren't they? Henrik took pains to assure us that he and Konrad were not. Montaigne expressed his horror at the thought. But the famous pairs of antiquity, Gilgamesh and Enkidu, Achilles and Patroclus, and David and Jonathan, had not been troubled by it. From the ancient acquiescence to same-sex desire[1] to the modern denials people have sought to explain the attraction between two friends, especially the possibility that erotic attraction may play its devilish role.

Objections arise from diverse quarters. For Aristotle an erotic bond, being a relationship of pleasure, would represent a lesser form of friendship. For a Christian writer, such as Aelred, any suggestion of sexual yearning would be unholy. To the contemporary eye sexual longing between two men raises the specter of homosexuality, branding them indelibly. The penchant for labeling makes people believe that lust reveals inner truth. But beyond the tortured issue of identity, the eroticization of friendship disturbs us, as we deem friendship and sexuality antithetical. The introduction of the sexual seems to transform the relationship, blurring the boundary between these two categories, whether the two friends are of the same or a different gender.[2]

We want to keep the erotic urges separate from the ethical judgments. Consider a tongue-in-cheek conversation in Mario Vargas Llosa's comic novel, *Aunt Julia and the Script-Writer*. Although the topic is not friendship per se, it reveals how the imaginative and the procreative impulses are mutually exclusive in the same way that friendship and the erotic are distinct categories. A wildly successful writer of popular radio dramas, Pedro Camacho is not very sympathetic to the plight of the young narrator, Mario, who has fallen in love with his thirty-year-old and recently divorced Aunt Julia. The Bolivian scriptwriter has no time for personal entanglements. "Do you think that it's possible to produce offspring and stories at the same time?," Camacho asks. "Do you think that it would be possible to do what I do if women sapped my energy" (1982, 159)? For Pedro Camacho there is no overlap between sexuality and art. Modern society tends to look at friendship in a similar way, preferring to keep it separate from sexuality.

Passion and Ancient Days

Classical thinkers, such as Aeschylus, Xenophon, and Plato, on the other hand, took it for granted that eros inspired friendship. They presumed, for instance, the existence of a bodily relationship between Achilles and Patroclus but differed solely over what role each hero played in this relationship. Although we don't have the extant work, secondary evidence suggests that Aeschylus had written a play called *The Myrmidons* in which he represented a sexual bond between Achilles and Patroclus. In Plato's *Symposium* Phaedrus criticizes Aeschylus for misrepresenting the attachment between the two heroes. The participants in the symposium disagreed over who was the lover or *erastes* (older and active) and who the beloved or *eromenos* (younger and passive).[3] Phaedrus chastises Aeschylus for not casting Achilles as the *eromenos* when, he claims, Homer represents him as younger and more attractive than Patroclus (Plato 1989, 180a). Phaedrus praises Achilles for avenging Patroclus's death, all the time knowing that he would die after killing Hector. In other words, Phaedrus finds it remarkable that Achilles, the *eromenos*, would sacrifice himself for Patroclus, the *erastes*. He is surprised by Achilles's devotion because he understands the friendship in the pederastic scheme of classical Greece.[4] The *Iliad*, however, portrays this as a bond of love and affection rather than of power.

Phaedrus's speech presumes the presence of the erotic longing in friendship, refusing to divorce trust from lust, the narrative of companionship from the narrative of courtship. What he does, in a sense, is offer an explanation for friendship: he says we search for the friend because we find in him something lacking in ourselves. Indeed, Plato traces the source of friendship in the well of longing, in contrast to Aristotle who locates it in our sociability and commitment to the common good.[5] In *Lysis*, the dialogue on pederastic love, Socrates states that desire is a cause of friendship. We wish for what we don't have (Plato 1979, 221d). Plato offers an argument of utility, seeing in our desire for what is lacking, rather than in commitment to reciprocal virtue, the root of human attachments.[6]

Desire presupposes need and the origin of that need is loss.[7] By focusing on longing Plato humanizes friendship, locating the foundation of companionship in our deficiencies rather than in our quest for abstract integrity. When Socrates speaks of friendship with his interlocutors, Lysis and Menexus, he talks about "passionate love" and "belonging." Erotic longing implies that we are partial beings who strive to become whole by surrendering ourselves to another person.[8] We acknowledge that we are separate, always in search of another person to fulfill us. But we also recognize the need for reciprocity, namely, the other person finds in us something that she or he lacks.

Friendship then undermines the possibility of self-sufficiency in human relations. Attraction toward the other implies interaction with him. "Who is sufficient," Socrates says, "would be in want of nothing in accordance with his sufficiency." Such a person, he then adds, would neither treasure nor love anything. "And whoever doesn't love is not a friend" (Plato 1989, 215a–b). We are human insofar as we accept simultaneously our separateness and our desire to embrace another person. We derive nourishment from the friendship even if we never achieve it ideally.

A similar description emerges in Plato's *Symposium*, the account of a dinner given by the poet Agathon for Socrates, Alcibiades, Aristophanes, and other companions.[9] The text is composed of speeches on love given by the guests. The comedian Aristophanes offers the most memorable disquisition according to which love yokes together two distinct people into one unit. Eros, Aristophanes explains, is the human force that makes us seek our other half, someone who complements us and who promises what we are lacking. Aristophanes builds his theory on a myth of an androgynous human ancestor who was severed into female and male parts. He contends that Zeus, having sundered humans in two, took pity on them and moved their genitals from the inside to the outside of their bodies. Since that original division people have longed for reunion with their other half. When a person meets this other, "something wonderful happens: the two are struck from their senses by love, by a sense of belonging to one another and by desire" (Plato 1989, 192c). When woman and man commingle, women are able to bear children. But when man and man embrace, "they have the satisfaction of intercourse" (191d). For Aristophanes, love is "the name for our pursuit of wholeness, for our desire to be complete" (192d).[10]

The emphasis on desire brings love down to the lived experiences of people. Indeed, this conception of love as jubilation lies closer to the modern understanding of love as exultation than does Aristotle's conception of love as a dignifying force. Aristophanes says that desire introduces something "wonderful" to relationships, an energy that can often be nonproductive.[11] Indeed, after the embrace, the two "return to their jobs, and look after their other needs in life" (191d). Love, as magnetic attraction, offers people a brief respite from everyday activities. We seek love for no other reason than that it is there and we are human.

Love then can be nonutilitarian in the same way that art is. Although not overtly, Aristophanes's narrative points to the aesthetic understanding of love as impractical, self-validating activity. It is not a coincidence that, as an artist, he is permitted the greatest latitude in departing from the conventional discussions of the topic, thereby providing the most idiosyncratic speech in the symposium. He treats love almost as a defamiliarizing force in human affairs, much as the Russian formalists described the function of literature: it intensifies our awareness of the world around us by encouraging us to concentrate on the daily objects we routinely gloss over. Like literature, love turns the quotidian briefly into something extraordinary, after which we return to our regular toils. Love is a force that, as Shelley said of poetry, "lifts the veil from the hidden beauty of the world, and makes familiar objects be as if they were not familiar" (Shelley 1890, 13).

Or to put it another way, love makes small things bigger. The formerly East German writer Christa Wolf brought attention to the relationship between the ethics and aesthetics of friendship by emphasizing the power of writing to magnify. In her novel *The Quest for Christa T*, she explores the capacity of both art and love to amplify life. "Writing means making things large" (Wolf 1970, 168), the narrator states, a phrase she repeats frequently. Implied throughout is the sense that "friendship means making things large," showing one more time the implicit dialogue between friendship and fiction. It is through the letters and diaries that the narrator comes to understand Christa T., a woman she met at the university before World War II but who had died of leukemia at the age of thirty. In charting her fascination with Christa T, the narrator goes on a quest to comprehend and also resurrect her dead friend. Rather than a traditional plot-driven, postmortem novel, it turns into a philosophical introspection on friendship, the narrative propelled by the narrator's desire to discover more and more about her friend.

Of course, the act of retrieving Christa T's writings resurrects a life. But it also shows that writing is a dialogic process between author and reader, the self and the friend, through which both get to know the other. It compels us to recognize the presence and power of the other. Although the making of art may seem like a solitary process, it requires the consumer, that is, the friend. This novel, like the *Epic of Gilgamesh*, understands that friendship is a conversation, a dialogue that forces us to question our self-sufficiency. Although friendship encourages secession from the world, it also obliges the self to negotiate with the other, as my analysis of *A Passage to India* and *The Adventures of Huckleberry Finn* shows. This is the paradox: withdrawal into their relationship requires that the two friends puncture their respective personal autonomy. Aristotle argues as much. It is said, he claims, that self-sufficient people are blessed and have no need for friends; "for they have things that are good, and therefore being self-sufficient need nothing further while a friend, being another self, furnishes what a man cannot provide by his own effort" (1984, 1169b3–8). In reality friendship is antithetical to self-reliance.

When we cherish the friend we take a trip into the territory of the human, a state that tempts us out of the delusion of solipsism: I cannot know myself without you. Indeed, you show me that I am just a question entangled with other questions. Enkidu provides the earliest example of how this socialization works. Although rescued from his beastly subsistence by the harlot, he becomes a member of society with Gilgamesh's companionship. There is something transcendent about this process of solidarity. Knowing that we are bound to another person and through that person to others, we can somehow overcome our own finitude.[12] We are no longer one but at least two people, connected to others in empathic interdependence. And this linkage is brought about by the need we have for others.

This, I think, also differentiates friendship from sexual love. Of course, it is not always possible to differentiate the two. But generally friendship is not motivated by the need to possess, not propelled by the wild jubilation that drives Anna Karenina in her self-destructive attachment to Count Alexis Vronsky. Rather than scaling the Himalayan peaks of sexuality, friendship is satisfied with softer, more temperate hills. Consider the first encounter between Nick Carraway and Jay Gatsby. Carraway describes his fascination with the mysterious millionaire: "It was one of those rare smiles with a quality of eternal reassurance, that you come across four or five times in life. It faced ... the whole external world for an instance, and then concentrated on *you* with an irresistible prejudice in your favor. It understood you just as far as you wanted to be understood, believed in you as you would like to believe in yourself, and assured you that it has precisely the impression of you, that, at your best, you hoped to convey" (Fitzgerald [1925] 1953, 48). This passage suggests that, rather than heading toward proprietorship of the other, friendship looks for complementarity. Carraway finds Gatsby "gorgeous." But what moves him toward his neighbor is Gatsby's "heightened sensitivity to the promises of life," and his "extraordinary gift for hope" and a "romantic readiness" (2). The world does not end with Gatsby; it begins with him, and Carraway wishes to be part of it, even if tangentially. It is this reciprocity that distinguishes his joy from the exultation that Anna feels on meeting Vronsky.

In Carmen Laforet's dark, debut work *Nada* (1945), one of the most important novels in post-Civil War Spain, the poverty-stricken Andrea, who has just arrived in Barcelona after the civil war, is similarly smitten by the affluent Ena. Her friend offers all that the grotesque relatives of Calle de Aribau can't: "Ena provided everything. This chafed in a disagreeable way. All the happiness I enjoyed during the time seemed somehow diminished by my obsession with reciprocating her consideration. Until then no one had shown me so much affection" (2007, 52). Andrea is obsessed less with Ena than with correcting the imbalance in the relationship. She seeks to redress this disparity with a gift, searching for her most precious possession, a "handkerchief of magnificent old lace that my grandmother had sent me on the day of my first communion." Even if this gift, which causes an argument with her comically creepy aunt, Angustias, can never counterbalance Ena's tenderness, it is telling that for Andrea equality is a prime consideration.

Romantic Friendship

Nineteenth-century writers in Europe and the United States would have probably recognized the bond between Ena and Andrea as a romantic friendship, a form of association that flourished at the time. An attachment mostly of youth, it blossomed before the onset of marriage and was characterized by erotic ambiguity, loyalty, idealization, and undying love.[13] In the Victorian period romantic friendship was considered an ennobling association. The young David, for instance, in Charles Dickens's bildungsroman *David Copperfield*, is enamored of and idealizes the older boy, James Steerforth, at the Salem House boarding school from whom he must part after his mother's death. Reunited with the dashing and self-possessed Steerforth years later, David yearns for an intimate connection: "I soon fell asleep in a blissful condition, and dreamed of ancient Rome, Steerforth and friendship" (Dickens [1850] 1996, 298). Steerforth himself wishes to rise to David's ideal. "Daisy [his nickname for David], if anything should ever separate us, you must think of me at my best, old boy" (443).[14] Ultimately, he falls from Aristotelian loftiness, having seduced and abandoned Emily, the sister of Daniel Pegotty, a fisherman in Yarmouth and brother of David's former housekeeper, Miss Pegotty. David's discovery of Steerforth's "unworthiness" (461) constitutes one more step in his coming of age, with friendship serving here as a path of self-discovery rather than a destination.

The forerunner of this relationship is, no doubt, the famous bond between Montaigne and La Boétie. It is the first time that two men, with self-defined subjectivities, attempt a "perfect" union, ideal in the Aristotelian sense but also erotic in the Platonic. Montaigne speaks of falling in love with La Boétie, of finding the right soul mate, of forming a companionship that is self-validating. In many ways the two friends are centuries ahead of their time, more like characters in an early nineteenth-century novel about courtship. Theirs is a romance, a marriage of sorts so real that now it seems fictional, a creation of a Jane Austen. Michel and Etienne are modern *avant la lettre*, their relationship exhibiting the hallmarks of romantic friendship: mutually confessional and erotic. And because it is erotic, it must prove that it is not sexual.

"The other, licentious Greek love is justly abhorred by our morality," Montaigne says. It is a sentiment that appears almost verbatim in subsequent literary treatments. In Forster's posthumous *Maurice*, the tutor who enjoys reading the *Symposium* with his young students asks them to omit the references to the "unspeakable vice of the Greeks" (Forster 1971, 51). And in *Embers*, Henrik observes, as we have seen, that "perhaps buried deep in every relationship between two people is some tiny spark of erotic attraction" and immediately adds that this allure is different "from the affairs of those driven by morbid impulses" to satisfy themselves sexually with members of their own sex (Màrai 2002, 108).

From Montaigne on friends begin to exhibit "homosexual panic," the fear that others suspect them of homosexuality.[15] They have to demonstrate that they are not deviants just because they are friends. Rather than diminishing in our times through the acceptance of homosexuality, this presumption that same-sex friends may be gay has actually heightened. Indeed, the more visible homosexuality becomes the more unsure the majority is about its meaning and the more it affects relations between men.[16] Recent sociological research indicates that the terror of being labeled queer permeates American masculinity, with "that's so gay" being the most frequent jab among American young men.[17]

Friendship as Retreat

Romantic friendship occurred as much among women as among men. Indeed, it had as one of its sources the relationship between two aristocratic women who became renowned for no other reason than their notorious relationship. The story of the Ladies of Llangollen dramatizes the link between friendship and fiction. Eleanor Butler, an Anglo-Irish aristocrat, twenty-nine, and Sarah Ponsonby, her neighbor, thirteen, met in 1768 with hopes of living together in a country retreat. Rather than be compelled to marry against their wills, they fled together in 1778, in what was feared by their families to be an elopement. Terrified of a scandal, their respective families hunted them down and brought them back home, their virtue intact since the cohabitation did not involve men. But they escaped again two years later and settled in Plas Newydd, near the Welsh town of Llangollen, where they lived for the next fifty years in relative isolation, creating an aesthetic refuge and delineating a new type of friendship. The two women withdrew into their Welsh cottage where they came to represent the "retirement" from society into nature so celebrated by the Romantics.[18] In this retreat they spent time exclusively together, gardening, learning languages, reading, writing letters, recording their diaries, walking, painting, and renovating their cottage.

Almost two centuries before mass media made celebrity possible, the two Irish women became famous for being famous. Although themselves neither artists nor writers, they were visited by such luminaries of the poetic world as William Wordsworth, Shelley, Byron, and Sir Walter Scott. Even the Duke of Wellington paid them a visit.[19] Although they accomplished nothing extraordinary to justify their reputation, they exemplified a new sensibility—romantic friendship, celebrating an attachment that was to become pervasive among middle-and upper-class women (and men) in the next two centuries.

More than signifying shared activities, romantic friendship was physically intimate and sensual, exhibiting many characteristics that we now associate with sexuality.[20] Although it is plausible to think that the relationship between Sarah and Eleanor was more sexual than not, the written record draws a veil over this point. But the sexual nature of their attachment was less of a concern for their contemporaries. Women of the time revered the Ladies for challenging male authority, carving out a separate female retreat, and for placing love above financial security.[21] The lives of the Ladies manifested the ideals of the Romantic individual—personal happiness, social autonomy, and absolute devotion to inner truth.

Other women emulated the values espoused by the Ladies of Llangollen. Diaries, letters, and journals from the nineteenth century show women developing a segregated world of same-sex friendships, cut off from the universe of men.[22] These documents show that historically women have placed greater emphasis on self-awareness and intimacy in their interpersonal relations, leading their lives in the confines of the home.[23] Their identity was formed within sequestered spheres of family and friendship, whereas men were able to bridge their private and public selves more easily.

Independence from men entailed the creation of a separate living arrangement, like the one depicted in the utopian novel *Millenium Hall* by Sarah Scott.[24] When asked by a visitor why women would isolate themselves from society, Mrs. Mancel, a resident, responds that they seek an ideal society rather than Hobbes's state of war. She says, "What I understand by society is a state of mutual confidence, reciprocal services, and correspondent affections" (Scott [1762] 1995, 111). She describes a community held together by shared activities and interconnecting sentiments, striving for rational "communication and improvement" as well as the "social comforts of friendship" (110).

The utopia they created in Millenium Hall was, like that in the Ladies' Plas Newydd, as much physical as literary. Indeed, both places manifested the interdependence of ethics and aesthetics, fiction and friendship. The extensive gardens the Ladies of Llangollen had developed, along with the elaborate gothic features they added to their cottage, enhanced the artistic dimension of their relationship. Indeed, "the ladies created a work of art, their life," incorporating the two principles of eighteenth-century aesthetic theory: the sublime (of the wild Welsh countryside) and the beautiful (of their house and garden). Their feminine pastoral space contrasted with the untamed nature and hostile society outside.[25] Although the two women did not produce self-conscious art, their aesthetic partnership provides an early example of a link that would develop later between artistic collaboration and homosociality.[26]

After the example of the Ladies, romantic friends fell in love with each other, courted and confirmed their love with declarations of marriage, and experienced emotional and physical intimacy. Indeed, women were allowed to kiss, fondle, and caress each other, though stopping short of overt sexual relations.[27] Middle-class women developed these intense relationships before marriage with other women because, for the most part, contact with men was limited, especially in the eighteenth century. In most cases, these relationships continued well after marriage. Husbands accepted their wives' passionate devotion to their women friends.

Romantic friendship allowed women to achieve a seamless bond, much like that described by Montaigne, a mingling of souls.[28] And its hold on women reached into the twentieth century. The wish of Lily Briscoe in

Virginia Woolf's *To the Lighthouse* to unite and become one with Mrs. Ramsay is a case in point: "Could loving, as people called it, make her and Mrs. Ramsay one? For it was not knowledge but unity that she desired . . . intimacy itself, which is knowledge" (Woolf 1927, 79). Today relationships like that between Lily Briscoe and Mrs. Ramsay and between the Ladies of Llangollen would not flourish as easily because sexual taboos have limited the possibility of homosocial ties.[29] Moreover, they would be assumed to be lesbian.

It is worth comparing the fluidity of romantic friendships with the firm ontology built in the founding lesbian novel in English, Radclyffe Hall's *The Well of Loneliness* (1928). Its heroine, Stephen Gordon, longs to return with her lover, Mary Llewellyn, to Morton, her country estate, from which she has been banned by her mother following Stephen's acknowledgment of her "inversion." She yearns for the country seclusion so popularized by the Ladies of Llangollen. But Stephen is driven by the exigencies of sexuality, an insistent drive for internal ratification, rather than just the needs of romance. She says to her mother about her first affair with an American woman, Angela Crossby: "If I could have married her and brought her home—I wanted to bring her here to Morton. . . . I don't know what I am; no one's ever told me that I'm different and yet I know that I am different" (1956, 201). Through this confession, Stephen expresses her imperative to explore and liberate her sexual self, posing a question of essence. Passion equals self and the task of this self is to discover its roots in passion. The argument is circular, like all declarations of identity, be they of sexuality, race, ethnicity, or nationalism. It is not the well of loneliness but of identity that saturates the narrative. Stephen announces the existence of a new type of person, hitherto unacknowledged, and no longer beholden to dissimulation and an "intolerable quagmire of lies and deceit" (234).

Stephen embraces the discourse of liberation to fight against secrecy, disgust, and oppression: "As for those who were ashamed to declare themselves, lying low for the sake of a peaceful existence, she utterly despised such of them as had brains; they were traitors to themselves and their fellows, she insisted" (406). A revolutionary cry for recognition of the self, these sentiments don't express the dynamic of friendship, which depends on and thrives in dissimulation, the ongoing negotiation between the self and a fiction. The politics of identity, on the other hand, is foremost an attack on dissembling.

Of course, it is often difficult to make rigid distinctions in human affairs as physical intimacy could quite easily slide into sexual contact. Conceptually speaking, romantic friendship does not end, like a historical chronograph, giving way to homosexuality. Love and sexuality are intertwined. Yet, it is clear that *The Well of Loneliness*, like *Maurice*, opens the curtains to a category of being whose raison d'être is its sexual difference. We can better understand romantic relationships among women (and indeed among men) in the nineteenth century if we abandon the strict divisions between homosexuality and heterosexuality. Marriage and homosociality were intertwined and women had available to them a continuum of emotional and sexual possibilities with other women.[30] At the very least, society was much more receptive to different modes of living, even if it did not condone erotic attachments among women.[31] It recognized friendship as a bond comparable to kinship and conjugal love.[32]

Of Male Bonding

Romantic friendship thrived among men in the eighteenth and nineteenth centuries, allowing the possibility of homoerotic ties that are inconceivable today. A case in point is John André, whose fatal appeal to other men highlights an openness that permitted men to speak of their attractions to one another. Born in 1750 in England, he was executed by American forces as a British spy thirty years later. This execution brought forth issues that, while seemingly contentious today, were endemic to male subjectivity at the time: the link between loyalty and beauty, the frank expression of eroticism, and the dialogue between aesthetic collaboration and companionship.

Like the Ladies of Llangollen, John André's life unfolded like literature. Indeed, he seems to have been a literary character, a Billy Budd, before Herman Melville's creation. The historical record attests that his "masculine beauty" and his extraordinary charisma made all men love him. Like Billy Budd, "a virtue went out of him" that compelled men to admire and try to save him (Melville 1962, 47). He was fluent in a many languages, painted, and wrote poetry—a sensitive, intelligent, and versatile man well suited to the nuances of romantic friendship.

Arriving in 1774 in Canada as a lieutenant with the Royal Fusiliers, he was captured by American forces a year later. While a prisoner in

Lancaster, Pennsylvania, he was permitted to billet with the family of a Quaker, Caleb Cope. While there, the twenty-five-year-old André developed a friendship with Cope's thirteen-year-old son, John, whom he taught drawing. With their relationship deepening, the two resolved to move to London and spend the rest of their lives together, like the Ladies of Llangollen.[33] After he was transferred from Lancaster to Carlisle, Pennsylvania, André carried on a correspondence with Cope Sr. in which he often discussed his son, asking permission to take John to England and assume responsibility for his education.[34] In these letters he expresses his desires to continue teaching John: "I shall be happy if an Occasion shall offer of my giving your son some farther hints in the Art for which he was so happy a turn." André asks the elder Cope to send greetings to his family "but particularly to your son, my disciple."[35]

In 1776 he was freed in a prisoner exchange. But four years later he was captured wearing an American uniform, charged with being a spy, convicted, and sentenced to death by hanging. During the days of the trial and just before his execution, the prisoner seemed to captivate those around him, both by his extraordinary beauty and his character. Many men fell under his Tadzio-like spell, including Alexander Hamilton, Washington's aide-de-camp.[36] His biographer, Winthrop Sargent, writes that friend and foe praised André's beatific kindness toward and understanding of his captors and lamented his imminent end (Sargent 1871). The qualities mirror the saintly radiance exuded by Billy Budd at the scene of his execution when he uttered the final words: "God bless Captain Vere!" (Melville 1962, 123). What was "phenomenal" about Billy Budd's death was the stillness of the hanging body that did not display any "spasmodic movement" (125). This unnatural immobility seems to suggest something holy and calm about his end.

In many ways John André is Billy Budd. "From the few days of intimate intercourse I had with him," wrote one American officer, "I became so deeply attached to Major André that I could remember no instance where my affections were so fully absorbed by any man." Another confessed that André was "the handsomest man I ever laid my eyes on."[37] Many tried to intervene on his behalf, including Hamilton himself. But Washington was not to be moved. On the day of his hanging, Hamilton drafted a ten-page letter to his friend John Laurens, giving an account of the execution.[38] "Never perhaps did any man suffer death with more justice, or deserve it less," Hamilton wrote. The Marquis de Lafayette, who like many other men openly wept at the execution, later characterized Hamilton's description of André's imprisonment and death as a "masterpiece of literary talents and amiable sensibility."[39] Caleb Crain notes that Hamilton's account "may be the earliest instance in the young republic" of literary ambition. "It is a piece of writing that aspires to represent a man's feelings for another man" (2001, 9). Literary composition granted these men the liberty to express themselves in a way not possible in ordinary discourse. Men wrote about "what they felt for one another" and "in the process they created literature" (13).[40]

As we witnessed in the *Epic of Gilgamesh* and the *Iliad*, the birth of a literature coincides with the story of friendship, in this case a tale of masculine love and imaginative collaboration. Hamilton's literary letter was the product of his bond with André and Laurens, inspired by the former and written for the latter. John André was an artist himself and his young companion, John Cope, had similar ambitions. There is an overlap also between ethics and aesthetics, with *eros* enhancing *philia* and *philia* heightening *eros*.[41]

Literature gives license for the description of a relationship that ultimately can't be made to conform to social reproduction. Male attraction arouses fears of sedition, whether in the courts of Uruk, the tent of Agamemnon, or in Washington's office. Alexander Hamilton, an adviser to the country's founding father, sided with love and beauty over patriotism and duty. Through the discourse of romantic friendship he tried to comprehend and then to save John André, a man whom Washington held to be a treacherous spy. The case of John André demonstrates how romantic friendship can stimulate contradictory emotions: we love the friend but the friend has to die because we love him. And his death inspires narrative that can be understood as fiction.

Perhaps we can best understand André's life as literature. Although there is no evidence that Melville knew of John André, his writing provides insights into the intricate link between life and art. "The symmetry of form attainable in pure fiction cannot so readily be achieved in a narration essentially having less to do with fable than with fact. Truth uncompromisingly told will always have its ragged edge," says the narrator of *Billy Budd* (Melville 1962, 128). And he adds that "the story ends with his life." But in real life the story has an antecedent that seems as fictional as the fable so that we don't know which "narration" is more "finished," the actual or the fictional one.

Literature and friendship are similar in another fundamental way I hinted at earlier; being ambiguous, they are precarious. In friendship we are not always sure whether the other is a companion, a lover, an associate, a comrade-in-arms, or a blood brother. If the rise of literature narrates the tale of friendship, it is because literature and friendship trade in this uncertainty. At the same time, the story of John André narrates some of the fundamental themes of literature: youth, heart-stopping good looks, untimely death, execution, betrayal, and unbending political authority.[42] We respond to it with a mixture of dread and sympathy, attempting to mind read the motivations of the leading characters: Why was André so civil and painfully understanding to his executioners, displaying an "uncomplaining acquiescence," as Melville says of Billy Budd (Melville 1962, 45)? How could so many manly men around him succumb to his unfailing virtue and his vulnerable physique? And why was Washington alone so unfeeling, his ears plugged to the siren songs of beauty, youth, and goodness?

The friend has to die because he is a foe. While romantic friendship may have represented an egalitarian union, fundamental to democratic society, it could also shake that society by confounding men's hearts and minds. If so, is the friend executed because he is a friend, threatening the cohesion of the body politic? That is to say, is he put to death because, being supremely literary, he is able to seduce men to place themselves in the shoes of another? Does André achieve what the friend is supposed to do, introduce ambiguity in the relationship between fact and fiction?

Romantic friendship did not take its last breath on the gallows with André; it thrived for decades on American soil. Most young men had a close intimate friend. And we have a number of famous pairs, including Daniel Webster and James Herrey Bingham and, of course, Abraham Lincoln and Joshua Speed. This type of friendship, as I have shown, represented a metaphor for the union of citizens during the American Revolution and for decades afterwards. Not itself the subject of a cause, say the liberation from (political or sexual) oppression, it remained a relation rather than an essence.

But romantic friendship began to disappear after the Civil War. The intimate correspondence, the warm touch, the friendly embrace, and the contours of the masculine form in bed that were a source of comfort eventually became a cause of distress or perhaps disgust. Arousing suspicion about unnatural desire, romantic friends became with each decade more conscious of shame and ridicule. What eventually won out was romantic love first between men and women and then, in the twentieth century, after much struggle, between members of the same gender. But there does not seem to be a place for romantic friendship in romantic love, the ultimate aim of which remains carnal fulfillment. In a society that overvalues sexual relations and that prefers materialist explanations for human nature, friendship seems both unfitting and unsettling.

We can outline the transition from the softness of romantic friendship to the hardness of today's relations by looking at the life of Mark Twain (Samuel Clemens). By the 1880s men had abandoned the intimacy and sentimental connections of early America and their own childhoods and came to embrace notions of male-male bonds that were closer to our own. Yet they remembered the more fluid emotional attachments of their youth. Clemens's friend David Twichell, for instance, described such tenderness in letters to his father during the Civil War. Reporting his response to the death of a young soldier, Twichell writes, "I feel a sob choking me as I write now, for I tell you, Father, this boy had a strange hold on me." After the battle at Gettysburg, he confesses that before leaving boy in the field hospital "I gave the little hero . . . a kiss of true love."[43]

This rhetoric became unthinkable as the century came to an end. The more malleable homosociality of earlier decades disappeared in favor of a more rigid manliness.[44] Men's emotions came increasingly to focus on their wives rather than on their male friends. The opportunities and need for male friendship began to shrink against the background of changes in the workplace and the household.

The Fiction of Intimacy

It is literature that shows perhaps why this is so, why society pulled men away from the ambivalence of romantic friendship into the fixity of conjugal union. Specifically, one early scene in Melville's *Moby Dick* demonstrates why the messiness of classification eventually gave way to certainty. Melville's novel has an epic sweep, as it follows the larger-than-life struggle between Captain Ahab and Moby Dick. But the narrative often descends from its Homeric heights to explore minute stories of touching tenderness, like the meeting between Diomedes and Glaucon.[45]

Such is the scene one morning when Ishmael, having just arrived in the whaling town of New Bedford, Massachusetts, wakes up in his hotel to find a stranger in his bed. This experience, I argued earlier, was not at all unusual, the sharing of beds by brothers, friends, and strangers being a necessity of space and money. Boys became accustomed to sleeping with their brothers and then with their roommates in college, and with strangers when traveling. So did soldiers. Physically intimacy between men was economically enforced and privacy was not available.[46] Before central heating the male body lying next to you was a source of warmth.[47] Men, in short, were familiar with the scent and touch of other men. Undoubtedly, some may have felt a "sexual piquancy" lying next to another man.[48]

Melville certainly highlights the ambiguous nature of these frequent encounters. The two strangers have suddenly become man and wife as Ishmael wakes up to discover an "affectionate arm." He and the stranger, who he learns is called Queequeg, are sleeping "socially," having become "bosom buddies." As he gradually opens his eyes, he realizes that "you had almost thought I had been his wife" (Melville 1956, 40). Try as he might, Ishmael can't unlock Queequeg's "bridegroom clasp," which is hugging him so "tightly" (41). And Ishmael comes to appreciate the advantages of an unheated room. In order to appreciate warmth, he reflects, some part of your body must be cold. And this coldness forces you to snuggle up to the body next to you. "For this reason a sleeping apartment should never be furnished with a fire, which is one of the luxurious discomforts of the rich" (61).

Although the discourse of romantic friendship was available to Melville—language he no doubt had used in letters and diaries as had other contemporaneous men[49]—he chooses to cast the embrace in the form of the conjugal couple. The touch here seems to be more than a touch. And literature appears to explore the implications of desire that transcend the acceptable limits of male companionship. Or was romantic friendship always unclassifiable?

The tone of the narrative voice in this section is one of an ingénue, of a young man setting out on an adventure on the high seas. This expansiveness of the first-person account allows an openness to strangeness, in this case both to new experiences and to foreigners. Although the practice of sleeping with strangers in hotels was not uncommon, few contemporaries would have described it as a male-female relationship, even in the ironic, distanced mode of the narrator who becomes the metaphorical wife to a "savage." But this is what the narrator does. And their marriage is formalized on the second night: when their smoke was over, "he pressed his forehead against mine, clasped me round the waist, and henceforth we were married" (59). Even though Ishmael considers the "unbecomingness of his hugging a fellow male in that matrimonial sort of style," he does not push the body away. The distancing mode of his narrative hides his inner pleasure at the fictitious marriage, making acceptable the tight embrace of their bosoms. Indeed, Queequeg's matter-of-factness, his straightness, contrasts with "Ishmael's longing for him" and makes this bonding seem sexual.[50]

Here dissimulation is necessary. The constant give and take between the real embrace and the make-believe marriage allows this scene a peculiar reality. We have then a happy combination of Aristotle's disinterested companionship with Plato's erotic longing. However, they become committed not to reciprocal virtue but to each other, as Queequeg will become Ishmael's shipmate on the *Pequod*. What are they? Friends? Shipmates? Lovers? The relationship is not easily graspable.

But could we not say this of the characters in real life? What was the bond between John Cope and John André and between Alexander Hamilton and John André? We have less here what Derrida calls "virile homosexuality" than the feminization of male longing or at least the release of male desire from the strictures of marriage and the duties of kinship. Romantic friendship presented an acceptable category to make sense of and deal with same-sex desire. But the honest probing of the literary text shows how vague this relationship was and how confounding of norms. And it did this before the discourse on homosexuality cast same-sex attraction into a tension between clandestine and suppressed behavior and dominant and acceptable modes of practice. The discourse of identity defines dissembling as a crime, an attack on the romantic soul's inner truth, as my discussions of *Maurice* and *The Well of Loneliness* have shown.

What makes possible the feminization of the male, white narrator? First, we can say it's the otherness of his bedmate. Intimacy is always easier, less risky or embarrassing, with social inferiors or with animals. People may show tenderness to pets or children that they don't express with their equals. Disparities of class or race also make possible the breaking of sexual taboos. An obvious example is Lady Chatterley's affair with Oliver Mellors, her husband's gamekeeper. His earthy masculinity excites Lady Chatterley in a way none of the aristocratic men, including her husband, the handicapped veteran Sir Gordon, can. It is not the affair per se that shocks society but Lady Chatterley's violation of class boundaries. Through Mellors she loses her embarrassment over sex and gains the possibility of pleasure for the first time: "She felt, now, she had come to the real bedrock of her nature, and was essentially shameless" (Lawrence 1959, 280).

This is also true of *Maurice*. The real scandal arises less from the mixing of bodily fluids than of social hierarchy. Maurice attains true love with the gamekeeper, Alec Scudder, rather than the aristocratic Clive. Indeed, Clive finds Maurice's relationship with Scudder "grotesque" because "intimacy with any social inferior was unthinkable to him" (Forster 1971, 242). Finally, both women lovers of the aristocratic Stephen Gordon in *The Well of Loneliness* are middle class. These books also demonstrate how we reach our "authentic" self by violating conventions. Although both *Maurice* and *The Well of Loneliness* are conservative in terms of politics and aesthetics—not celebrating sexual dissidence like Oscar Wilde and Constantine P. Cavafy—they see the liberation of the self in homosexual desire, discovering truth by turning away from customs.[51]

Ishmael and Queequeg are not interested in violating social norms, striving for a friendship rather than an ontology. Queequeg's exoticism enables the caress between the two men. But in the previous examples the overthrowing of conventions establishes a new identity: a free femininity against a dogmatic patriarchy in *Lady Chatterley's Lover* and homosexual ontology against a violent, heterosexual order in *Maurice* and *The Well of Loneliness*.

Ishmael characterizes Queequeg as an unfamiliar creature, "neither caterpillar nor butterfly," a description of strangeness that illustrates their relationship (Melville 1956, 42). And he rationalizes his passive surrender to Queequeg like a person tacitly accepting the unorthodox practices in a foreign land.[52] When in Polynesia, do as the Polynesians![53] But since he is still in New Bedford, he needs the escape made possible by the inventions of art, by the "confabulations" (60) they tell each other in bed. The coziness of their embrace is realized in the netherland of fiction.

The bedroom becomes for them an aesthetic refuge from the outside world—much like the whimsical house designed by the Ladies of

Llangollen—where they can put into practice a romantic and very physical friendship between a white man and a "savage." And in the bed they exchange mutual confidences so vital to friendship. "There is no place like a bed for confidential disclosures between friends" and, he adds, between man and wife. "Thus, then, in our heart's honeymoon, lay I and Queequeg—a cozy and loving pair" (61).

Contemporaneous readers would probably not have imputed homoerotic motives to these acts because men, as I noted earlier, were accustomed to sharing beds with other men, because the partner was foreign to New England society, and because the described acts took place in fiction. Literature translated them through the distance of irony into a marriage, rendering the extraordinary normal. Literature offered American men the dispensation to articulate erotic sentiments.[54] Metaphors, styles, and the language of poetry and novels, in other words, made possible the expression of erotic longing. The masculine embrace became allowable when converted by the literary experience into a marriage.

Friendship requires fantasy, making acceptable the "marriage," with Queequeg "affectionately throwing his brown tattooed legs over mine; . . . so entirely sociable free and easy were we" (60). Literature refracts and eroticizes the everyday experience of romantic friendship, Ishmael and his "fellow man," both undressed and hugging tightly in bed. And Queequeg himself is imaginary, both in being a literary character and in coming from the invented island of Kokovoko in the South Pacific, which does not exist in the same way that New Bedford does. Ishmael himself recognizes that in a "countryman" such a "sudden flame of friendship" would be "distrusted." But in this "simple savage those old rules would not apply" (59).

The intimacy between Ishmael and Queequeg is enabled by fiction and it also disrupts the "rules" of acceptable relations at the time. The "free and easy" manner of the bedroom embrace reminds us of Jim and Huck floating "free and easy" downriver (Twain 2000, 177). The narrator experiences Queequeg as a make-believe husband, a creation of his own desire for a bosom friend with whom he could have a "matrimonial" cuddle. And in art his feminization becomes feasible. We have an embrace of sorts: romantic friendship = marriage = fiction = romantic friendship. In this exchange between illusion and actuality we can't easily differentiate the normal from the extraordinary, with Ishmael's relationship with

Queequeg being a dialogue between life and art, between a real person and an abstraction of that person.

Men in Love?

With the gradual banishment of romantic friendship from the social order and its association with shame at the end of the nineteenth century, it found hospitality again in literature. If writing makes things large, then literature's function here is to bring friendship back from exile, if only momentarily. There is an irony. Although friendship witnessed literature's birth, literature now laments the passing of romantic friendship.

How else can we interpret the sorrowful ending of D. H. Lawrence's *Women in Love* (1921) other than as a dirge for a lost ideal? The novel expresses many of the anxieties arising from male bonding. Rupert Birkin and his wife, Ursula, have returned to the Tyrol to retrieve the body of Birkin's best friend, Gerald Crich, who has committed suicide by walking through the Alpine landscape and then freezing to death in the snow. Gerald's suicide is partly provoked by his increasingly destructive relationship with Gudrun Brangwen, Ursula's sister, and her dalliance with the homosexual and nihilistic sculptor Loerke. But his inability of opening up to Gudrun has to do with his overall difficulty in resolving his many contradictions, male intimacy being one of them.

Lawrence's work recasts the romantic story that sees marriage as the ultimate aim of fiction by treating friendship as a competitor to matrimony. In this, *Women in Love* defamiliarizes the traditional plot narrative of the nineteenth-century novel, which treats friendship as a bona-fide subject infrequently.[55] To the extent that it figures in nineteenth-century writing, say, Elizabeth Gaskell's *Wives and Daughters* ([1866] 1996), friendship is incidental to the plot structure of wedlock. In Gaskell's novel, the friendship between Molly Gibson and her stepsister, Cynthia, is secondary to the plans of Molly's stepmother to have them both stand before the altar. The title itself announces the work's thematic preoccupation. The same is true in Charlotte Brontë's *Shirley* ([1849] 1979). The relationship between the impoverished Caroline Helstone and the heiress, Shirley Keeldar, only serves the greater purpose of each woman's courtship, consummated with a double wedding ceremony at the work's end. Although valued as a social good, in both works friendship plays second violin to the dominant melody of marriage. Similarly, in Henry James's *The American* ([1877] 1971) the comradeship between the prosperous American businessman, Christopher Newman, and the French nobleman, Valentin Bellegarde, is subordinated to the courtship between Newman and Bellegarde's sister, Claire. Indeed, the latter helps the former in facilitating the marriage.

In *Women in Love*, by contrast, the love narrative between Birkin and Ursula and between Gerald and Gudrun is unsettled by the development of a friendship between Birkin and Gerald. The challenge that the two men face, however, is that they possess neither the language nor the conventions of the romantic friendships of the previous century. How can they foster an intimate tie that seemed so self-evident to men from Montaigne to Alexander Hamilton? They resort to a literary imagining of sorts, the possibility of fashioning a medieval blood brotherhood, yearning for the rules and norms of a ritualized friendship. In the seemingly unlimited freedom of the twentieth century, they crave the laws, ceremonies, and material expectations of tradition.[56]

The novel reveals the challenge facing friends in modern society. Because friendship is independent from the medical, legal, and psychological regulation that homosexuality is subjected to, Birkin and Gerald are free to create the relationship they want. But without contemporaneous models of and language of friendship, they turn to an invented, mythical time, just like the two boys in Màrai's *Embers*.

Early on in the novel, before their love affairs with the two sisters take root, Birkin, the more adventurous of the two, propose a *Blutbrüderschaft* (ritual brotherhood) when Gerald visits him at his sickbed. He suggests that they build something that was taken for granted centuries earlier. When an institution becomes self-conscious, as Hegel says of art, then it seems to have exhausted itself. This seems true of friendship in the novel. If men have become aware of the shame in male intimacy, they are obliged to return to a much older institution in order to justify, or get away with, this attachment. Birkin, who "had been loving Gerald all along and all along denying it," proposes a medieval form of comradeship to validate the "problem of love and eternal conjunction between men" (Lawrence 1976, 198–99). Rejecting the necessity of wounds and blood as obsolete, Birkin suggests that "we ought to swear to love each other, you and I, implicitly and perfectly, finally, without any possibility of going back on it" (199).

Looking at Gerald with "happy eyes," he pleads but Gerald keeps his reserve, asking for more time to understand this suggestion better. Birkin's offer of knightly fellowship somehow sanctions a desire that, as Tennyson said, cannot be named. Much like the economic "pretext" in *Zorba the Greek*, this ancient form of manly exchange makes (modern) male intimacy palatable. It soothes the uneasiness of male same-sex interaction that in Tennyson could be imagined as communion with the dead. But Lawrence also needs the trope of combat, as he does medieval ritual, to convert the English mates into Roland and Oliver.

So literature provides here not only the home for friendship but also the instrument for its imagining. Lawrence's novel dramatizes literature's function of highlighting the border between actuality and illusion, so vividly enacted in the aptly named chapter "Gladiatorial," when Birkin proposes a naked wrestling match with Gerald. The physical contest, as we will see in "Brokeback Mountain," is based on a traditional premise that men become friends through fighting—a theme as old as the *Epic of Gilgamesh*. In this case, however, the physical struggle heightens the sensual excitement. The pressing of one body on the other and the grappling of muscles turn the fight into an erotic play between simulation and reality.

The language of this scene, bursting with hyperbole and raw power, transposes the rubbing of sweaty bodies in Gerald's room onto ancient Rome. Birkin, the weaker of the two, somehow manages to subdue Gerald on the floor, "to penetrate into Gerald's more solid, more diffuse body" (262). At the end of the match, lying almost unconscious on top of Gerald's exhausted frame, Birkin is jolted by the "hammer-stroke" knocking outside of the room. Incapable of getting up, he realizes "it was his own heart beating." Then with their hands momentarily clasping, they get up to normality, the momentary escape from the world having ended. "We are mentally, spiritually intimate," Birkin pleads again, "therefore we should be more or less physically intimate too" (265). Gerald agrees: "It was rather wonderful to me."[57] Here the competition between men is not, as Hobbes would argue, for honor or glory but actually for physical union. Men make war to lie naked next to one another.

What takes place here? A youthful and guileless wrestling match? Is it intercourse through metaphor or metaphor as intercourse? Have the two men become, like Ishmael and Queequeg, husband and wife? Have they crossed the bounds of friendship, romantic or not? As in Melville, the figural language of literature allows the interpenetration of illusion into reality. Have they achieved in this imaginary realm male intimacy that is both emotional and physical?[58] This wrestling bout, this ancient trope where the match turns erotic/sexual, is an expression of masculine desire rather than of sexual essence. For Lawrence highlights the love struggle between the two manly men against Loerke, the decadent homosexual (and, thus, the outsider of heterosexuality), the "vice" the "real" men scorn and fear.

This sense of "wonderful" male bonding is anticipated in Lawrence's first novel, *The White Peacock* (1911), an idealized narrative set in the countryside of the Midlands that has been airbrushed of soot. Told in the first person, it follows Cyril Beardsall, a lanky and dreamy youth, and his growing infatuation with George Saxton, the son of a neighboring farmer. Upon entering their farmhouse, Cyril observes George with a book in his hands: "He looked up as I entered, and I loved him when he looked up at me, and as he lingered on his quiet 'Hullo!' His eyes were beautifully eloquent—as eloquent as a kiss" (Lawrence 1966, 97). There is an adolescent naïveté, a total absence of the infiltrative aggression of the wrestling match, though there is a parallel between Gerald and George (both of whom deteriorate in the course of the narratives), on the one hand, and Birkin and Cyril, on the other. This fascination becomes quasi physical the day Cyril joins George in a swim. After their frolic in the pond, they climb out to dry themselves, each eyeing the other: "He was well proportioned, and naturally of handsome physique, heavily limbed." Cyril takes pleasure in observing George dry himself and George himself knows how much Cyril "admired the noble, white fruitfulness of his form" (245).[59] Lost in a trance, Cyril forgets to rub himself, so George begins to wipe him, "as if I were a child, or rather, a woman he loved and did not fear." At one point, to get a better grip, George puts his arm around Cyril, pressing himself upon his friend, "and the sweetness of the touch of our naked bodies one against the other was superb." This physical convergence, so reminiscent of the embrace between Queequeg and Ishmael, seems to satisfy some "vague, indecipherable yearning" of their souls: "When he rubbed me all warm, he let me go, and we looked at each other with eyes of still laughter, and our love was perfect for a moment, more perfect than any love I have known since, either for man or woman" (245).[60]

The language of this scene, romanticized and ingenuous, anticipates the forever-spring sentiments of the first half of Evelyn Waugh's *Brideshead*

Revisited, entitled "Et in Arcadia Ego"—the first and only time Charles Ryder encounters love. Recounting the day he visited Sebastian's house, Charles remembers the "cloudless day in June when the ditches were creamy with meadowsweet and the air heavy with the scents of summer" (Waugh 1960, 29). Both novels showcase the freedom of postadolescent romantic friendship. The absence of self-consciousness in *The White Peacock* describes the love between George and Cyril as self-evident and unthreatened by grit and guilt. Nevertheless, it necessitates the banishment of women from this idyll. George's sister, Emily, who laughs at them from the water's edge, flees their manly paradise after getting splashed by Cyril. Friendship necessitates a social escape even in youth. And it is this bucolic potential that Gerald and particularly Birkin try to achieve through the violence of the wrestling match. In both cases, with the idealized imagery of *The White Peacock* yielding to the disenchanted sentiments of *Women in Love*, the Arcadia of friendship eventually leads to Hades. And it certainly puts the men into conflict with the women in their lives.

Homoeroticism seems to heighten the distance between men and women. The ambiguity of a desire that does not seek total possession, that does not end in social reproduction, and that does not express itself in a sexual identity, unsettles social categories. Gudrun and Loerke go off together, leaving Gerald to die alone in the snow. The gay man can become friends with a woman. Male homosexuality can coexist with femininity as a separate identity. But does male-male longing have a place within a male-female universe? Can a dialogic mode coexist with human essences? Can a man love a man exactly as he can love his wife?[61] Or is sexuality so one-sided that it can bear either a friend or a wife but not both?

So the narrative closes off inconclusively, much like the *Lysis*, that is, with the inconclusiveness of male friendship. Disturbed by Birkin's strong attachment to Gerald, Ursula wonders if she was enough for him. "You are all women to me," he responds. "But I wanted a man friend, as eternal as you and I are eternal." Troubled further by his answer, she presses him to reassure her that she satisfies him completely. But for Birkin to be "really happy," he wanted "another kind of love." Ursula can't understand. "It's an obstinacy, a theory, a perversity. . . . You can't have two kinds of love. Why should you? . . . You can't have it because it's false, impossible" (473).[62] To which Birkin responds with the last line of the novel—"I don't believe it"—a line that strikes like a horse's hoof in Chandrapore.

Even in death this "kind of love" is impossible. Lawrence's narrative is not an elegy to Gerald in the way that "In Memoriam" is an aesthetic remembering and restructuring. There is a finality to Gerald's suicide much like Myris's untimely death in Cavafy's dramatic monologue "Myris. Alexandria 400 AD." There the speaker flees the Christian home of his recently departed friend, terrified that the Christianity of Myris's relatives would seize his memory of Myris. The poem mourns as much the passing of paganism as a way of life as of a living person (Cavafy 1975, 155). So Lawrence's novel is an elegy to romantic friendship as a historically situated way of life. Gerald's suicide is a logical outcome perhaps of a time that fears friendship as a pathology, as a competitor to marriage, and as a sign of veiled homosexuality. The decisiveness of death only emphasizes the indecisiveness of Birkin and Gerald's bond. What was their friendship exactly? Part filial, party comradely, part brotherly, part erotic, part conjugal? A mosaic of these qualities? A thicket of twisted tensions? Hence Ursula's dismay and lack of comprehension.

The fraternity that Birkin and Gerald strive for includes femininity. In their final conversation Birkin makes the case quite clearly that he aspired to a love with Gerald as absolute as that with Ursula. But the work ends by pointing to what would be a main thrust of modern life—friendship as an opponent to matrimony. It also anticipates the rise of homosexual identity against which friendship now will be compared. If Lawrence's novel explicitly announces a struggle between male friendship and marriage, it quietly forecasts a conflict between friendship and the new politics of identity. If friendship has to square off against the productivity of conjugal love, it must also confront the tendency in the twentieth century to conceive of sexuality as ontology. Faced with the prescriptions of heterosexuality and the potential stigma of homosexuality, what emerges is a hard, unbending masculinity that aspires to self-sufficiency.

The New Autonomy

Ernest Hemingway's *The Sun Also Rises*, published a couple of years after *Women in Love*, provides a lucid illustration of the new masculinity, framed by feminism, on the one hand, and an oblique homosexuality, on the other. Hemingway's prose, sparse, emotionally neutral, quasi journalistic, mirrors the detached (mostly American) expatriates living in Paris after World War I. If the main protagonist, James Barnes, fails to make an intimate connection with Lady Brett Ashley, he does not even attempt to with either Robert Cohn or Bill Gordon, his male friends. In fact, Barnes is not at all preoccupied by his relationships to either Cohn or Gordon, his main concern being his inability to settle down with Brett.

The normal guys, who pursue women in this novel, show none of the softness we saw in diaries and letters of the previous century or from World War I. Friendship in the text figures neither as a metaphor for political coexistence, as in *Passage to India* or *The Adventures of Huckleberry Finn*, nor for erotic interaction, as in *Women in Love*. In fact, friendship becomes almost indiscernible, no longer a topic of conscious concern. It's not certain whether this invisibility suggests contentment with the institution of friendship or simply indifference. And what does friendship mean for these men? It seems to signify the sharing of activities, like attending bull fights, asserting a brawny masculinity, and competing over women, but not the romantic relations of the nineteenth century nor the passionate entanglements described by Montaigne or Kazantzakis. More often than not men don't seem to yearn for such attachments, having neither the language for mutual revelation nor the desire for emotional ties with other men. The characters in Hemingway's novel manifest both the decline of romantic friendship and the appearance of self-sufficient male subjectivity as a social ideal. With the erection of barriers between men and the removal of barriers between men and women, marriage offered men their best opportunity for intimacy. And men built their friendships with men through companionship and shared pastimes.[63]

We see this turn in the friendship that develops between an American and an Englishman in Graham Greene's *The Quiet American* (1955). The youthful, callow American, Alden Pyle, meets the veteran and much older British journalist, Thomas Fowler, in a Saigon café. Pyle is taken by the cosmopolitan, albeit more cynical Fowler, following him around town, suggesting meetings. Fowler, the narrator, is pleased by if somewhat wary of the American's homegrown naïveté, his desire to install democracy in war-torn Vietnam. Pyle quite clearly "imposed" the friendship from the beginning; Pyle's "lips expressed with even more fervor the strength of his affection and of his admiration— God save the mark—for me" (106).

The low-key nature of their relationship turns very aggressive when Pyle falls in love with Phuong, Fowler's young Vietnamese girlfriend. Here the trope of manly struggle, in the midst of a deadly war, is transmuted into a fight over a woman. Pyle offers her his youth, a wedding ring, and the promise of an American visa, while the already married Fowler can give her little in return, other than an uncertain future in French-controlled Saigon. The relationship between Fowler and Pyle remains tenuous, unequal, promoted more by the American and tolerated by the British journalist, even though Pyle saves Fowler's life. At the end, it is the cynic Fowler who gets disillusioned with Pyle's idealism when he unearths the consequences of the American's plans. In his attempt to promote democracy Pyle has involved himself with a political faction that has planted a car bomb in Saigon with many civilian casualties. Fowler indecisively participates in Pyle's assassination by a shadowy resistance group. The novel ends on an uncertain note that captures the state of their friendship: "I thought of the first day and Pyle sitting beside me at the Continental, with his eye on the soda-fountain across the way. Everything had gone right with me since he had died, but how I wished there existed someone to whom I could say that I was sorry" (247). Fowler remains friendless, though he keeps his girl.

This emotional disconnection seethes through Saul Bellow's magisterial *Humboldt's Gift* (1975), a novel that spans from 1930 to 1970 and covers topics from the place of poetry in American society to the decline of marriage. Among other things, it deals with the traumatic relationship between Charlie Citrine, a successful poet and essayist from Chicago, and von Humboldt Fleischer, Citrine's self-destructive mentor. The novel, in part, dramatizes Citrine's fascination with Humboldt, ever since he read the latter's collection of poems and borrowed money to visit the great poet in Greenwich Village. Thus one of the main topics is his attempt to re-create Humboldt after the latter's death by recalling memories and scouring the poet's diaries, notes, letters, and published works, a task resembling the narrator's reconstruction of Christa in Wolf's *Christa T.* The "gift" in the title refers to the papers bequeathed to Citrine in Humboldt's will. Among them is the suggestion for a movie script based on Humboldt's life (Bellow 1975, 346).

Here we have again the example of friendship as a memorial, or rather the recasting of friendship into an aesthetic act. The friend attempts to re-create the dead comrade through the devices of fiction. As taken as Citrine was by Humboldt when he was alive, he becomes obsessed with him after his death. Mourning for the friend, I have argued, involves the recognition of the loss of the other half. "I've been attached to Humboldt for nearly forty years. It's been an ecstatic connection. The hope of having poetry—the joy of knowing the kind of man that created poetry" (Bellow 1975, 477). On the one hand, this is a very successful friendship, having lasted for four decades and having been nourished by a mutual commitment to lyric. Citrine recognizes Humboldt's great disappointment in not having created "some high work." He knows Humboldt was capable of composing such verse; he was the person who could "express a sense of life," who could "find out the truths of nature," using the opportunities time offers. "When those opportunities are great, then there's love and friendship between all who are in the same enterprise. When the opportunities are smaller, there's spite and rage, insanity" (477).

On the other hand, their relationship, Citrine seems to say, also manifests wrath and malice. The language both men use to express their devotion is hard-hitting. They compete with one another, often denigrating each other. Theirs is a tough-guy relationship by men who pursue their "broads."[64] The trope of war turns into an equivocal skirmish. Whereas in previous novels and poems men struggled to gain more intimacy, both physical and emotional, here the aim of the contest is uncertain. What is it that they are after?

Friendship, I have argued, requires an act of dissimulation. A person attempts to stand in the shoes of the friend through the powers of the imagination. Empathy comes about through an act of aesthetic projection. But Citrine says that the ethical and poetical faculties seem to be weak in their time. His age provides the opportunities neither for great friendship nor for great poetry. In their situation Citrine finds "heartbreak and madness," because poets have to dream, he quips to his girlfriend, Renata, "and dreaming in American is no cinch" (312).

So we are left with two strands in the novel: the withering of male intimacy and the shriveling of poetry. The novel charts both the near impossibility of great poetry in America and indirectly—because Citrine only alludes to it—the near impossibility of great friendship. The barriers to poetry are connected to the obstacles facing friendship, showing one more time the intersection between the language of aesthetics and the language of ethics. The characters don't need to dissemble about their friendship, as in the case, say, of *Zorba the Greek*. They don't have to create a pretext for intimacy as in *Moby Dick*. While the text mourns the dire situation of poetry in America, it indirectly laments the similar fate of friendship. But the dirge for friendship is nearly inaudible, taking place almost in the background of other events and reflections. Friendship is not worthy of being a literary topic, not even a secondary one as, in Victorian literature, a stepping-stone toward the altar. To save itself, the novel grabs on to manly heterosexuality.

A Queer Embrace

It is nearly impossible for friendship today to escape the polarization between heterosexuality and homosexuality. What has not been noticed is how this binary tension leaves so little scope for fiction. That is to say, the modern proclivity to fix identity—national, ethnic, religious, or sexual—at the core of individual being has turned dissembling into a pathology. The task of any person is now to express her or his core of truth. This Romantic ideology curbs behavioral possibilities available in the past because it sees sexuality as both a product and an expression of ontology. The ambiguous nature of friendship confronts the rigidity of choice.

Try as E. Annie Proulx might, her story "Brokeback Mountain" cannot escape the conflict between being gay and straight. Perhaps this is why it moves unknowingly toward death, even though the reader picks up the elegiac tone in the first paragraph. Originally published in the *New Yorker* (1997), it was made into a feature film by Ang Lee in 2005. The story's narrative appeal comes from the author's decision to use the conventions of a heterosexual romance to describe the attachment between two cowboys, Ennis Del Mar and Jack Twist.[65] The erotic energy, displaced in Lawrence as a mythological, knightly tale, becomes real and raw. And Proulx's writing is folksy and raunchy, using the argot and metaphors of the ranch. The horses here don't veer off, forever separating Dr. Aziz from Mr. Fielding. Friendship no longer has to be imagined as an ahistorical blood brotherhood or as a marriage. There is no need for pretext, for play or ruse.

Having met in 1963 herding sheep on Brokeback Mountain in Wyoming, Jack and Ennis reunite again a couple of years later, after they both have married and had children. Unable to live together or apart, they carry on an adulterous affair for twenty years, meeting intermittingly for fishing and camping trips.[66] The story's originality lies in turning their union into the homoerotic version of Tristan and Isolde and of Vis and Ramin.[67] The results are equally tragic, with Jack killed beside the highway while changing a flat tire.

The story begins with an epitaph of sorts, with Ennis, divorced and isolated, thinking back to Brokeback Mountain, the site of those halcyon days of youthful apostasy. He has been dreaming of Jack recently, trying to reconstruct the summer they met on top of the world. It is a retrospective approach, like so many elegies, constructed on the antithesis between an empty present and a full past. But there is neither mourning nor any commemoration. It is a lament of silence as the wordless Ennis can't find the right expression. Everything seems so inconclusive to him, "an open space between what he knew and what he tried to believe" (Proulx 2000, 285). Jack's death, which embraces the narrative from start to finish, further heightens the open-ended but self-contradictory aspect of their relationship. "Nothing ended, nothing begun, nothing resolved" (278).

To be sure, theirs is a tale of fractured intimacy, of thwarted love stretching over half their lives. Yet, while that of Tristan and Isolde's infidelity can be spoken about, their attachment has no name. So if Isolde's death becomes a cautionary tale against betrayal, Jack's demise is equivocal. He dies in and because of ambiguity, the conflicts running through "another kind of love." This confusion comes out in the image of their flocks running into the sheep of another herder that summer on the mountain, and the two young men rushing to sort them out. "In a disquieting way everything seemed mixed" (262). For the rest of their lives, they try to sort themselves out. What were they, after all: friends, lovers, husbands, gay, straight, cowboys, sheepherders, fathers? "I'm not no queer," Ennis mumbles, "and Jack jumps in with 'Me neither'" (262). It's the same conundrum.

Did they or didn't they? There is no doubt they did. But are they queer? Proulx's story continues the long tradition of regarding friendship as an inconstant bond, torn apart by internal struggles and struck down by suspicion or enmity. Yet, unlike other texts that play out this contradiction, hers seems at one point to veer off the parallel railway ties, balancing itself on one side of the track. Her narrative steps into essentialism, a move reproduced by Lee's film, and by its public reception and the critics' approach to the film.[68]

It is not that the friendship itself becomes an identity but rather that it is translated into a gay romance. The dissidence of friendship then is decoded into a homosexuality, which one could celebrate or deride. Although the narrative presents the two men as caught in two ways of life, one with each other and another with their families, it also expresses an implicit need to cut through the tension and to see Ennis and Jack as repressed gay men who, if they had lived in more enlightened times, would have settled together on a ranch. As Ennis learns the nature of Jack's death from his wife, he wonders if Jack had been the victim of an antigay hate crime. No, it was not an accident, he fears, "they got him with the tire iron" because he was different (279). Ennis thinks back to an admonitory story related to him by his father of an old ranch hand who had met such a fate. "They'd took a tire iron to him, spurred him up, drug him around by his dick until it pulled off" (270). The friend passes away not because he is a friend but because he is gay, whose sense of self is branded on him by everyone, friend and foe alike. The buddy dies, in other words, because social mores are inflexible.

Stamping their friendship as homosexual satisfies the conceptual hunger for sorting out people like sheep. And, of course, the death, either by accident or design, further reinforces the social tendency to see homoerotic desire as deviant. Male erotic attachments, as I have argued, tend to be expressed in elegy form. We seem to understand these associations in terms of loss and death rather than, say, of happiness and optimism.[69] To interpret the story as being about gay cowboys is further to reinforce this tradition. If, in the past, the friend passed away because of the muddles of male intimacy, now he must be killed because he is deviant. So we have here friendship as suppressed gender identity and misogyny: they cheat on themselves and on their wives about their true identity, participating in a double crime.

But Ennis and Jack don't see their relationship so simplistically. Ennis himself says: "I was sitting up here all that time tryin to figure out if I was—? I know I ain't. I mean here we both got wives and kids, right?" (268). He expresses their irreconcilability—their "situation," as they called it. In the twenty years since Brokeback Mountain they have been trying to deal with the pulls of this predicament. That is to say, their relationship asks us to think about the link between homoeroticism and marriage, male same-sex desire and domesticity. Can one love another man and be a father? Can one be physically intimate with another man while still being a husband? Birkin raised these very issues directly with his spouse. But the novel ended interrogatively. The answer now seems uninhibitedly negative. Essentialism requires that both men be gay, that they express their sexuality as a way of life, and that they fight against their own subjugation. It opposes them to domesticity, as a no longer hated but proud and open other. In so doing, it limits the affective possibilities available to Ennis and Jack, flexible modes of being that Tennyson and Hallam, Queequeg and Ishmael could assume, along with the heroes of epics past.[70] Essentialism paradoxically clamps down on one side of love as it simultaneously liberates another.

If a tire iron had indeed struck Jack by the highway, it was the rod of conceptual rigidity that regards sexuality as a seal of identity, branded upon people's skins. In killing Jack the story reveals the modern impulse to make passion reveal inner secrets. It accepts the binary opposition ascribed by the murderer. This is why the story became for many readers and viewers a narrative of identity. Jack and Ennis can't be friends because—*for the modern reader*—they have to be gay. The erotic (and sexual) vagueness that bestrides Achilles and Patroclus, Gilgamesh and Enkidu, Queequeg and Ishmael, Birkin and Gerald collapses, transposed into a unidirectional path toward truth. This does not mean that actual people, in this case, gay men, can't form friendships. Nothing could be further from the truth. The journalist Andrew Sullivan observes that gay men, because of their social marginalization, have sought out friends and have developed friendship networks that only women are otherwise capable of (1998, 230). It is our proclivity to privilege sexuality as an expression of essential meaning that is the issue here. In this sense, the story reveals indirectly that love is a greater social menace than sexuality to the modern sensibility.[71] And in so doing it challenges readers and moviegoers: Can male friends fall in love with each other? Can they engage in a sexual affair and still be conventionally masculine? Does their affection then expose a hidden reality about them and about their community?

Yet, despite all the uproar, there is in a sense little that is shocking about the story: two nineteen-year-old cowboys spending a summer on a lonesome mountain discover mutual sexual attraction. Those with experience of cowboy culture would hardly be surprised with the couplings on the plains: young men isolated from women and their families for long periods in the company of animals and guns.[72] And the western film, as a genre, captures and plays with same-sex attraction. It portrays a heroic masculinity obsessed with guns in a landscape almost devoid of women and kinship. "Brokeback Mountain" brings attention to the "mutual masculine longing and homoerotic posturing." Loneliness in the western is always resolved by another cowboy rather than by a woman.[73]

But the essentialism implicit in the story and film and explicit in the public reception of both ultimately frustrate our imagining different modes of behaving, feeling, and being. It opens but ultimately closes the window to possibilities beyond identity: if you love another man you must be gay. For a more nuanced view of gender and friendship I turn to two recent examples, one in fiction and the other in real life.

Let me start with the literary example, *Gods and Monsters* by Christopher Bram. Based on the life of James Whale, the British director of such horror film classics as *Frankenstein*, the work is set in the heady and unbuttoned Los Angeles of the 1950s. It also introduces the fictional character of Clay Boone, a handsome ex-Marine who works in the garden of the convalescent and aged director. The gay filmmaker is so captivated by the gorgeous physique of the gardener that he pays him to model for his sketches. At first, the homophobic Clay is reluctant but agrees to sit fully clothed. He needs to be in control of his body and of his words, not wanting to step out of the social role he has been assigned: the tough, emotionally inarticulate, nonbonding soldier. But one night, listening to Whale's nightmarish account of his World War I experience and fearing that they might induce another stroke in Whale, Clay tosses off his comforting script of both warrior and model. He erases the lines he has drawn between distance and closeness, homosexuality and heterosexuality, fantasy and reality. He is "ashamed" at being moved by the old man's experiences yet fearful for his employer. The only way he can imagine to "snatch" Whale from his past is to drop his towel. "His body acts on impulse before his mind makes sense of it" (Bram 2005, 240). In a sense, he sacrifices himself or, rather, his self-control.

By exposing his nakedness, he shortens the remoteness to Whale that he had so prized. He does so with the aim of restoring some order to their lives. This to a certain extent is the function of sacrifice. Ancient societies reinstated peace and balance in the social order by ritual murder.[74] In Boone's case, the sacrifice is a Christian (or post-Christian) act of ceding the body for the spirit. It seeks release from the turmoil that the relationship with Whale has thrown him into. By surrendering his clothes, surprising as it is to both of them, Clay no longer regards himself as an autonomous person with respect to Whale, but as a man in inner communication with another. What is important here is not the You or the I, the straight or the gay, the hale gardener and sickly director but the exchange taking place between them. This relation exceeds the completeness each represents.

Boone, for instance, has never had an intimate relationship with anyone before. He has slept with women and he has bonded with his buddies in the Marines. But he has never been entangled with another human being in an intense way. And he certainly has no social protocols to lead him in a close relationship with another man, gay or straight. For this, he needs the power of the imagination to see himself and his relationship in a different way. He becomes his own fiction writer, the author of his own short story.

Although the ending of the novel seems contrived and implausible, it shows friendship as risk taking, an action that entails both the revision of roles and destinies and the invention of new channels of communicating. Indeed, Clay is "amazed to discover" himself full of "tenderness and sorrowful awe," and capable of feeling so contradictorily toward another man (252). In the morning, having discovered Whale's body floating in the pool, the victim of a suicide, Clay knows that he will carry Whale's death with him, despite the fact that they had known each other for only two weeks (270–71).[75] Later, at the funeral, the narrator notes that only the "husky, young" yardman lingers to "watch the masons cement a marble square over the little urn" (273). His world has changed because he has surrendered to the chaos of friendship with the most unlikely person, a gay, English director over thirty years his senior. This tacit consent makes him exude a faint aura at the funeral, as if he were the only true "mourner" there.

Of course, this escape from the gravity of identity is made possible by literature. In actuality, life itself can be very literary, offering people the velocity to transcend social limits. I have in mind a group of women in a Greek town that consciously defies easy categorization. Known among themselves as *parea* (company or group), this collection of seventy women, who were studied by ethnographer Elisabeth Kirtsoglou, embraces a gender that is not "constitutive of identity."[76] Although many of them are married with children, or have never considered sexual relations outside of this group of women, they see themselves as neither lesbian nor heterosexual. Typical is the story told by Nena. On the one hand, Nena says that her friend/partner, Stasa, gives her everything she could ever imagine from a man: "affection, love, understanding, erotic fulfillment, company, stimulation, joy" (Kirtsoglou 2004, 142). But on the other, she claims not to be attracted to women but only to Stasa; the person, in other words, rather than the category. Loving women for her and her cohort does not imply being committed to a particular mode of identification. Rather, exploiting the blurriness of friendship, Nena and Stasa maintain their relationship even if it means guarding it to keep it private.

The women keep their *parea* secret not out of shame but out of fear that the outside society would put upon them the straitjacket of identity. As Maro says to the author, to those outside "things are 'either'—'or'." They, on the other hand, strive for a utopian society, an attempt to chart an alternative path. And it is with this in mind that they allow Kirtsoglou to write the ethnography. As one informant tells the author, "write about the *parea* and let the world know that somewhere there exist some women who dare imagine a different life." A different life for them signifies the freedom to maintain two or three different selves, which a moralizing society would condemn as hypocrisy. "I am split between three places, three roles, almost three selves," confesses Carolina as she describes her life at home with her son and husband, at the beauty salon, and with the *parea*. The author herself is astonished to see Carolina return home at 6:00 a.m. from the bar, kiss her husband good morning, make her son's lunch, sleep a few hours, and then drive to her salon.[77] What permits this Dr. Jekyll/Mr. Hyde mask-switching is the capaciousness of both friendship and marriage, that is, that women are allowed intense relations with other women while remaining "faithful" to their husbands.[78]

It is an openness to the porous nature of family, affection, sexuality, marriage, and friendship that "Brokeback Mountain" touches yet cannot tolerate. In this case, literature seems less daring than life itself. But death saves the story from closing in on itself. At the end, the narrative loops back to the beginning. We are still in the realm of fiction, returning to where we started. Ennis is staring at a postcard of Brokeback Mountain and the two shirts, his and Jack's, hanging over each other, much like

Achilles and Patroclus wearing the same armor, two bodies indivisible. To be sure, the fact that both heroes could wear the same breastplates and helmets indicates the similarity of their builds. And so it is with these two shirts, a memento of a bonding that had taken place twenty years earlier. The two had been involved in a wrestling match with Ennis getting a bloody nose that stained his shirt. And now Ennis discovers the two shirts in a back recess of Jack's closet when he visits Jack's house after his death. Evidently Jack had kept them, one hanging over the other, as a hidden testament. The shirts attain the closeness that eluded the two men in life and they come to resemble the intermingling bones and ashes of two fallen heroes in an amphora.

Although the postmodern story strips the relationship of the martial metaphors in the epic, it accepts the ancient idea that friendship prospers in the underworld where it cannot play havoc with the fences set up by the living. So mourning is what awaits Ennis, who is unable to find consolation on the "grieving plain" (284). He is a shepherd crying for his Lycidas in this modern, western pastoral. "If you can't change it, you've got to stand it," he once said to Jack. Although Ennis wants to fulfill Jack's wish to have his ashes scattered on Brokeback Mountain, Jack's father doesn't allow it. The contrariety that can't be named cannot be. The friend dies. Categories are maintained. But the friend can't really be killed forever. He reappears in another story, coming back each spring to restore chaos to life. "The leprous corpse exhales itself in flowers of gentle breath" (Shelley 1984, 20.172–73). We want the friend to live so as to disturb our need for categories.

AFTERWORD

Digital Friends

> There is no harder prison than writing verse,
> what's poetry, if it is worth its salt,
> but a phrase men can pass from hand to mouth?
> —DEREK WALCOTT, "FOREST OF EUROPE"

Is friendship, like poetry, dead? When poems and novels lament friendship as much as a fallen hero, do they suggest that it's no longer viable? Is literature morbid in its obsession with the dying friend?

Outside of literature it is possible to find flourishing literary relationships. Mary McCarthy and Hannah Arendt come to mind. They met in 1944 and continued a warm friendship for thirty years. Upon Arendt's death in 1974 McCarthy put aside a book she was finishing to edit and annotate Arendt's unfinished Gifford lectures that were published as *The Life of the Mind*. It was a friendship that sustained them both. When Arendt's husband, Heinrich Blücher, died in 1970, Arendt asked those gathered in her apartment, "How am I to live now?"[1] Although the question may have been rhetorical, the answer was clear—through companionship, especially with McCarthy.

McCarthy flew in from Paris the next day. After she returned to Europe, they spoke on the phone every other week at a time when international calls were costly. Their thirty-year-old correspondence attests to a remarkable commitment.[2] The subjects of these letters, as one can imagine, are vast, ranging from their writing, to McCarthy's husbands, travel, literature, politics, gifts, disappointments at reviews, and contemporary events, like the Eichmann trial that Arendt covered for the *New Yorker* or McCarthy's trip to Hanoi and her reports from the Watergate hearings that appeared in the *New York Review of Books*. They miss each other's physical presence: "I'm writing you this note," McCarthy remarks, "because my heart is full of emotion and I want to talk." At one point, Arendt, not given normally to intimacy, says, "Oh Mary, how I wish you were here and how tired I am of this letter writing " (Brightman 1995, 107).[3]

Two most unlikely friends, separated by two continents, their gender, and social standing, Tennessee Williams and the Russian émigré actress Maria St. Just corresponded for nearly forty years until the playwright's death. Having met in 1948 at John Gielgud's house, they wrote to each other nearly every month. They talked about her acting, his plays and movies, his travels, the leading luminaries of the theatrical world, his depressions, his lovers, and his fears about his fading career. The letters, gossipy, emotional, funny, trivial, and indiscreet, demonstrated the constancy of a relationship. "Rome lacks your presence as do most places where you have been and gone," he writes in 1955.[4] He needs her and "the dignity of London," he confesses, in order to get through the latest Broadway production. "Your letters bring me back to life." And she in turn reassures him that "you are my family, and the very deep love and affection and respect I bear for you has never diminished over the years. If you are in trouble and unhappy, you must feel that you are not alone." When Williams died, he entrusted his estate and his sister Rose, who suffered from mental illness, to Maria St. Just. Although he knew many cultural literati of his time, from Luchino Visconti and Franco Zeffirelli, to Gore Vidal and Truman Capote, to Clare Bloom and Marlon Brando, the person he felt closest to was a woman who lived in England.[5]

People make friends. But what is the quality of these friendships? What are the boundaries? What are the claims? I argued that friendship did not disappear in modernity, as some sociologists had feared. On the contrary, rationalization and differentiation created more opportunities for intimacy. Although traditional relations, such as blood brotherhoods, gradually withered away, a new type of friendship emerged that seemed to stem from individual desire and to be held together by ties of self-revelation. By definition, these new bonds were weaker, no longer supported by a floor of rules, rituals, and gift exchange. The twentieth-century novels, poems, and short stories examined here allude to these transformations, especially in male bonding. But it is fitting to ask whether literature's portrayal is on the mark or overly pessimistic.

Whither Friendship?

As I noted earlier, research on friendship has begun only in the last few decades. These investigations, however, indicate that American men have anxieties about male intimacy and that they are most comfortable in companionably shared activities. A recent survey of men across ages, classes, and racial groups in the United States revealed that 60 percent of the respondents reported that they had enough friends, 25 percent not enough, and 15 percent were unsure. This represents a high number of men claiming to have fulfilling relationships. What do these friendships entail? On the whole, they involve pastimes such as playing or watching sports, talking on the phone, using e-mail or social networking sites, volunteering, going to bars, or meeting for a meal. At the same time, most men confessed to not wanting much emotional intimacy with their male friends.[6] Physical closeness or the voicing of personal concerns provoked fear of being labeled gay. And this anxiety cut across ages, classes, and racial groups. The topics of masculinity and homosexuality arose in nearly all the interviews. On this point the findings seem contradictory. On the one hand, men claimed to have enough companions. On the other, they acknowledged their difficulties in making friends due to the lack of role models, the terror of seeming vulnerable, and the reluctance to appear gay or effeminate.[7]

What also emerges from these studies is that friendship is no longer seen as an social or personal ideal. Americans seems to view male achievement as occurring primarily in the areas of family, virility, and work. Rarely do they "gauge a man in terms of his success as a friend."[8] This is a significant but underappreciated insight into how friendship ranks in society today. The pressure placed on men at the end of the nineteenth century to differentiate their behavior from that of women and homosexuals also removed friendship from the attributes of an accomplished man. Men want friends. But they live in a society that worships competition, that glorifies what

Aristotle defined as friendships of utility, and that sexualizes physical and emotional closeness. American society no longer elevates deep, intimate friendship among adult men as a value in the way it did in the eighteenth and nineteenth centuries.

In order to understand why men today may not yearn for a relationship that was considered ordinary a hundred years ago, we might look at the socialization of boys. A study has shown that boys and girls in early adolescence have equally intense emotional friendships. But boys begin to lose their friends after they are sixteen, a process that continues to old age. The slide in the number of friends occurs across classes, ethnic, and racial groups. Between the ages of twelve and fourteen, boys have close relationships with other boys and speak of their love unselfconsciously. They value friendships not only for collective activities but also for sharing secrets and for revealing feelings.[9] Much to the surprise of the researchers, boys manifest intricate social skills and the ability to speak about their emotions. But this all changes around middle adolescence when boys begin to fear and distrust their peers and are less willing to seek intimacy with other boys. They also speak of being lonely and depressed. The story of growing up male is the story of loss and increasingly emotional disengagement with other boys and men.[10] As a result, men "learn to do without friends," and they learn to suppress the need.[11]

What explanation do boys give for these developments? Unsurprisingly, the same as provided by the literary documents. The appearance of the girlfriend is the main reason boys themselves list for their growing distance from their buddies. They give up their male friends in pursuit of romantic love, which has been idealized in American society since the end of the nineteenth century.[12] Homophobia is another obvious motivation. The boys pepper their conversations with the phrase "no homo" so as to preempt any gay aspersions being cast on them (220). This phrase suggests both that homosexual panic still reigns and that boys and men regard emotional intimacy as a manifestation of sexuality (or that homosexuals are the only ones capable of such connection with other men).

Other factors for the reduction in the number of friendships are the ones usually cited: the mobility of American society, pressures of work and family life, and the conventions of masculinity.[13] What remains unacknowledged, however, is that American society itself discourages male friendship after adolescence. Boys grow up in a world that expects men to have buddies—in sports or chess—while women are allowed to possess sensitive companions. At the same time society segregates emotions from cognition and endows these divisions with gendered personalities,[14] exaggerating, in this way, the gap between men. As a result, people come to believe that men and women have separate capacities for forming relationships. But there is nothing ontological about these characteristics. Boys are perfectly capable of intimacy, as were men of previous centuries.[15] The difference between now and the past is that today boys are conditioned to distance themselves from their own capacities and inclinations.

And when boys turn to popular culture they find rampant phobia about male-to-male closeness. On the one hand, movies, television series, and videos have embraced friendship in the last thirty years. The couples of the *Honeymooners*, *I Love Lucy*, and *The Dick Van Dyke Show* have given way to the single friends sharing both living spaces and everyday activities. From Sheriff Andy Taylor and his deputy Barney Fife on *The Andy Griffith Show* to *Starsky and Hutch* to Miles and Jack, the wine-loving buddies of the film *Sideways*, friends are shown depending on each other. Characters in television shows like the *Mary Tyler Moore Show*, *Friends*, *Frasier*, *Sex and the City*, *Scrubs*, *Gilmore Girls*, *How I Met Your Mother*, and movies like *Bridesmaids* turn to their friends rather than to spouses or family for support. Although many of the protagonists still aspire to marriage, they realize that it is not the reachable goal it once seemed. As a result, it is friendship that these characters embrace, even as they are careful to differentiate friendship from same-sex affection.

The friendships in popular culture rarely stray from the prescribed paths of masculine and feminine self-representation. And when they do, as in episodes of *Friends* or *Scrubs* that explore more physical expressions of male intimacy, the resolutions safely return the viewer to the heterosexual hug.[16] Seldom is there a twist to this tale as in *Casablanca* (1942) where the boy stays with his friend rather than going off with the girl. Rick Blaine (played by Humphrey Bogart) loses his love, Ilsa Lund (played by Ingrid Bergman), having given up his own escape from Casablanca to ensure her flight to Lisbon with her husband. But he ends up with an unusual companion. When Captain Louis Renault (Claude Rains) suggests that Rick and he abandon Casablanca and join the Free French in Brazzaville (capital of the French Congo), Rick responds with that wry line—"Louis, I think this is the beginning of a beautiful friendship." Although the remark may be ironic, it is significant that Rick disappears into the fog with his buddy rather than riding off alone like the gunslinger Shane.

Quite often popular culture expresses anxiety about male companionship. A case in point is the riotous episode from the television show *Friends* entitled "The One with the Nap Partners." In many respects, the scene is similar to the conjugal embrace between Ishmael and Queequeg. Joey and Ross wake up from a blissful slumber to discover that they were napping together, Ross snuggling against Joey. Their beatific expressions turn to horror once they realize that Ross is on top of Joey, his hand on his buddy's chest. They are dumfounded with embarrassment. "We fell asleep, that is all," Ross assures his pal. Joey promises not to talk about the unnameable act. As he reaches out to shake his friend's hand, he is admonished with the suddenly self-conscious demand, "No touch." In a later scene Joey confesses that it was the best nap he had ever had. When pushed, Ross agrees, a remarkable admission today but, as we have seen, not so in previous times.

"But it's over, Joey," Ross insists. Joey, on the other hand, wants to experience the embrace again. "It's weird," Ross cries as he steps out of the room. Later in a bar Joey winks at his friend that he will be upstairs taking a nap. The episode ends with Ross lying in Joey's arms, content and peaceful. "It was a great nap," they mumble to each other. But as the camera pans away, we see the other roommates staring at them, baffled and displeased. Sensing their presence, Joey jumps up, hollering, "Dude, what the hell are you doing?" It is all over. The chorus has passed judgment. There is no dissimulation possible, no pretense to marriage (Melville) or medieval ritual (Lawrence). Although much has changed since *Moby Dick*, pals still want to sleep next to each other. But that sleep has taken on a troubling connotation. "Weird" means queer.

Even the suggestion of male physicality provokes trepidation in Eminem's disturbing song "Stan." Introduced by the haunting lyrics of Dido and the roar of thunder, in the background we hear Stan, one of Slim Shady's (Eminem's first stage name) fans, a man desperate to communicate with his idol. In a frantic note, Stan confesses that he adores Slim, that he has Slim's name tattooed across his chest, and that he wants an autograph for his younger brother. He draws parallels between his own life and Slim's. Although Stan has a girlfriend, the real object of his affection is Slim, manifesting here a hip-hop version of the Patroclus and Achilles dynamic. "My girlfriend's jealous cause I talk about you 24/7 / But she don't know you like I do Slim, no one does." He begs Slim to call him, saying, "We should be together." But he never hears from the singer. So in one last, desperate cassette recording, he rejects his idol, shouting that his girlfriend is tied up in the trunk (we hear her screaming). He hollers: "I love you Slim, we coulda been together, think about it / You ruined it now." At that point Stan discovers that the bridge in front of him is out as he hits the brakes.

Slim finally writes, not knowing that Stan and his girlfriend are dead, advising Stan to get "counseling," astonishingly conventional guidance from a rebel. But he recoils at his fan's outward affection: "And what's this shit about us meant to be together? / That type of shit'll make me not want us to meet each other."[17] Whereas Dido's lyrics are soft, Eminem's rhymes hammer the listener, dramatizing the homoerotic relation between fan and celebrity—the hunger of the fan for affection and the endless desire of the star for adulation. Stan yearns for a male friend just like the suicidal Gerald in *Women in Love*. But Slim's platitudes seem insufficient to the tragedy that has already taken place. At the same time, Slim's reaction to Stan's erotic inferences shows the weight of masculine stereotyping in popular culture. The antiauthoritarian Eminem, the working class refusenik who succeeded, as he boasted, in black music, can't turn his rhymes against American manliness. The message seems to be that tough guys don't touch each other.

This appears also to be the directive in Anthony Swofford's memoir, *Jarhead*, an honest and raw chronicle of his experience in the Gulf War. The writing, thoughtful and visceral, attests to the martial masculinity of the time. This brand of virility imprints itself on the text like the tattoos fixed into the flesh of new recruits. Thus there is little of the caressing tenderness toward fellow soldiers evident in the writings from the American Civil War and World War I. This is particularly true in the chapter dealing with the death of Troy, Swofford's former fellow Marine who was killed in a car accident in Michigan and who had stopped Swofford from committing suicide during the war. Distressed at his early passing, Swofford and his buddies buy a bottle of liquor after the funeral service and go to a bar where they begin to fight with the locals, shattering bottles, throwing chairs, breaking skulls: "We cried as we beat them, we called them sons of bitches and civilian fucks and motherfucking whores and we didn't stop until the police arrived" (Swofford 2003, 81).

Never portraying himself as a war hero, Swofford writes his book in "despair over the likelihood" of another war being declared and of "further atrocities." He apologizes to future mothers: "This will never end. Sorry" (254–55). And in the course of his book, he subjects God, country, and family to sharp critique. But he rarely thrusts his bayonet into the maleness that motivates both his narrative and the identity of the men around him.[18] Once the fighting finally begins and he puts on his gas mask, he weeps from fear but primarily from the realization that "I'm finally in combat. I've pissed my pants, but only a bit" (190). Masculinity here triumphs as an unscrutinized way of life and an inscrutable trope.

Whatsapp with Friendship?

Is Swofford wrong in the way he behaves with his buddies? Obviously there is no correct or incorrect friendship. Nor was there ever a time of perfect friendship. But in comparison with the past, our society seems to have less time for it. Always a luxury, friendship has become more so today. In his famous sociological study, Robert D. Putnam concluded that friendship is less of a priority for people: "We are spending significantly less time nowadays with friends and neighbors than we used to." The time people devote to their neighbors has fallen by 30 percent. Simultaneously, the frequency of invitations of friends for dinner declined appreciably between 1975 and 1999. "The practice of entertaining friends . . . seems to be vanishing entirely."[19]

Putnam looked at the impact of technology, in his case television, on social relationships.[20] For a considerable part of the previous century television competed for free time. Now, of course, it's the Internet that pulls our attention. In the blink of an eye we have gone from a world of two types of media (the first run mostly by professionals and broadcast to an audience with the second constituting private conversations) to a world where the two converge.[21] We are encouraged to think about our lives and act them out through digital technologies. And we increasingly organize our lives and think about our relationships with and through digital technologies. There seems to be no existence possible outside of the Net.[22] To communicate through the Internet, to purchase goods on the Web, to write a blog, to contribute to networking sites is to participate in a new subjectivity. In other words, to partake in electronic communication is to invest yourself with social relevance. If you are under thirty and live in a Western industrialized economy, you have no choice but to enter the network.[23]

In one respect the formation of social links is not new. Society has always been networked, as it has always been global.[24] What is different today is the intensity and saturation power of the network both as reality and metaphor. The network constitutes the new organizing impulse of society, affecting the economy, politics, culture, and personal experience.[25] If communication is the sharing of meaning through the exchange of information, then communication takes place today in vertigo-inducing speed and volume.[26]

But what seems to be affecting our personal relations, such as friendship, is the confluence taking place between communication and consumerism. Our sense of self seems to be now for sale.[27] The Internet unites the human need to connect (i.e., to make friends) with the commercial propensity for profit.[28] Rather than turning people into commodities or friends into goods, the Web converts the instinct to open up to people into a sellable good. Of course friends have partaken in economic exchange since the time of Diomedes and Glaucus. Treating someone to a movie, sharing a restaurant bill, getting married, and raising children are activities that entail "extensive production, consumption, distribution, and transfer of assets."[29] In other words, friendship could never be distinct from the overall economy. But there is a twist to the new situation.

Let us look at the example of two friends going out for a coffee in the 1980s. Their togetherness had been made possible, to a certain extent, by the payment for goods they consumed. But what transpired between them during their time together remained confidential. And at the end, they had to decide how to pay for the bill. Money made their intimacy possible.[30] Today, however, intimacy makes money. Our desire to fashion bonds with others becomes a feast for firms seeking the information we voluntarily make public. The secrets we guarded in the past now become fruit for profit. Google and Facebook hoard our intimate details from date of birth, to marital status, to tastes, and political affiliations. They capitalize on this information and thus target the audience for advertising.[31] Our reading habits, the sites we visit, and the films we watch are constantly under surveillance, and we submit to it as a trade-off for staying connected for free.[32] Our friendships, once sacrosanct, turn into an object of public and commercial scrutiny.

There is a historical irony here. Money, as Georg Simmel noted a century ago, has been a great leveler, bringing people together indirectly from disparate parts of the world in temporary and tenuous links. Although these individuals won't ever meet, on any particular day their tie to other people has been made possible by financial exchanges in real or electronic form. And now friendship is a source of fortune, making money circulate with the expansion of the network. In this process the Internet converts Aristotle's category of friendship of pleasure into an instrumental relationship—profit for Facebook.

What does friendship mean when one can boast a thousand friends? In one respect, nothing. No one claims that all the "friends" are friends. Perhaps the question only reflects the anxiety felt toward new technologies by an older generation. It raises doubts, in other words, about network friendship by undermining its authenticity: we assure ourselves of what is real by defining it as face-to-face communication. It is worth remembering that every new mode of communication has appeared initially threatening because it brought people together who were not physically present. All technologies of information from the epistle on have been disembodied, rupturing the connection between message delivery and shared space.[33] People feared that the telephone, for instance, would reduce intimacy and lead to interruptions at home. Although some of these predictions have been borne out, on the whole the telephone has been a boon to social relations, supplementing rather than supplanting social dealings.

Similar patterns seem to be developing with digital communications.[34] At the core, online social networking tends to reflect offline interaction. Not surprisingly, these online networks don't seem to enhance our relationship to our core group.[35] Of course, Facebook has redefined friendship by permitting people to maintain ties among a larger field of individuals, enabling the creation of dense webs with massive amounts of file sharing. It has achieved efficiencies in relationships not possible before. But no one pretends that it is a vehicle for warmth.

Inauthentic Selves?

Yet it would be wrong to argue that relationships made or maintained online cannot be genuine.[36] In part, our fears about the effect of Facebook, texting, and instant messaging on friendship have to do with distress about the impact of the Internet on intimacy. We clearly have a bias for direct encounter and fear the distancing mode of technology. We wonder: Does it undermine friendship? Do people prefer texting to talking? Are we dealing with a real person on the other side of the screen or a profile? What are the social and emotional implications when all the patrons in a café are communicating in a solitary fashion with someone far away? At the same time, what can intimacy signify when the details of a friend's life are revealed forever in a blog or on YouTube?[37] Is it important any longer?

Preliminary research shows that most relationships maintained by social network sites are weak. These sites are effective in keeping people posted rather than maintaining deep relationships.[38] But is it ultimately wrong that some people prefer texting to talking? The disembodying quality of writing does not make it less able to communicate love. People, after all, have maintained intimate relationship through letters for centuries and often over great distances. But the letter presupposed one addressee, whereas the confessional blog or the post on YouTube can be seen by hundreds if not thousands of people. There is a frictionless and quick progression from one medium to the other. So if we made friends in the past by withdrawing from the world, we make friends today by opening ourselves to it. At the very least, what is created is a different sense of the public, not the mass targets of radio and television but an aggregate of private spheres.[39]

Is there a digital flattening taking place in this process? Are we losing a sense of individuality? As Jaron Lanier (one of the inventors of virtual reality) points out, the Internet promotes conformity of expression, organizing people according to rigid protocols (2010, 48, 68).[40] Friends present their profiles in the templates available to them. The question he poses, whether we are being defined by our own software, echoes Marshall McLuhan's insight that the communicative tools we have shaped, shape us afterwards (1964). Is friendship conditioned by the protocols of Facebook and Twitter the same way that it was determined by the codes of letter writing?

From Private to Public

What is happening right now is much more profound than Facebook or Twitter. It's the gradual reversal of a centuries-long process from a public to an increasingly private world.[41] The wall between these two aspects of the self has to a certain extent defined the way we have organized our lives in modernity, from politics to relationships. Indeed, we have regarded friendship as a withdrawal from the struggles and demands of politics and the market even if this secession could never be fully realized, as *A Passage to India, Huckleberry Finn*, and "Moscóv-Selím" have demonstrated.

The digitalization of life is reshaping our understanding of the private-political divide, reconfiguring our sense of friendship while enabling new forms of political engagement. At the same time, politics has entered the home. Or, rather, people are able to practice politics without leaving their (no-longer) personal space.[42] The mobile features of converged media enable people to fill out protest petitions online, monitor the activities of politicians, join like-minded discussion groups, write blogs, post videos on YouTube, and come together on the streets via messages posted on Twitter and Facebook. Although this may seem civic engagement "lite" to some, we have to accept that monitoring constitutes one aspect of citizenship: "monitorial citizens" are no better or worse than citizens of previous eras.[43] They understand their duty as staying informed about politics so as to contribute more effectively to public administration. So while the individual appears physically alone in front of a screen, she or he is not necessarily isolated.

What does friendship mean in this hybrid space in which our traditional definitions no longer obtain? Is secession, so vital to friendship, possible or even desirable from the network? Can you free yourself from the Internet in order to pursue love? Or do the algorithms of network communication impose their own prohibitions and commandments? Moreover, what does warmth signify in the strobe flashes of self-revelation? What do you say to your close friend that is different from the mass self-communication you posted on Facebook?

Yet, people still have the need to talk to someone. In the last scene of *The Social Network*, the 2010 movie dealing with the founding of Facebook, Mark Zuckerberg (played by Jesse Eisenberg) finds himself alone in an office. He cuts a pitiful figure. Having established Facebook as a major shaper of social life, he seems isolated and friendless. So what does he do? He refreshes his "friend" request to his former girlfriend. Despite the dysfunction and sociopathy, he, the destroyer of personal friendships, covets a snippet of intimacy, even in digital form.

Georg Simmel accurately predicted about a century ago that modern individuals confront a surfeit of information that provokes in them a sense of melancholy. Although Simmel could never have imagined the dense, stimuli-drenched grids of the Internet age, he would have understood the sadness of excess. The sorrow today is not that of the romantic sublime, of Caspar David Friedrich's solitary figure gazing into the expanse of the seas. It's not the grandeur of nature that we fail to comprehend but the unending flickers of self-diffusion and of dense connection—images of new shoes, snippets of love affairs, shots from the beach, friending requests, opinions, and evites—an extension and makeover of social relations. We are confronted with the splendor of minutiae, of infinitely expanding entropy. But we cannot help but operate in and experience our lives in this digital universe, given that we are a companionate and cooperative species.

Is this why we have made friendship—the relationship we seek outside of kinship, beyond the market and the political arena—the hub of the social network? Is it a wonder that the metaphor and the term we have used to make sense of the new digital world is friendship? Our impulses for the future may also take us back to the past, to the inauguration of literature. The *Epic of Gilgamesh* sang of a friendship. The two heroes humanized the world by their comradeship. Literature and friendship took their baby steps together. And so it is with the Internet. A convergence is taking place between the power of the Internet to bring people together and the capacities in literature to foster empathic understanding in people. The talent to jump from one place to another and to imagine another place, person, or situation is literary. Literature invites us to enter the minds of other people, to conjure up places we don't know, and to enter worlds that are not real. In short, it enhances our capacities to foster links with others beyond our doorstep.[44]

The magic of the Internet is to create and multiply these connections. It helps bring about not only global projects of common effort, such as Wikipedia, but also the large grid of friends. People pool their resources for collective endeavors as they also seek human contact. The Internet is giving them new ways of looking at human behavior that I have called here literary and that I have defined as the aptitude to think our way into the minds of other people. This reality presupposes the fundamental human desire for connectedness and empathy. It assumes that human beings are an affectionate and cooperative species rather than just aggressive and self-interested.

Of course, the Internet can spread hatred as well as freedom. Along with the invitation for shared information, there are also calls for terror. But we will disappear as a species, and take other forms of life down with us, if we obsess only about our failings. Concentrating on destructive characteristics blocks from view the possibilities that can arise when we recognize life as a chain of solidarity with other beings. This is the connected world of the Net, which is a literary world. It is not a galaxy of fiction but a universe linked by fiction—by our abilities to imagine alternate realities, to conjure what other people might be feeling, to be mindful of them, to identify ourselves with them, and to change society. We can solve our global problems more effectively if we envision more vividly our ties to other human beings.

We are all friends now.

Notes

Introduction

1. Pigliucci 2012, 177.
2. Hiss 2010, 12.
3. Keats 2001, 43. Actually Keats was wrong. It was Balboa who stared out at the Pacific from a peak in Darien.
4. Byron [1809] 1982, 30.
5. On friendship in children and early adolescence, see Bukowski, Newcomb, and Hartup 1996.
6. Parker-Pope 2009. Both Fred Pfeil's *White Guys* (1995) and Michael Kimmel's *Guyland* (2008) devote virtually no space to friendship. Recent works on friendship almost in unison lament the paucity of research within the respective field (e.g., Konstan 1997, 174). Anthony Giddens's *The Transformation of Intimacy* (1992), Zygmunt Bauman's *Liquid Love* (2003), and Eve Kosofsky Sedgwick's *Epistemology of the Closet* (1990) hardly mention it.
7. Kierkegaard 1995, 58.
8. Rahe 1992, 266.
9. Hobbes [1642] 1983, 43.
10. Locke 1995, 320. See Yenor 2003.
11. Today, "when we move beyond the intimate ties of love and family, the most important claims upon us seem not to be those of friendship so much as broader and more abstract or universal claims" (Pangle 2003, 3).
12. Booth 1988, 171.

13. *Science* 309, July 1, 2005, 19, 93; Bowles and Gintis 2011, 6.

14. Rifkin (2009) presents a modern version of Adam Smith's view of moral and social interdependence as expressed in *The Theory of Moral Sentiments*. See also David Cannadine's *The Undivided Past: Humanity beyond Our Differences* (2013) and Robert Axelrod's *The Evolution of Cooperation* (1984).

15. Harman 2010, 3. In a four-thousand-year-old grave in Vietnam, scholars discovered the remains of a man who had been paralyzed from the waist down. Suffering from Klippel-Feil disease, he had been looked after by those around him. This and other sites show that cooperation and care have been part of human societies for a long time (Gorman 2012, D1).

16. Bowles and Gintis 2011, 2. Born for social learning, our species acquired systems of collaboration early on that enabled the sharing of knowledge (Pagel 2012, 46, 70, 72). See also Matthew D. Lieberman's *Social: Why Our Brains Are Wired to Connect* (2013).

17. Harman 2011, 326, 125. This is contestable, as Zahavi and Zahavi (1997) note.

18. Bowles and Gintis 2011, 195.

19. Frans de Waal believes that humans, like all primates, are preprogrammed to ensure cooperation and hence survival as a group (2009, 111, 198).

20. Zahavi and Zahavi 1997, 165, 225.

21. Pinker 2011, 574, 175. Pinker's *The Better Angels of Our Nature: Why Violence Has Declined* lends further proof to this view of humans as an accommodating species. For my critique of Pinker, see http://arcade.stanford.edu/literature-and-end-of-violence.

22. Hunt 2007, 29. On the Athenian drinking song, see Athenaeus 2012, 5.694d–3.

23. The story is based on a historical event—fifteen hundred central European Jews were prevented by the British from landing in Jaifa (in Palestine, now Israel) and were sent as prisoners to the island of Mauritius.

24. Bowles and Gintis 2011, 200.

25. Rifkin 2009, 3.

26. In *The Necessary Nation* I argue that nationalism and ethnicity could mobilize people to action. And in *Fiction Agonistes: In Defense of Literature* I try to demonstrate the role literature plays in determining our relationship to reality.

27. Arendt 1968, 26.

28. The novel as genre itself deals with identity, the two being interrelated. Brooks 2011, 10. On the proliferation of memoirs, see Jurecic 2012.

29. Barry Kemp, the excavator of the ancient Egyptian city of Amarna, writes that the Egyptians experienced life as partly material and partly imaginary: "Eternity was a nervous voyaging through an imagined universe—an Otherworld—that the Egyptians seem to have recognized was actually within themselves" (2012, 238).

30. Fantasy, the evolutionary biologist Robert Trivers argues, is part of our biology. "We create an artificial world and then choose to live in it" (2011, 109). Trivers traces the talent to dupe and the ability to detect the lie to the actions of simple viruses.

31. Shirky 2010, 119. Apache, the world's most widely used Web server, was designed by Brian Behlendorf and is freely available to users to copy and enhance.

32. See Christakis and Fowler on networking man (2009, 222, 31, 296).

33. The concept of romantic love was an invention of the seventeenth century when it replaced the courtly love of the late Middle Ages and the Renaissance (Passerini 1999, 1). See also de Rougemont (1956).

34. Giddens 1992, 184.

35. Stone 1977, 686.

36. Cherlin 2009, 140. Only 16 percent of young people in the United States see children as the goal of marriage. Even weddings themselves are regarded as celebrations of the couple, controlled by the bride and groom, rather than as a conjoining of two families.

37. Arendt 1998, 22

38. Early hunter-gatherers were more cooperative and willing to learn from one another than say, chimpanzees. This tendency toward collaboration and social acquisition pushed early humans toward a different evolutionary path (Wade 2011, A3).

39. Bakhtin 1984, 287; Hölderlin 1967, 438.

1. The Politics of Friendship

1. Forster 1951, 68. Alasdair MacIntyre rightly points out that the Aristotelian view of community, as a common project, is alien to the modern liberal perspective (1981, 146). See also Hutter 1978.

2. Arendt 1968, 24–25.

3. See *The Politics of Friendship* (1997) by Jacques Derrida, for a critique of the philosophical tradition on friendship. Derrida grounds his investigation on a phrase attributed to Aristotle and cited by the leading philosophical texts on the topic, "O my friends, there is no friend" (1997, 1). (See Salkever 2008, 64, and Heller 1998, 6). Derrida rejects this tradition because it is ruled by the ideal of "reciprocity." This "Greco-Roman model" is defined by "homological, immanentist, finitist—and rather politist—concord" (290).

4. Currie 2010, iv. Aristotle's distinction between history and poetry may be relevant here. The poet's function, he says, is "to describe, not the thing that has happened but a kind of thing that might happen," while that of the historian is to "describe the thing that has been" (1451a35–1451b6).

5. Derrida argues that the philosophical paradigm carries within itself "the power to become infinite and dissymmetrical." Thus Montaigne deconstructs this model when he "breaks with the reciprocity and discreetly introduces . . . heterology, transcendence, dissymmetry, and infinity" (1997, 291), achieving a messianic ideal of friendship as waiting. This is a surprising claim, for Montaigne actually undoes the otherness of Aristotle's definition by presenting friendship as a perfect union of self and other. Since Derrida does not engage with the literary representation of friendship, he cannot see how literature deconstructs friendship as it also constructs it.

6. Pangle 2003, 153. Pangle says that Aristotle's paradoxical expression differs from the command in Matthew 22:39 to "love thy neighbor as thyself."

7. The "alterity" inherent in friendship approximates Emmanuel Lévinas's conception of the other: "We recognize the other as resembling us, but exterior to us" (1987, 75). But Lévinas weakens the political significance of this alterity by placing it in a messianic context of mystery and expectation: "The relationship with the other is a relationship with a Mystery." It is a mystery because it can't be known or anticipated: "The future is what is not grasped, what befalls us and lays hold of us. The other is the future. The very relationship with the other is the relationship with the future" (77).

8. "The Other is what I myself am not. The Other is this, not because of the Other's character, or physiognomy, or psychology, but because of the Other's very alterity" (Lévinas 1987, 83). Lévinas characterizes alterity as a "non-reciprocal relationship" (83). Our relationship with the other is not a "harmonious relationship of communion, or a sympathy through which we put ourselves in the other's place" (75). He removes it from the present by projecting it into the future: "I have tried to find the temporal transcendence of the present towards the mystery of the future" (94).

9. Interestingly, Plato explores in this dialogue not what friendship is but how it arises (Rhodes 2008, 35). Socrates concludes, "But what he who is a friend is we have not yet been able to discover" (Plato 1979, 223b). This is an aporetic ending to Socrates's original question: "I don't even know the manner in which one person becomes the friend of another" (212a). This textual impasse in *Lysis* shows the structural ambivalence of friendship.

10. With justification Derrida sees in our desire for union the perils of appropriation, the right to property" (1997, 64). Citing Friedrich Nietzsche's term *Habsucht* (force of love), he rejects the "Greco-Roman model" for instilling a proprietary lust with respect to the other—hence

his validation of an ethics of solitude. But Derrida misunderstands the importance of reciprocity in this "model."

11. This is, according to A. W. Price, a central insight of the *Lysis* (1989, 12, 39). Even if mutuality is present, however, it may be asymmetrical.

12. Scheler 1970, 70–71. Agnes Heller says something similar: "My friend receives my freedom, as I receive his" (1998, 11). Derrida, in outlining his own version of friendship as a perpetual waiting "friendship to come" and in privileging "solitude" (1997, 306, 54–55), undervalues what Greek philosophy attempted to accomplish: to pose the question of how we live together. Democracy, for Derrida, "remains to come." He asks whether it's "possible to open up to the 'come' of a certain democracy which is no longer an insult to the friendship we have striven to think beyond the homo-fraternal and phallogocentric schema" (306)?

13. Simon Baron-Cohen's definition is helpful: "Empathy is our ability to identify what someone is thinking or feeling and to respond to their thoughts and feelings with an appropriate emotion." It has, in other words, two stages, recognition and response (2011, 16). The terms empathy and sympathy are often used interchangeably in popular discourse. I try to distinguish between them. In empathy, "we feel what we believe to be the emotions of others," such as the expression "I feel your pain." In sympathy, we feel compassion for the person, as in "I feel pity for your pain" (S. Keen 2007, 5). On the emotion of compassion, see Berlant 2004, Chandler 2013, and Nussbaum 2001. For the early and definitive study, see Scheler [1913] 1970.

14. I try to show this at greater length in *Fiction Agonistes: In Defense of Literature*.

15. Wayne C. Booth argues that all stories, from the realist to the most experimental, can be viewed as companions. They begin with an invitation to spend time and engage with friends (1988, 175). Readers form friendships with characters and with the implied authors who reveal themselves to the audience (179–80). Martha Nussbaum adds that we yield to the demands of the story, making moral and social assessments (1997, 100–101).

16. M. Smith 1995, 18, 31.

17. Ibid., 82.

18. Nussbaum 2001, 22.

19. This is the view of Martha Nussbaum: "Narrative imagination is an essential preparation for moral interaction. Habits of empathy and conjecture conduce a certain type of citizenship" (1997, 90). She then makes a direct connection between narrative and moral commitment: "It is impossible to care about the characters [in Sophocles, Dickens, George Eliot] and their well-being in the way the text invites, without having some very definite political and core interests awakened in oneself—interests, for example, in the just treatment of workers and in the reform of education" (104). The literary imagination develops compassion and compassion is essential for civic responsibility (99). Jonathan Gottschall makes extraordinary claims about the power of stories to encourage people to behave ethically and to change the world (2012, 134, 198). For my critique of Gottschall, see http://arcade.stanford.edu/tyranny-of-stories. See also Palumbo-Liu 2012.

20. Adorno said Brecht "found that to give his political position artistic expression it was necessary to distance himself from that social reality at which his works took aim" ([1958] 1997, 226).

21. But can't "realist" works heighten the audience's critical disposition as well? For instance, can't readers be engaged with injustice in Harper Lee's *To Kill a Mockingbird* or Harriet Beecher Stowe's *Uncle Tom's Cabin*, to cite two popular works? My intention here is not to create a neat distinction between mimetic and nonmimetic works or to demonstrate the superiority of the latter over the former.

22. Defamiliarization is a term coined by Russian formalists to express the distancing effect that fiction produces in readers, by obliging them to stop, look, and listen, paying attention to what they may have missed.

23. Nussbaum overlooks the existence of novels as art, works of fiction operating according to literary conventions. Thus while Nussbaum calls for critical reading she means critical in the moral sense, namely that we should read works that give voice to underprivileged groups (1997, 100). Although a novel may deal with the experience of middle-class women (Virginia Woolf), she cautions that it may render working-class people invisible (101)

24. Suzanne Keen's research into reader response demonstrates that readers, particularly "middle-brow" readers, value and actively seek their identification with fictional characters. But this goal does not *automatically* yield good citizenship. The theory of empathetic understanding cannot be used as a justification for the place of literature in society (S. Keen 2007, vii, 145, 62). Nussbaum's position stems from the humanist belief in the ameliorative powers of culture, that art yields personal and social improvement.

25. Nagel 1970, 83, 88. See also Cavell 1969.

26. Scheler 1970, 58, 65, 98.

27. Dana Munteanu argues that this conciliatory thought was central to the way Aristotle and other classical thinkers understood the spectator's response to tragedy: I am bound with the character in our common response to anguish (2012, 136).

28. An example of mind-reading would go like this: Did she raise her eyebrows because she did not understand, because she is hurt, because she has a headache, or because she was thinking of yesterday's argument?

29. See Zunshine 2010, 117, and Zunshine 2006, 25.

30. In other words, people like comparing real things and their representation in art. Aristotle also understood the centrality of *phantasia* (imagination) in the emotions of pity and fear that spectators feel in response to the characters' plight (see Munteanu 2012, 96).

31. Evolutionary theorists have traced the origins of play to two hundred million years ago with the dawn of mammals. Konner 2010, 502.

32. Ibid., 502.

33. Schaeffer 2010, xv.

34. Eisner 2002, 5. Let me cite a brief example here. In Daniel Defoe's *Moll Flanders* (1722) the eponymous protagonist, dissatisfied with her social situation, imagines a different reality for herself, as a "gentlewoman" rather than as a servant. Being a gentlewoman means for her "to be able to work for herself" and not to go into "service" (Defoe 2005, 12). Through the imagination she can visualize a life of economic and social autonomy and thereby strive to achieve it.

35. Dehaene 2009, 315.

36. Interestingly, Dehaene believes that we are not hardwired for this function. That is to say, it was not genetically determined but resulted from a change in circuitry that was already present. The human brain can convert some of its parts to new uses, such as writing (2009, 8). This is what he calls the "reading paradox," namely that our genes have not evolved to enable us to read. Rather the capacity to read grew out of constraints in the brain circuits (8). See here Damasio 2010.

37. Currie 1995, 151. Booth argues that the value of fiction is to provide a "cost-free offer of trial runs" (Booth 1988, 485).

38. The primatologist Frans de Waal contends that primates are capable of mind-reading, a capacity that allows them to identify with fellow creatures (2009,108, 223).

39. Currie 1995, 157, 161. Not everyone believes that simulation is an essential part of understanding others. Sophie Ratcliffe promotes the "theory-theory" approach. We develop theories about ways in which others behave and use these theories to predict behavior (2008, 44). Carroll is also critical of simulation theory (2001). The controversy between simulation and theory-theory theorists goes beyond the scope of my study.

40. Currie and Ravenscroft 2002, 203; Nussbaum 2001, 327.

41. Vermeule 2010, 40–41.

42. Immanuel Kant makes a similar argument with respect to the aesthetic judgment: when we judge an object, we compare "our judgment with the possible rather than the actual judgment of others, and by putting ourselves in the place of any other man, by abstracting from the limitations which contingently attach to our own judgment" (2000, 170).

43. Smith regarded shared feeling as a spontaneous mechanism for public cohesion. He saw public morality as a universe of simulative acts by which people attempted to imagine how others feel in particular circumstances.

44. John Ruskin understood this connection between empathy and the ability to imagine others, believing the imagination to be a "moral factor." Human beings require imagination to stir their sympathies: "People would instantly care for others as well as for themselves if only they could *imagine* others as well as themselves" (1893, 232).

45. Currie 1990, 24; Eisner 2002, 3. Percy Bysshe Shelley linked imagination and morality in his theory of poetry: "A man, to be greatly good, must imagine intensely and comprehensively; he must put himself in the place of another and of many others; the pains and pleasures of his species must become his own. The great instrument of the moral good is the imagination; and poetry administers to the effect by acting upon the cause" (1890, 14).

46. The Israeli novelist David Grossman poses a similar question in his account of his three-month travel assignment through the West Bank in 1988. At one point he asks himself of some settlers: "I am very curious to see if they can imagine themselves in their Arab neighbors' places" (1988, 37).

47. Although it is essential that we place ourselves in the position of fellow human beings, this may not be enough. We need to judge that cruelty as wrong. As Scheler pointed out, the sadistic man is motivated in his actions exactly by his recognition of the pain he is causing (1970, 13). Nazis knew the conditions in the cattle cars and may have taken pleasure in imagining Jews confined inside them. In a sense we need both, the imagination to see ourselves as the victim (not to objectify the person as other) and the critical function to judge the brutality as immoral.

48. Although they meet in a mosque, religion per se does not play a great role in the novel. Yet, as Peter Jeffreys argues, Forster incorporated many sacred traditions in the text, interested as he was in Sufi and Hindu versions of friendship. In the passages that he quotes, the friend is evoked in a mystical manner (2005, 121–29).

49. This, of course, is in direct opposition to Mrs. Moore's son, Ronnie, who is shocked to learn that his mother had been associating with a Moslem. When she tells him that she met a "nice doctor," he assumes him to be English (Forster 1924, 29–30).

50. I will discuss this in chapter 3.

51. Schaeffer calls fiction a "shared ludic feint" (2010, 236)

52. The need for equality in friendship is dramatized in the 2010 historical film *The King's Speech*, which documents the friendship between Prince Albert (the future king George VI) and his speech therapist, the Australian Lionel Logue. In order to be treated for stuttering, the prince comes to Logue's practice stripped of all authority and allows himself to be addressed as Bertie. The parity achieved between a royal and a commoner enables an unlikely bond.

53. The editorial remark by the narrator tells us that Orientals often mistake hospitality for intimacy (152).

54. For Forster, the cave comes to represent India itself, a muddle, an impenetrable mystery. But, of course, it is not a riddle for local inhabitants. Moreover, the narrative logic of the courtroom needs the dazed female protagonist. Although Miss Quested makes the incendiary accusations, she comes to realize Dr. Aziz's innocence under cross-examination. Both she and India appear very confused and confusing to the male actors.

55. Wadell 1989, 58.

56. The narrative logic reaches its peak inside the courtroom as the charges of rape are withdrawn and then loses some energy, unable to yoke together successfully the story of friendship with that of nationalism. But Forster still has to resolve the conflict between Aziz and Fielding.

57. I am referring here to Derrida's position discussed earlier.

58. One wonders—from the outlook of the imaginary grace conjured by fiction—whether Aziz and Fielding are still looking for each other, to undo the rift torn by the horses, God, and mortal hatred.

59. The novel shows that Maurice's love for a member of the working class is more shocking to Clive and others than that the object of that love was a man: "Intimacy with a social inferior was unthinkable to him" (Forster 1983, 242). Maurice himself realizes that he has "gone outside his class" (207).

60. Carpenter (1844–1929), a founder of the Labour Party, published the first text defending homosexuality, *Homogenic Love* (1885). Another pamphlet, *Love's Coming of Age*, circulated one year later (see Beauman 1994, 205–6). Forster writes that he conceived *Maurice* during a visit to Millthorpe in 1913. He recalls the exact moment of conception when Merrill touched "my backside—gently and just above the buttocks. . . . The sensation was unusual and I still remember it, as I remember the position of a long vanished tooth" (Forster 1971, 249). We should keep in mind that homosexuality was illegal at the time.

61. This saying forms the scaffolding of Derrida's study of friendship.

62. "Bon, who for a year and a half now had been watching Henry ape his clothing and speech, who for a year and a half now had seen himself as the object of that complete and abnegant devotion which only a youth, never a woman, gives to another youth or a man" (107).

63. Compare this twist with the real-life situation of Alfred Tennyson and Arthur Hallam, who becomes the lover of Tennyson's sister. Could the homoerotic attraction between Tennyson and Hallam resolve itself only through this potential marriage? The poem, as I argue in the next chapter, contains many references to the matrimony of the friend. The most famous example of homoeroticism projected onto a sister is in Evelyn Waugh's *Brideshead Revisited* where Charles, following Sebastian's collapse into alcoholism, falls in love with Sebastian's sister, Julia, to whom he characterizes Sebastian as a forerunner.

64. In Lessing's *Nathan the Wise* there is similar confusion of identities. Recha, a Christian, raised by a Jew, discovers both that she and her Christian lover, the Templar, are not only Moslems but also brother and sister.

65. Godbeer 2009, 9, 10.

66. Crain 2001, 5.

67. Of course, this was an exclusionary effort that denied citizenship to slaves, indigenous people, and women. Believing that friendship is a social bond does not preclude belief in other forms of adhesion. There are many reasons why a society holds together, ideological as well as material.

68. Godbeer 2009, 153.

69. Godbeer 2009, 13, 117, 193, 164.

70. Taussig 2002, 44, 45.

71. For earlier conceptions of friendship in England, see Shannon 2002 and Tadmor 2001.

72. Eleni Leontsini (2013) makes this very point with respect to Aristotle.

73. This makes Derrida's rejection of reciprocity in friendship puzzling. For how can one build a voluntary relationship other than on the basis of reciprocity? Although Derrida points to a conflict between respect for the other and the social order, he gives the issue of social coexistence little attention despite his stated objective of examining the politics of friendship. Derrida calls for a new model of politics, away from that which places friendship as the model for social relations. Yet he says very little about this democracy to come beyond gesturing "toward an uncertain

future." He returns to these questions in other works (http://www.livingphilosophy.org/Derrida-politics-friendship.htm). In a deconstructive study of literary friendship Leela Gandhi dismisses the Aristotelian tradition for basing friendship on "filiation" and "similitude" (2006, 27). For critiques of Derrida, see McGowan 1991, Schweitzer 2006, and S. White 1991.

74. Godbeer 2009, 196.

75. Messent 2009, 21–21, 24.

76. Other novels also interrogate the reigning model of male friendship: consider the relationship between the white Ishmael and the Polynesian islander Queequeg in *Moby Dick* (1851) and the white Hawkeye and the Mohican Chingachgook in *The Last of the Mohicans* (1826). See Schweitzer 2006.

77. On the application of Aristotle's notion of friendship to modern society, see Bentley 2013.

78. Even in the first sentence, James Phelan notes, Twain emphasizes the tensions of the novel between fact and fiction, aesthetic representation and reality (2005, 1).

79. In his autobiography, *Black Boy*, Richard Wright tells how dissemblance was a necessary survival trait in the segregated South. Lying in order to get access to the library, young Wright comes to discover how the "imaginative constructions" of novels parallel the dissimulation he had to practice in his own life in order to live (1937, 227).

80. It is astounding that Helen sees herself as an object of glory, usually the attribute of men who fight to win praise. Because she is almost divine, Helen appropriates what is normally a masculine right. Of women only Medea, a foreigner and a sorceress, claims (in Euripides's fifth-century drama) the fame of a man. "I'd sooner stand behind a shield / three times in battle than give birth once," she declares to Jason, who himself recognizes Medea's renown in Greece: "Would you have been famous back where you came from, / on the very edge of the world?" (Euripides 2008, 250–51, 540–41). Here Medea contravenes the Greek ideal of womanhood, which is to resign herself to the private realm. The greatest glory of a woman, Pericles announces in his Funerary Oration, is to not be talked about by men (Thucydides 1982, book 2, sec. 45).

2. Mourning Becomes Friendship

1. This seems in contrast to portrayals in popular culture. In the 1942 film *Casablanca* Rick Blaine and Captain Renault saunter into the misty night as Rick utters the memorable line: "Louis, I think this is the beginning of a beautiful friendship." Similarly, in *Butch Cassidy and the Sundance Kid* (1969), the two criminals are frozen alive in the last freeze-frame, though they are about to be shot dead in Bolivia. It is as if the film wanted to suspend them for posterity as buddies in crime rather than as corpses.

2. In preparation for his own journey into Hades, Aeneas enumerates the heroes who preceded him. He himself is in search for his dead father, Anchises. "Teach me the way," he says to the Sibyl, "open the holy doors. / For through the fire, a thousand spears behind us, / I carried him upon these shoulders" (Virgil 1972, 6.150–53). Christ also belongs to this list of heroes but his is part of another, more complex story.

3. Harrison 2003, ix.

4. Sacks 1985, 2.

5. Heilke 2008, 166.

6. The Canadian poet Derrek Hines highlights the friendship theme in his reworking of the epic. After the wrestling match with Enkidu, he has the hero come to this insight: "Gilgamesh takes one heady step, two: / living for the first time / for someone else" (2002, 15). Hines suggests that in friendship we are obliged to recognize the possibility of other lives and other perspectives. Later in the lament for Enkidu, Gilgamesh asks, "how am I to know myself without you?" (46).

7. Walls 2001, 14.

8. Ibid., 53.

9. Ackerman 2005, 71. See also the study by Jean-Fabrice Nardelli (2007), which is largely a commentary on Ackerman's book. Theodore Ziolkowski has shown that many modern poets and fiction writers, attracted to the "gay" Gilgamesh, have found inspiration in the homoerotic relationship between the two heroes (2011, 91).

10. Heilke 2008, 166.

11. Calasso 1993, 214.

12. Ackerman 2005, 121.

13. Ibid., 193.

14. Ibid., 222.

15. In book 24 of the *Odyssey*, as we follow the souls of the slaughtered suitors descend into Hades, we overhear Agamemnon tell Achilles that the Greeks picked the bones from the pyre and placed them in an amphora: "In that vase, / Achilles here, lie your pale bones mixed / with mild Patroclus' bones, who died before you" (24.86–89).

16. Davidson 2007, 297.

17. Madeline Miller portrays them as gay in her novel, *The Song of Achilles* (2012). (For a critique, see http://arcade.stanford.edu/blogs/brokeback-mount-olympus-being-gay-iliad).

18. While on the *Symposium*, I mention briefly the erotic tension that Alcibiades, a participant in the symposium, reports to exist between himself and Socrates who nevertheless spurned his beauty (Plato 1989, 219c). It is significant here that this love began in battle when Socrates saved Alcibiades's life (220e).

19. See here the works of Philippe Ariès, 1962 and 1974.

20. There is a sense of memento mori in the literary treatment of friendship. It is the realization that occurs to Ishmael early in *Moby Dick* when he visits the Whaleman's Chapel in New Bedford. As he reads the tombstones, he reflects: "Ye know not the desolation that broods in bosoms like these. What bitter blanks in those black-bordered marbles, which cover no ashes! What despair in these immovable inscriptions" (Melville 1956, 48). And then he realizes that "the same fate may be thine."

21. Jaeger 1999, 36–37.

22. Ailes 1999, 217. As C. Stephen Jaeger reminds us, medieval poets, historians, and writers were indifferent to what we call private life (1999, 18).

23. In *Tristan* the friendship between Tristan and Kaherdin is secondary in importance to the love between Tristan and Iseult (Isolde). But the two fighters are portrayed as brothers in arms, loyal to each other. At the end of his life, Tristan goes to Kaherdin, seeking solace. "Kaherdin wept beside him. They wept their good comradeship, broken so soon" (Anon. 2005, 83). In *Prose Lancelot* the male bonding is so intimate that it verges on the homoerotic (Hyatte 1994, 102).

24. Stretter 2003, 234, 240, 242. Stretter argues that by the fourteenth century, in English literature at least, male-female erotic love had become a central thematic preoccupation. In Chaucer's *A Knight's Tale*, friendship is no match for sexual desire (Stretter 2003, 234). This triumph of erotic love has continued almost uncontested. What also persists, as we shall see in D. H. Lawrence's *Women in Love*, is the conflict between male-male and male-female bonding, transposed after the seventeenth century into a struggle between friendship and marriage.

25. See Cole, for instance. See my discussion of Wilfred Owen's "Strange Friendship" in chapter 1.

26. Das 2005, 25, 118.

27. Lilly 1993, 74.

28. What challenged this Victorian heterosexuality after the war was less sexual dissidence than the memories the soldiers brought back of these relationships (Das 2005, 136). We should also

bear in mind that World War I poets contributed to the debunking of traditional ideas of patriotism and heroism (Caesar 1993, 22).

29. Lilly 1993, 64. I return to this topic in my discussion of Annie Proulx's story, "Brokeback Mountain," in chapter 4.

30. In Fussell 1975, 274.

31. Kaplan 2006, 106.

32. This type of activity has been documented by anthropologists. See the collection of essays, *Ritualized Homosexuality in Melanesia* (Herdt 1984), and Spain 1992.

33. This is perhaps what Derrida means when he says that we identify friendship after death. "Many thanks be given to death. It is thanks to death that friendship can be declared. Never before, never otherwise" (1997, 302).

34. Montaigne devoted himself to his friend and to friendship while also maintaining a general misanthropic stance toward society. See Edyvane 2013.

35. See Abel 1981, 415.

36. Platt 1998, 54.

37. There is a feeling here that, although the person departs, his work survives. This sense of art's immortality in conjunction with friendship receives an early treatment in Callimachus's epigram on his friend, the Hellenistic poet Heraclitus. News of Heraclitus's death brings memories of late-night conversations with him. But the finality of death is tempered by art's longevity: "Your nightingales live on; on these Hades, that steals all away, will not set his hand" (Acosta-Hughes 2010, 4).

38. Schaefer 1998.

39. The reference is to the *Aeneid* (6.1177–82), when Aeneas, visiting the underworld, catches sight of Marcellus (42–23 BCE), nephew and son-in-law of Augustus, a young man of great promise who was expected to succeed Augustus.

40. The classic case of this resignation is Seneca's death in 65 CE, as recorded by Tacitus in the *Annals*. Ordered to commit suicide (or else be executed by Nero, his former pupil), Seneca slits his wrists. But because bleeding is slow on account of his age, he takes poison, and when this too fails, he chooses to suffocate in a steam room. During this protracted process, Seneca maintains his Stoic nobility, fading away with dignity and discipline (Tacitus 2008, 15.60–65).

41. Although Ariès claims that these approaches were historically separate, in Montaigne they seem identical. Ariès argues that the latter, "la mort de toi," actually appeared a century after Montaigne and manifested a new cult of commemoration of graves, monuments, poems, and the like. I believe Montaigne actually shows the nascent signs of this phenomenon.

42. The simplicity of this line is paralleled in the image of the trees of Cambridge from Abraham Cowley's (1618–67) poem, "On the Death of Mr. William Hervey" (Van Dyke 1907, 80–86):

Ye fields of Cambridge, our dear Cambridge, say
Have ye not seen us walking every day?
Was there a tree about which did not know
The love betwixt us two?

43. Queen Victoria, who had appointed Tennyson poet laureate in 1853 upon Wordsworth's death, and who herself mourned for forty years the loss of her husband, Prince Albert, told Tennyson that she kept it along with a copy of the Bible on her bedside table.

44. Caraveli 1986, 173, 187.

45. Ibid., 172, 175.

46. Alexiou 1974, 156, 185.

47. Holst-Warhaft 1992, 67, 97. See also Danforth 1982. A product of the rural tradition, the laments have all but disappeared in cities. Ethnographers document pressures on women, from friends and relatives, to cease their practice. Eugenia Fakinou's novel, *The Seventh Garment*,

documents in literary form the passing of this ritual tradition (1991). Nouri Gana investigates how the lament has been adopted by postcolonial fiction (2011).

48. See Jusdanis 2010.

49. Indeed, Tennyson chooses the tetrameter, the meter of songs and nursery rhymes, rather than the pentameter, the meter of epic. Even his rhyming scheme, *abba*, differs from the standard stanza of *abab*. Thus we have a line like "That loss is common would not make / My own less bitter, rather more" (VI, 5). This should be compared with Gray's heroic pentameter that marches with decorum and restraint: "The ploughman homeward plods his weary way, / And leaves the world to darkness and to me" ("Elegy Written in A Country Church-Yard"). Tennyson chose a difficult form, which, in its very difficulty, forces him to confront the resistance of reality.

50. I combine the two forms for convenience though there are differences between them, not least in the former being written and the latter oral. Whereas the elegy is seen as a commemoration of the dead, the ritual lament centers on the pain of the bereaved (Holst-Warhaft 1992, 97).

51. Shaw 1994, 50.

52. "The ordinary capacity of women is inadequate for that communion of fellowship which is the nurse of this sacred bond; nor does their soul seem firm enough to endure the strain of so tight and durable a knot" (190).

53. George E. Haggerty says this of the elegies of Thomas Gray, which he interprets as an early strategy in dealing with the sensibility of the closet. And the poet identifies love with loss in an attempt to come to terms with the impossibility of expressing openly the desire. Haggerty does point, however, to the fluid border between sexuality and friendship in the eighteenth century (1999, 122, 26).

54. Curr 2002, 166.

55. For an analysis of the dying kiss, see chapter 3 of Das's *Touch and Intimacy in First World War Literature* (2005). On the subject of the touch see Ritzenberg 2013.

56. Ramazani 1994, 3.

57. Milton is credited with restoring the elegiac form by revising the classical elegy (Sacks 1985, 118).

58. At the very least, the myth of Orpheus emphasizes the power of song to conquer death. Orpheus used his musical and poetic talents to win entry into the underworld and bring back his beloved. Of course, he failed in this quest.

59. See here a parallel line from Fulke Greville's (1554–1628) poem, "Elegy on the Death of Sidney" (attributed also to Sir Edward Dyer): "Sidney is dead, dead is my friend, dead is the world's delight." It commemorates his friend and poet, Sir Phillip Sidney, who died at thirty-two, and ends with the sonorous line: "Salute the stones that keep the bones that held so good a mind" (Van Dyke 1907, 49–51).

60. Shelley alludes to this line: "Our love, our hope, our sorrow, is not dead" ("Adonais," 10, 84).

61. Fully twenty-three stanzas draw from the elegies by Bion and Moschus (Shelley 1984, 7).

62. In the *Preface* Shelley expresses his frustration at the "savage criticism" that greeted the appearance of "Endymion" in 1817 and which Shelley blames for the onset of the consumption that killed Keats (1984, 26).

63. M. Putnam 1986, 137.

64. E. Smith 1977, 4.

65. This goes to show that consolation is illusory, with the elegy, like the ritual lament, forcing the mourner to confront his or her inconsolability. See Gana 2011, 180.

66. Kübler-Ross 1969, 161.

67. In his autobiography, *Report to Greco* (1965), Kazantzakis devotes a chapter to the writing of the novel.

68. Greek critics have often dismissed Kazantzakis because of his formal conservatism (see Tziovas 2009).

69. "Mnemosino," stemming from the ancient Greek "mnema" (a memorial, monument, remembrance of a dead person), is a funerary practice, combining Christian and pre-Christian rituals and celebrated at chronological intervals after the death, in church and at the cemetery. A plate of boiled wheat berries, elaborately decorated on the surface with sugar and almonds in the form of a cross, is offered to participants.

3. Duty and Desire

1. Francis Bacon, finding himself on the cusp of modernity, understood this liberty of friendship when he wrote that a man could speak to his son as a father, to his wife as a husband, "whereas a friend may speak as the case requires, and not as it sorteth with the person" (1860, 174).

2. Herman 1987, 7–10.

3. The grandfathers traded a war belt for a golden cup. But the narrator says that Zeus took away Glaucus's wits, making him offer gold for bronze armor, one hundred cattle's worth for nine. The narrator's comments show the influence of trade on rituals of *xenia*. In trade, "numerical equivalence of value is of the essence," whereas in friendship value is not supposed to be quantified (Seaford 2004, 34). Zeus, who guarantees *xenia*, robs Glaucus of his senses, so that the unequal swap of gifts would not get in the way of *philia*. Today we still feel discomfort at mixing friendship with money. We are conscious of unreciprocated dinner invitations, for instance.

4. Harm done to friends and violation of hospitality were themes of Greek literature and show how much Greeks were concerned with reciprocity (Belfiore 2000, xvi).

5. Konstan 1997, 2, 82. This observation holds true as well for the relationship between Jonathan and David in the book of Samuel and that between Gilgamesh and Enkidu in the *Epic of Gilgamesh*. See also the famous friendship in early Christianity between Gregory Nazianzen (330–390 CE) and Basil the Great (330–379 CE) who, along with John Chrysostom, were known as the Great Hierarchs of the Eastern Church (Manoussakis 2013).

6. MacIntyre 1981, 146.

7. Price 1989, 130.

8. Cicero believed that friendship was a "subject that everyone ought to think about" (Cicero 1971, 1.4). The issue had a self-evident and universal significance that seems foreign today.

9. Epistle IX in Pakaluk 1991, 121.

10. Ethan J. Leib (2011) argues that we should see friendship as a matter of public policy. See also Sharp 1986, 12.

11. In Germany today the switch from the formal, *Sie*, to the informal, *Du*, is often accompanied with a bottle of champagne.

12. The possibility of sexuality in male friendship is always a controversial topic. In his study of friendship in early medieval English literature, David Clark cautions against privileging genital expression of erotic desire. We should not make assumptions about an erotic relation based solely on whether sexual activity is involved (2009, 16–17).

13. Bray 2003, 136, 15.

14. Ibid., 126.

15. Rapp 1997, 309–15.

16. Boswell 1994, 202–6. Boswell's position is controversial and not accepted by many specialists. On Byzantine friendship, see also Magdalino 1989, Mullen 1997, Mullett 1988, and Tinnefeld 1973.

17. On knighthood and ritual brotherhood, see also M. Keen 1984, which deals with the topic in the wider context of chivalry.

18. The twelfth century particularly represents a great flowering of the discourse on friendship, not seen since the classical period.

19. Haseldine 1996, 193. Cicero's was one of the most popular classical texts on friendship in the medieval period. Others were *Lysis, Phaedrus,* and *Symposium* by Plato, and *The Nicomachean Ethics* by Aristotle (Lochman, López, and Hudson 2010, 3).

20. Jaeger 1999, 27. As Søren Kierkegaard notes, Christianity "has thrust love and friendship from the throne and set something far higher in their place" (1995, 59). For Kierkegaard earthly love is partial while Christian love is universal.

21. There were no surviving sources on monastic friendship from the period between 850 and 1050 (Hyatte 1994, 47). Brian Partick McGuire observes that, in contrast to Aristotle, early Christianity saw community and friendship as rivals (1988, xli). See also White 1992 and Rader 1983. Male friendship was celebrated in the secular tradition of poetry, in works such as the *Song of Roland, Prose Lancelot, The Quest of the Holy Grail,* and *The Romance of Tristan and Iseult.* These texts depart from the *amicitia Christiana* in describing a passionate male bonding that approximates that of ancient heroes.

22. The question remains whether these gestures and rhetoric manifest, as Boswell believes, evidence for same-sex love among the monks. McGuire (1988) and Ailes (1999) disagree. Cautioning against viewing these letters through our modern understanding of personal correspondence as self-revelation, they place them in the rhetorical tradition on brotherly love and life in the service of God.

23. Haseldine 1999, 253.

24. Jaeger 1999, 113.

25. It is significant that Christianity ascribed kinship terms to interpersonal relations. People become brothers and sisters, rather than friends, bound together in a wider family. And all of humanity became the offspring of God.

26. Bonds built by necessity or tradition did not necessarily yield empathy and affection (Jamieson 1998, 17).

27. See also Guido Ruggiero's *Machiavelli in Love: Sex, Self, and Society in the Italian Renaissance* (2007).

28. Indeed, we should compare Montaigne's characterization of friendship with the description of art by Karl Philipp Moritz (1756–93), a father of modern aesthetics. Five years before Immanuel Kant's *Critique of Judgment,* Moritz published an essay that portrayed art as self-contained and its pleasure disinterested. A beautiful object, he argued, constitutes "a totality in itself" and affords pleasure "for its own sake" ([1785] 2012, 97). It does not have "its purpose outside itself and exists not for the perfection of something else but for its own perfection" (98).

29. Luhmann 1986, 12.

30. Silver 1997, 45, 48.

31 Adam Smith pointed to the shared feelings that for him were responsible for the maintenance of social order. Friendship, he states, arises "not from constrained sympathy . . . which has been rendered habitual; but from a natural sympathy, from an involuntary feeling that the persons to whom we attach ourselves are the natural and proper objects of esteem and approbation" (1976, 224–25). The faculty of the imagination, according to Smith, allows us to conjure up the sentiments and judgments of others (1976, 109–10).

32. Luhmann 1986, 17, 19.

33. Stone 1977, 325. As "emotional revolutionaries," women have paved the way for interpersonal egalitarianism, and for "pure" relationships and a "plastic sexuality," freed from the needs of reproduction (Giddens 1992, 130, 182). Paradoxically, this may have made marriage less stable. Looking at arranged marriages in Java, Walter L. Williams found that because "love" was not the ostensible reason for the union, the marriage itself seemed to be removed from the vagaries of choice, desire, and fulfillment (1992).

34. Bray 2003, 150–55.

35. It is roughly at this time that we see in Europe the creation of the concept of family. An idea unknown in the Middle Ages, it developed in western Europe between the fifteenth and eighteenth

centuries. Around the seventeenth century people began to withdraw within the family and to shield themselves against a society increasingly seen as intrusive and hostile (Ariès 1962, 406).

36. If individuals were struggling to determine the conditions for their own association in public, they were following a similar direction in private—that is, negotiating their personal ties as equals (Giddens 1992, 185). Aristotle and Cicero understood the importance of equality in friendships but took only men into account.

37. While he remains on Crete, his friend Stavridakis struggles in the Caucasus region, orchestrating the removal of Greeks who are facing perdition at the hands of the Kurds after World War I.

38. Intimate friendship, like Aristotle's ideal friendship, separates itself from instrumentalist motives. But can relationships be completely free of economic design? Decisions, like sharing a house or going out to dinner, involve financial negotiation.

39. This confession about the difficulties both men had in expressing love to each other raises a question about intimacy and equality. Do we find it harder to express our love to our coevals, preferring those who are younger or older, or even our pets?

40. In chapter 4 I discuss how the narrator in *Moby Dick* compares his friendship with the Polynesian Queequeg to a marriage.

41. See my earlier discussion in chapter 1.

42. This is not necessarily the case in eighteenth-century fiction. A case in point is Defoe's *Moll Flanders* (1722), in which the protagonist, Moll Flanders, having been born in Newgate prison, resolves as a child not to end up in the same state as her mother. Seeing herself as a social outcast, she knows that "to be friendless is the worst condition, next to being in want, that a woman can be reduced to" (2005, 117). So she resolves to gain autonomy through marriage. In the course of her life she goes through five marriages and one incestuous union with her half brother. But the momentum of the narrative is not romance and marriage per se but social and economic survival in a heartless world. See also John Cleland's pornographic *Fanny Hill* ([1772] 1985).

43. In these passages, the text, like Thomas Mann's *Magic Mountain*, mixes genres, often incorporating philosophy. Henrik, a military man not given to introspection, speaks like Socrates, giving readers the sense that they are studying *Phaedrus* rather than a novel.

4. Friends and Lovers

1. I prefer the usage of "same-sex" rather than "homosexual" for premodern societies. What Allen S. Frantzen says of Anglo-Saxon society applies to antiquity too: sexual acts did not signify behavioral traits or identity (1998, 4).

2. For this reason people seem uneasy in undertaking cross-gender friendships, especially if they are already married (Rubin 1985, 149). Many societies distrust a relationship between a man and a woman that does not have the ultimate goal of courtship and marriage (Bell 1981, 95).

3. In the asymmetrical schema of unequal relations, the *eromenos* was not supposed to love the *erastes* nor gain pleasure from intercourse. The categories of *erastes* and *eromenos* conveyed stages of life rather than a lifestyle. The *eromenos* would become an *erastes* to another *eromenos* when he grew older. We should caution against searching in this pederastic relationship for a metaphor for Athenian society, seeing, for instance, political relations as matters of activity and passivity. See Davidson 2007.

4. This practice of transgenerational homosexuality, by which an older man passes on learning to an apprentice through a sexual act, has existed in many parts of the world. The institution is justified by the belief that the boy won't mature unless semen is implanted in his body by an adult (Greenberg 1988, 20). Anthropologists regard it as part of the initiatory process of sexuality (Herdt 1984, 2).

5. Aristotle does not treat the erotic as a separate topic but classifies it under the friendship of pleasure, which occupies a lower rank in his stepladder of values. Only when both friends are equally given to goodness could they achieve true friendship. His idealization of friendship precludes his taking into account the magnetic pull of desire. Modern commentators have criticized him for this omission (Pangle 2003; Price 1989).

6. In Plato's *Symposium* the priestess, Diotima, does provide such a conception of love as our desire "to possess the good forever" (1989, 206a).

7. Price 1989, 12.

8. Bolotin 1979, 182.

9. The dialogue on friendship continues in the *Symposium* because the *Lysis* ends inconclusively: "But who is a friend we have not yet been able to discover" (223b).

10. This myth is similar to the story of Hermaphrodite in Ovid's *Metamorphoses* in which the Nymph is so aroused by the lovely Hermaphroditus bathing in the water that she dives into the pool, coils herself around him, and begs the gods never to part them. They grant this wish by melding the two, male and female, into one.

11. Although many of the speeches deal with erotic desire, the one given by Diotima (as cited by Socrates in his own speech) presents love as the pursuit of wisdom: "The beauty of people's souls is more valuable than the beauty of their bodies." Love for Diotima is our craving to give birth to beauty: "One goes always upwards for the sake of this Beauty" (Plato 1989, 210c, 211c). Since Socrates agrees with what she says, her views would seem to resemble his.

12. R. Goldberg 2006, 93.

13. See also Oliker 1998 and Oulton 2007.

14. At the same time, Steerforth distances himself from David, effeminizing him by calling him Daisy and seeing him like a little sister. When the boys go to bed on David's initial arrival at the school, Steerforth appears as his savior. "I'll take care of you," he reassures David, and then asks him if he has a sister: "'That's a pity,' said Steerforth. 'If you had had one, I should think she would have been a pretty, timid, little bright-eyed sort of girl. I should have liked to know her" (99). Is Steerforth projecting his homoerotic longings for the younger David on an imaginary sister? And when David learns that Miss Creakle, the headmaster's daughter, is in love with Steerforth, David understands why, thinking of his "nice voice, and his fine face, and his easy manner and his curling hair" (98). See Furneaux 2009, 125.

15. See Sedgwick 1985, 88–89.

16. Dollimore 1991, 30.

17. See Kimmel 2008, 48–50. See also my afterword. Of course, this remark may often be used ironically and thus may make fun of someone's level of tolerance.

18. Mavor 1971, xvi.

19. When an unfavorable article in the *General Evening Post* (July 24, 1770) hinted at the "perversity" of their relationship, the two women solicited the help of Edmund Burke (Mavor 1971, 134, 73–74).

20. Ibid., 81.

21. Vicinus 2004, 6, 29. Although the daughters of barons, their intolerant families offered them only a modest income.

22. Carol Smith-Rosenberg examines documents from nineteenth-century American society that show a convergence in the practice and understanding of romantic friendship between England and the United States (1975, 9).

23. Oliker 1989, 7.

24. Influenced by bluestocking feminism, the novel depicts a group of women devoted to self-improvement through conversation, reading, and writing. One of the leading members of

the bluestockings was Elizabeth Montagu (1718–1800), Sarah Scott's sister. On the impact of this movement on English literature and female subjectivity, see Eger 2010.

25. Vicinus 2004, 12.

26. See Wayne Koestenbaum's study on male literary collaboration as a homosocial activity (1989). On this literary collaboration from an earlier period, see Bald 1936.

27. It was commonly believed in the eighteenth and nineteenth centuries that upper-and middle-class women were asexual and that a lady would engage in sex only to gratify her husband or to procreate (Faderman 1981, 80, 152, 75).

28. Abel 1981, 415.

29. Smith-Rosenberg 1975, 29.

30. Marcus 2007, 13.

31. Holy Furneaux demonstrates this with respect to Dickens (2009, 9) in whose works she finds cases not only of same-sex male attraction but also of alternative conceptions of masculinity such as the desire to be a parent without reproducing, the need to nurse others, and the longing for nongenital intimacy (12). The best example is Dan Peggotty, the brother of Miss Peggotty, David Copperfield's housekeeper, who, as a bachelor, has adopted two children, Emily and Ham. Though living on a houseboat, this nonorthodox family is treated like a conventional household.

32. Marcus 2007, 27–29, 57. Yet, these relationships rarely were the topic of either philosophy or literature. Most of our information about female friendship from the eighteenth and nineteenth centuries comes from letters, journals, biographies, and autobiographies.

33. Crain 2001, 11.

34. John wished to join André but his father proved inflexible, denying his son an artist's life. As a result of his disappointment, John, the son of a Quaker, became an alcoholic and died of liver failure in 1803 in a Philadelphia hospital.

35. Sargent 1871, 95, 93.

36. André inspired support not only from the elite. Many newspaper accounts expressed outrage at the injustice of the execution (Crain 2001, 10). André's charms and magnetism seemed more threatening than the actual treachery of Benedict Arnold. George Washington refused to consider Hamilton's proposal to exchange André for Arnold, who had escaped on a British ship.

37. This beauty is evident in a self-portrait, now housed in the Yale University Art Gallery, that André sketched during his time in jail.

38. In Crain 2001, 8, 9. Note the effusive language Hamilton uses in his correspondence with Laurens: "Like a jealous lover when I thought you slighted my caresses, my affection was alarmed and my vanity piqued. I had almost resolved to lavish no more of them upon you" (in Crain 2001, 6). Although many critics believe their relationship was platonic, William Benemann thinks it was sexual. The absence of rigid distinctions between heterosexuality and homosexuality allowed an easy physicality and affection (2006, xv).

39. Crain 2001, 9.

40. Ibid., 9, 13.

41. For this reason it may not be helpful to ask whether John Cope and John André were America's first queer couple. We don't know if the relationship was sexual. Crain writes that their "story belongs to a different era, when stories like it were not necessarily rare" (13). Sodomy always constituted an abominable act in Europe and was regarded outside the realm of male friendship in the colonies as well (J. Goldberg 1992, 118). But just because an act is stigmatized does not mean it doesn't occur. Moreover, the absence of a word denoting a particular practice does not imply that people are not aware of that practice (Murray 2000, 6). But to characterize the story of André and Cope as sexual is to impose our own sexual obsessions on eighteenth-century society.

42. Melville began *Billy Budd* in 1886 but died in 1891 without finishing it. It was published posthumously in 1924. In *Passages*, a fictional account of Melville's life, Jay Parini muses on the possible real-life source of *Billy Budd*.

43. Messent 2009, 22.

44. Ibid., 29.

45. Unlike these two Homeric heroes, the protagonists in the novel don't exchange gifts. Queequeg offers gifts to Ishmael, the embalmed head he was carrying as well as half of his savings (fifteen silver dollars), whereas the American gives nothing in turn other than remonstrance at his embarrassment for receiving the gifts (59).

46. In the preindustrial United States privacy neither existed nor was valued in a substantial sense either among family members or friends (Oliker 1998, 22). Are we approaching this new interpenetration of the public and private with the new social media such as Facebook and Twitter? See the discussion in the final chapter.

47. Rotundo 1993, 84–85.

48. Benemann 2006, 265.

49. Instructive is Melville's tortured (and for him unfulfilled) relationship with Nathaniel Hawthorne. Upon receipt of Hawthorne's letter about *Moby Dick* (to whom he dedicated it), Melville writes (November 17, 1851) that "I feel pantheistic then—your heart beat in my ribs and mine in yours," emphasizing what was for him an emotional and physical union. He adds, "I should write a thousand—a million—a billion thoughts, all under the form of a letter to you" (Baym et al. 1989, 2149). On his friendship with Hawthorne, see Argersinger and Person 2008, Delbanco's biography (2005), and Parini's novelized treatment of Melville's life (2010).

50. Bryant 2010, 1051.

51. Poets and writers of the late nineteenth and early twentieth centuries, like Cavafy, celebrated the transgressive potential of homosexuality, seeing in the liberation of desire a way to a more authentic self. Writers in the twentieth century proposed the radical force of same-sex desire to undo social categories. André Gide's insights into sexual discrimination forced him to commit himself to resistance of all kinds (Dollimore 1991, 39). This radical model, however, can't be transferred to premodern societies because it connects same-sex relations of earlier eras with modern homosexual relations of opposition and dominance (Frantzen 1998, 13).

52. This decision mirrors Queequeg's surrender of his own fate to Ishmael, who he follows to Nantucket and aboard the *Pequod*.

53. Melville had direct experience with Polynesians during the eighteen months he had spent whaling in the South Pacific. He had boarded the ship *Acushnet* in New Bedford in 1841 and abandoned it in the Marquesas Islands, an experience that made its way into his first novel, *Typee* (1846).

54. Crain 2001, 152.

55. See Oulton 2007. Even when we turn to one of the precursors of the novel, say, to Daniel Defoe's *Moll Flanders* (1772), the narrative logic is still the same. Although Moll Flanders is not the typical ingénue of nineteenth-century fiction, she realizes that the only way to succeed in life is for her to get married to a man of fortune. So she uses all her ingenuity and trickery to achieve this end.

56. On the anthropology of ritualized friendship, see Brain 1976.

57. Joey and Ross of the television show *Friends* similarly agree that their nap together has been the best in their lives. See the discussion in the Afterword.

58. In his exquisite poem "Half an Hour" Cavafy suggests that sensual and aesthetic men can achieve pleasure that seems almost physical. The speaker, sitting in the bar with a man in front of him, imagines a sexual encounter that is nearly corporeal, helped by the "imagination" and by "magic alcohol" (1975, 191).

59. Compare here the homoerotic description of Oliver Mellors, Lady Chatterley's lover and gamekeeper on her husband's estate. As she walks through the woods, Lady Chatterley catches him bathing outside his hut: "She saw the clumsy breeches slipping down over the pure delicate, white loins, the bones showing a little, and the sense of aloneness, of a creature purely alone" (Lawrence 1959, 73).

60. This comparison with the love of a woman is as old as the Hebrew Bible and the *Epic of Gilgamesh*, as we have seen.

61. This is the question nagging the two friends in Tahar Ben Jelloun's Moroccan novel, *The Last Friend*. In a posthumous letter to Ali, Mamed writes that when "our wives appeared, there was a moment when we wavered, but we both hung on. They had a hard time accepting the strength of our friendship" (Ben Jelloun 2006, 179).

62. They have an honest conversation here that Julia and Charles don't in *Brideshead Revisited*: When they finally get into bed on the ocean liner taking them back to England, Julia asks why he had married. He wonders whether it was because he "missed" Sebastian. "'You loved him, didn't you,' Julia says. 'Oh, yes, he was the forerunner,' he responds." (1960, 284). Was Sebastian the precursor to the now true love or was he the real love and Julia the ersatz?

63. Sherrod 1987, 221. These literary findings are confirmed by sociological research I will examine in the afterword.

64. On mutual abuse in friendship, see Peachin 2001.

65. We have to ask whether the story would have garnered the same attention if it had been about a man and a woman or if the two heroes were self-consciously gay. A traditional melodrama about the transcendence of love, the story gains power by casting that love as ambiguous, challenging our conventional view of sexuality.

66. There is a parallel here in the life of E. M. Forster. The third great love of Forster's life, the one that lasted the longest, was Bob Buckingham, a working-class police officer whom Forster met in 1930 and with whom he had a sexual affair. The relationship not only continued but also intensified after Buckingham's marriage and lasted until Forster's death. Forster had become part of the family and May, Bob's wife, cared for him in his dying days (Beauman 1994, 347–48, 371).

67. Dick Davis argues that the adulterous love told in the medieval Persian poem *Vis and Ramin* was the precursor of the story of Tristan and Isolde (in Gorgani 2008, xxxiii).

68. The critical discussions in the press dealt primarily with its queer possibilities. Was this a gay film? Did it deal with closeted identity? Were Ennis and Jack homosexual? Or was Ennis gay only with Jack? Is love the same whether it's homosexual or heterosexual? Hardly anyone treated it as a case of eroticized friendship. On this critical reception, see William R. Handley's *The Brokeback Book* (2011).

69. Haggerty 2004, 387.

70. See in this respect Holly Furneaux's *Queer Dickens* (2009), which strives for an optimistic view of same-sex relations, wishing to see them as life-preserving rather than life-threatening, and criticizing the tendency to associate these attachments with violence and death (15). See also Russo 1981.

71. "Two men having sex threatens no one. Two men in love: that begins to threaten the very foundation of heterosexist culture." Haggerty 1999, 20.

72. Warren 2011.

73. J. Halberstam 2011, 190, 191.

74. Girard 2011, 27.

75. Whale performs an ancient sacrifice by killing the real body. Boone's attempt at redemption fails in the same way that Girard says actual scapegoat sacrifice provided only temporary relief from social tensions (Girard 2011, 27–28).

76. The author, Elisabeth Kirtsoglou, was herself a member of this *parea*, serving, in this way, as both participant and ethnographer (2004, 1).

77. Kirtsoglou 2004, 117, 15, 111–14.

78. This is also true of men. In his analysis of male friendship in a village on Lesbos, Evthimios Papataxiarchis finds that men maintain friendships with the emotional intensity of their marriages. These "friends of the heart" are so closely attached to each other that they refer to themselves as *koliti*, literally "stuck together." Remarkably, those men not fortunate to have such friends are considered strange (1991, 167). See Kennedy (1986) on women's friendship in Greece.

Afterword

1. Brightman 1995, 266.

2. On the place of letters in people's lives, see Thomas Mallon's comprehensive study, *Yours Ever: People and Their Letters* (2009).

3. Brightman 1995, 33, 107.

4. T. Williams 1990, 115.

5. David Halberstam begins his nonfiction chronicle *The Teammates: A Portrait of a Friendship* (2003) with a description of a thirteen-hundred-mile car trip by two aged baseball players, Dominic DiMaggio and Johnny Pesky, to visit their dying friend, baseball legend Ted Williams. The book recounts the sixty-year-old friendship of these players and Bobby Doerr, who could not make the journey because he was at home taking care of his ill wife. David Michaelis (1983) also sketches vivid profiles of eight very loyal friendships among men in the twentieth century, ranging from politicians (K. LeMoyne Billings and John F. Kennedy) to actors (John Belushi and Dan Aykroyd).

6. Informants in another survey of men over thirty-five revealed that they did not have or did not aspire to intimate male relationships. Stuart Miller, the author of the study, defines deep friendship as "the special relaxation and easiness we feel with a male friend. These are different from the deep comfort a woman lover can give. . . . With a male friend, we experience a serene excitement, a softening that thaws the shoulders" (1983, 11).

7. Greif 2009, 58, 66, 239.

8. Michaelis 1983, 9. In collecting the material for his portraits, Michaelis discovered not only the relative invisibility of friendship as scholarly topic but, more important, as social relationship.

9. Way 2011, 2, 11, 16.

10. Ibid., 18, 185, 208. Way reports personal anecdotes of men coming up to her after lectures to speak of their own lack of friends (271). I can confirm this myself. Learning of the subject of my work, men engaged me in conversation, often about their loss of friendships or their reliance on their wives' social circle. Wives have always provided men the opportunity to make contacts with their own circle of associates (Christakis and Fowler 2009, 87).

11. Seidler 1992, 15. In studies conducted in the early 1980s two-thirds of the young male respondents reported to have no close or best friends (Rubin 1985, 63).

12. In societies where arranged marriage is practiced and where the conjugal bond is not romanticized, friendships flourish after marriage. In Java, for instance, marriage is not expected to be emotionally intense and intimacies are maintained with best friends after the wedding (W. Williams 1992, 195). Among villagers on Lesbos, as I have noted, most men have just as emotionally passionate friendships with their male friends as with their wives (Papataxiarchis 1991). Those that don't have such friendships are considered antisocial.

13. On men's time constraints, see Cohen 1992.

14. Way 2011, 20, 263.

15. See also Hansen 1992.

16. In *Scrubs* both Turk and JD sing of their "guylove." http://www.youtube.com/watch?v=1L4L4Uv5rf0.

17. We get a different perspective in "I Need a Doctor," a song about friendship and sacrifice that is a collaborative effort by Eminem, his mentor Dr. Dre, and Skylar Grey. The piece begins with the musty voice of Skylar Grey, who sings the chorus. In the homage to Dr. Dre, Eminem confesses: "I don't think you realize what you mean to me, not the slightest clue / 'Cause me and you were like a crew / I was like your sidekick, you gon' either wanna fight me / When I get off this fucking mic or you gon' hug me." The song suggests that Dre saved Eminem's life and now he repays the obligation. http://www.youtube.com/watch?v=6m3vtWYCuMg.

18. In an examination of writings by American soldiers, Stacey Peebles concludes that though the soldiers express dissatisfaction with traditional gender roles, their attempts to draft

alternatives seem to fail (2011, 3). For a more nuanced portrayal of this masculinity, see Kevin Powers's novel *The Yellow Birds* (2012), which follows the ten-month sojourn of Privates Bartle and Murphy in Iraq.

19. R. Putnam 2000, 104, 105. Putnam has piled up mountains of statistics to show that Americans do not maintain the level of social links that they had earlier in the twentieth century. Not everyone agrees. Liz Spencer and Ray Pahl don't share Putnam's evaluations of current social trends, finding little evidence of social isolation among the people they interviewed (2006, 126, 199). Although Americans may not have the same connections with their neighbors, they are engaged in other contacts through previously unavailable social media.

20. He points to the spread of television viewing as a major factor in the reduction of social interconnectedness. In 1950 only 10 percent of American households owned a television but this number jumped to 90 percent by 1959, an astronomical increase (221).

21. Shirky 2010, 211. See also Coleman 2011.

22. Bauman argues that the objective of consumer culture was to make its lifestyle the "sole unquestionably approved choice"; a similar development is taking place in the fluid universe of the Net (2007, 14, 53). The world of consumers in the previous century is gradually yielding to the galaxy of networkers, spawning more networks. On the globalization of the Internet, see Farivar 2011 and Dimock 2011.

23. Since the Internet has been associated with the freedoms of both consumerism and of participatory democracy, it has become impervious to criticism. It is hard to point to destructive aspects of the Internet without appearing antimodern (Siegel 2008, 3).

24. Castells 2009, 21.

25. Castells 1996, 469; 2009, 54.

26. The network informs the global economy whose raw material seems to be information itself. What distinguishes our current technological revolution is less the centrality of knowledge than the application of such knowledge to the generation of further knowledge (Castells 1996, 32). On the inequalities of the new capitalism, see T. Miller 2007, Sennett 2006, and Klein 2007.

27. Bauman argues that the purpose of consumption is to raise the status of the consumers into sellable commodities (2007, 56).

28. Facebook does not produce goods in the way Toyota produces cars or like Apple makes computers. In 2011 Facebook employed only two thousand people (Brooks 2011, A27), an astonishingly small number given its global impact. In the winter of 2014 Facebook purchased the mobile message service, Whatsapp, for nearly 19 billion dollars. Yet Whatsapp employed only fifty-five individuals. Jaron Lanier's *Who Owns the Future* (2013) examines how Internet technology leads to the loss of jobs. Until now this technology has not generated wealth in the way that the invention of electricity did in the previous century.

29. Zelizer 2005, 291.

30. On the promises and pitfalls of Internet dating, see Kaufmann 2012.

31. Advertising remains the lifeblood of the Web economy (Lanier 2010, 82). Have individual artists profited, however? Everyone now wants free "content," what used to be called art. Our desire for free information may come at the expense of creativity. See Levine 2011 and Lanier 2013.

32. The Internet started in the 1960s as a project of the U.S. Department of Defense. Garret Keizer examines the gradual loss of privacy for the have-nots in the widening income disparities (2012). On digital surveillance, see Evgeny Mozorov (2011), who provides a reality check to Internet boosterism. Sennett described modern society as strangers duty bound to reciprocate each other's indifference (1974, 27). How off the mark does this seem today?

33. Baym 2010, 92.

34. Spencer and Pahl 2006, 34.

35. Christakis and Fowler 2009, 276. Tina Rosenberg examines how the power of the group, what she calls the "social cure," can tackle the world's problems, from overturning dictatorship in

Serbia to tackling teenage drinking in the United States. "What matters to us most is our relation-ships with fellow humans—the most commanding force for change" (2011, 95).

36. In *Alone Together: Why We Expect More from Technology and Less from Each Other* (2011), Sherry Turkle criticizes digital technologies for undermining authenticity. She details the darker side of the Internet—isolation, families eating dinner while staying online, obsessions with num-ber of Facebook friends, dependence on mobile phones. On intimacy and the new app generation, see Gardner and Davis 2013.

37. The tendency in the digital age to engage in mass communication of the self is not en-tirely new. A confessional streak has been present in American life for more than thirty years with a mountain of memoirs, autobiographies, and reality programs on television that have probed into hitherto inaccessible regions, including family intervention sessions, obsessions such as hoarding of animals, the travails of the morbidly obese.

38. Baym 2010, 134, 140.

39. D. Miller 2011, 170. Through the Net, everyone can become a celebrity for a second. See Gamson 2011.

40. There is a tension between the unlimited freedom the Internet offers individuals and the way it determines how that freedom is expressed. Users of Facebook express their individuality according to that corporation's paradigms, outsourcing their notion of self to algorithmic formulas (Lovink 2011, 34). Leib refers to the "undifferentiated nature of Internet personas" that are trace-able to the interface designs of the social network (2011, 2). The same reductionism exists in Wiki-pedia, which squeezes individual expression into a collective, anonymous style.

41. This process has been preoccupying social scientists for a century. About forty years ago Richard Sennett argued in *The End of Public Man* that capitalism has resulted in the withdrawal from publicity into the family (1974, 20).

42. Papacharissi 2010, 81, 133.

43. Ibid., 102.

44. What type of literature we will have in the future? The novel is still propelled by the tech-nology of print. We don't have, for instance, the novel equivalent of Wikipedia. If people were to create such a text, would it still be a novel? See Punday 2012. Fan fiction, narratives written by fans in response to actual fiction, is a new and expanding phenomenon. Analogous to Wikipedia, it may represent a window on the future.

Works Cited

Abel, Elizabeth, 1981. "(E)Merging Identities: The Dynamics of Female Friendship In Contemporary Fiction by Women." *Signs* 6, no. 3: 413–35.

Ackerman, Susan. 2005. *When Heroes Love: The Ambiguity of Eros in the Stories of Gilgamesh and David*. New York: Columbia University Press.

Acosta-Hughes, Benjamin. 2010. "Reflections: Two Letters, and Two Poets." *Dictynna* 8:1–8.

Adorno, Theodor W. [1958] 1997. *Aesthetic Theory*. Edited and translated by Robert Hullot-Kentor. Minneapolis: University of Minnesota Press.

Aelred of Rievaulx. 1974. *Spiritual Friendship*. Translated by Mary Eugenia Laker. Kalamazoo, MI: Cistercian Publications.

Ailes, M. J. 1999. "The Medieval Male Couple and the Language of Homosociality." In *Masculinity in Medieval Europe*, edited by Dawn M. Hadley. London: Longman.

Alexiou, Margaret. 1974. *The Ritual Lament in Greek Tradition*. Cambridge: Cambridge University Press.

Anon. 1957. *The Song of Roland*. Translated by Dorothy L. Sayers. New York: Penguin.

———. 1977. *A Choice of Anglo-Saxon Verse*. Selected and translated by Richard Hamer. London: Faber and Faber.

———. 2001. *The Epic of Gilgamesh*. Translated and edited by Benjamin R. Foster. New York: W W Norton.

——. 2005. *The Romance of Tristan and Iseult*. Retold by J. Bédier. Translated by Hilaire Belloc. Mineola, NY: Dover.

Appanah, Nathacha. 2010. *The Last Brother*. Translated by Geoffrey Strachan. Minneapolis: Graywolf Press.

Arendt, Hannah. 1968. *Men in Dark Times*. New York: Harcourt, Brace and World.

——. 1998. *The Human Condition*. 2nd ed. Chicago: University of Chicago Press.

Ariès, Philippe. 1962. *Centuries of Childhood: A Social History of Family Life*. Translated by Robert Baldick. New York: Knopf.

——. 1974. *Western Attitudes to Death: From the Middle Ages to the Present*. Baltimore: Johns Hopkins University Press.

Aristotle. 1984. *The Complete Works of Aristotle*. Vol. 2. Edited by Jonathan Barnes. Princeton: Princeton University Press.

Argersinger, Jana L, and Leland S. Person, eds. 2008. *Hawthorne and Melville: Writing a Relationship*. Athens: University of Georgia Press.

Athenaeus. 2012. *The Learned Banqueters*. Vol. 8. Translated by S. Douglas Olson. Cambridge: Harvard University Press.

Axelrod, Robert. 1984. *The Evolution of Cooperation*. New York: Basic Books.

Bacon, Francis. 1860. *The Works of Francis Bacon*. Vol. 12. Edited by James Spedding, Robert Leslie Ellis, and Douglas Denon Heath. Boston: Brown & Taggard.

Bakhtin, Mikhail. 1984. *Problems of Dostoevsky's Poetics*. Translated by Caryl Emerson. Minneapolis: University of Minnesota Press.

Bald, R. D., ed. 1936. *Literary Friendship in the Age of Wordsworth*. Cambridge: Cambridge University Press.

Baron-Cohen, Simon. 2011. *The Science of Evil: On Empathy and the Origins of Cruelty*. New York: Basic Books.

Bauman, Zygmunt. 2003. *Liquid Love: On the Frailty of Human Bonds*. Cambridge: Polity.

——. 2007. *Consuming Life*. Cambridge: Polity.

Baym, Nancy K. 2010. *Personal Connections in the Digital Age*. Cambridge: Polity.

Baym, Nina, et al. eds. 1989. *The Norton Anthology of American Literature*. Vol. 1, 3rd ed. New York: W. W. Norton.

Beauman, Nicola. 1994. *E. M. Forster: A Biography*. New York: Knopf.

Belfiore, Elizabeth S. 2000. *Murder among Friends: Violation of Philia in Greek Tragedy*. New York: Oxford University Press.

Bell, Robert R. 1981. *Worlds of Friendship*. Sage, CA: Beverly Hills.

Bellow, Saul. 1975. *Humboldt's Gift*. New York: Viking Press.

Benemann, William. 2006. *Male-Male Intimacy in Early America: Beyond Romantic Friendships*. New York: Haworth Press.

Ben Jelloun, Tahar. 2006. *The Last Friend*. Translated by Kevin Michel Capé and Hazel Rowley. New York: New Press.

Bentley, R. K. 2013. "Civic Friendship and Thin Citizenship." *Res Publica* 19:5–19.

Berlant, Lauren, ed. 2004. *Compassion: The Culture and Politics of an Emotion*. New York: Routledge.

Bion 1912. "The Lament for Adonis." In *The Greek Bucolic Poets*, translated by J. M. Edmonds. Cambridge: Harvard University Press.

Bolotin, David. 1979. *Plato's Dialogue on Friendship: An Interpretation of the* Lysis *with a New Translation*. Ithaca: Cornell University Press.

Booth, Wayne C. 1988. *The Company We Keep: An Ethics of Fiction*. Berkeley: University of California Press.

Boswell, John. 1994. *Same-Sex Unions in Premodern Europe*. New York: Villard Books.

Bowles, Samuel, and Herbert Gintis. 2011. *A Cooperative Species: Human Reciprocity and Its Evolution*. Princeton: Princeton University Press.

Brain, Robert. 1976. *Friends and Lovers*. New York: Basic Books.

Bram, Christopher. 2005. *Gods and Monsters*. New York: Harper Perennial.

Bray, Alan. 2003. *The Friend*. Chicago: University of Chicago Press.

Brecht, Bertolt. 1957. *Brecht on Theater: The Development of an Aesthetic*. Translated by John Willet. New York: Hill and Wang.

Brightman, Carol, ed. 1995. *Between Friends: The Correspondence of Hannah Arendt and Mary McCarthy, 1949–1975*. New York: Harcourt, Brace.

Brontë, Charlotte. 1979. *Shirley*. Oxford: Oxford University Press.

Brooks, David. 2011. "The Experience Economy." *New York Times*, February 15, A27.

Brooks, Peter. 2011. *Enigmas of Identity*. Princeton: Princeton University Press.

Brown, Donald E. 2000. "Human Universals and Their Implications." In *Being Universal: Anthropological Universality and Particularity in Transdisciplinary Perspectives*, edited by Neil Roughley. Berlin: Walter de Gruyter.

Bryant, John. 2010. "Rewriting *Moby-Dick*: Politics, Textual Identity, and the Revision Narrative." *PMLA* 125, no. 4: 1043–60.

Bukowski, William M., Andrew F. Newcomb, and Willard W. Hartup, eds. 1996. *The Company They Keep: Friendship in Childhood and Adolescence*. Cambridge: Cambridge University Press.

Byron, George Gordon. 1982. *Lord Byron: Selected Letters and Journals*. Edited by Leslie A. Marchand. Cambridge: Harvard University Press.

Caesar, Adrian. 1993. *Taking It Like a Man: Suffering, Sexuality, and the War Poets Brooke, Sassoon, Owen, Graves*. Manchester: Manchester University Press.

Calasso, Roberto. 1993. *The Marriage of Cadmus and Harmony*. Translated by Tim Parks. New York: Knopf.

Cannadine, David. 2013. *The Undivided Past: Humanity beyond Our Differences*. New York: Knopf.

Caraveli, Anna, 1986. "The Bitter Wounding: The Lament as Social Protest in Rural Greece." In *Gender and Power in Rural Greece*, edited by Jill Dubisch. Princeton: Princeton University Press.

Carroll, Noël. 2001. *Beyond Aesthetics: Philosophical Essays*. Cambridge: Cambridge University Press.

Castells, Manuel. 1996. *The Rise of the Network Society*. Oxford: Oxford University Press.

———. 2009. *Communication Power*. Oxford: Oxford University Press.

Cather, Willa. 1996. *Paul's Case and Other Stories*. New York: Dover Publications.

Cavafy, C. P. 1963. *Poiimata*. 2 vols. Edited by G. P. Savidis. Athens: Ikaros.

———. 1975. *C. P. Cavafy Collected Poems*. Translated by Edmund Keeley and Philip Sherrard and edited by George Savidis. Princeton: Princeton University Press.

——. 1977. *Anekdota Poiimata 1882–1923*. Athens: Ikaros.

Cavell, Stanley. 1969. *Must We Mean What We Say? A Book of Essays*. New York: Charles Scribner's Sons.

Chandler, James. 2013. *An Archaeology of Sympathy: The Sentimental Mode in Literature and Cinema*. Chicago: University of Chicago Press.

Cherlin, Andrew J. 2009. *The Marriage-Go-Round: The State of Marriage and the Family in America Today*. New York: Knopf.

Christakis, Nicholas A., and James H. Fowler. 2009. *Connected: The Surprising Power of Our Social Networks*. New York: Little Brown.

Cicero. 1971. *On Old Age and Friendship*. Translated by Frank O. Copley. Ann Arbor: University of Michigan Press.

Clark, David. 2009. *Between Medieval Men: Male Friendship and Desire in Early Medieval English Literature*. Oxford: Oxford University Press.

Cleland, John. 1985. *Fanny Hill or Memoirs of a Woman of Pleasure*. New York: Penguin.

Coetzee, J. M. 2003. *Elizabeth Costello*. New York: Viking.

Cohen, Theodore F. 1992. "Men's Families, Men's Friends: A Structural Analysis of Constraints on Men's Social Ties." In *Men's Friendship*, edited by Peter M. Nardi. Newbury Park, CA: Sage.

Cole, Sarah. 2003. *Modernism, Male Friendship, and the First World War*. Cambridge: Cambridge University Press.

Coleman, Beth. 2011. *Hello Avatar: Rise of the Networked Generation*. Cambridge, MA: MIT Press.

Crain, Caleb. 2001. *American Sympathy: Men, Friendship, and Literature in the New Nation*. New Haven: Yale University Press.

Curr, Matthew. 2002. *The Consolation of Otherness: The Male Love Elegy in Milton, Gray, and Tennyson*. Jefferson, NC: McFarland and Co.

Currie, Gregory. 1990. *The Nature of Fiction*. Cambridge: Cambridge University Press.

——. 1995. "Imagination and Simulation: Aesthetics Meets Cognitive Science." In *Mental Simulation: Evaluations and Applications*, edited by Martin Davies and Tony Stone. Oxford: Blackwell.

——. 2010. *Narratives and Narrators: A Philosophy of Stories*. Oxford: Oxford University Press.

Currie, Gregory, and Ian Ravenscroft. 2002. *Recreative Minds: Imagining in Philosophy and Psychology*. Oxford: Clarendon Press.

Damasio, Antonio. 2010. *Self Comes to Mind: Constructing the Conscious Brain*. New York: Pantheon.

Danforth, Loring M. 1982. *The Death Rituals of Rural Greece*. Princeton: Princeton University Press.

Das, Santanu. 2005. *Touch and Intimacy in First World War Literature*. Cambridge: Cambridge University Press.

Davidson, James. 2007. *The Greeks and Greek Love: A Radical Reappraisal of Greek Homosexuality*. London: Weidenfeld and Nicholson.

Defoe, Daniel. 2005. *The Fortunes and Misfortunes of the Famous Moll Flanders*. New York: Signet Classics.

Dehaene, Stanislas. 2009. *Reading in the Brain: The Science and Evolution of a Human Invention*. New York: Viking.

Delbanco, Andrew. 2005. *Melville: His World and Work*. New York: Knopf.

Deleuze, Gilles. 1993. *The Deleuze Reader*. Edited by Constantin V. Boundas. New York: Columbia University Press.

De Rougemont, Denis. 1956. *Love in the Western World*. Translated by Montgomery Belgion. New York: Pantheon.

Derrida, Jacques. 1997. *Politics of Friendship*. Translated by George Collins. London: Verso.

De Waal, Frans. 2009. *The Age of Empathy: Nature's Lessons for a Kinder Society*. New York: Harmony Books.

Dickens, Charles. 1996. *David Copperfield*. London: Penguin.

Dimock, Wai Chee. 2011. "World Literature on Facebook." *PMLA* 26, no. 3: 730–36.

Dollimore, Jonathan. 1991. *Sexual Dissidence: Augustine to Wilde, Freud to Foucault*. Oxford: Clarendon Press.

Dryden, John. 1972. *The Works of John Dryden*. Vol. 2. Edited by H. T. Swedenberg Jr. Berkeley: University of California Press.

Edyvane, Derek. 2013. "Rejecting Society: Misanthropy, Friendship and Montaigne." *Res Publica* 19:53–65.

Eger, Elizabeth. 2010. *Bluestockings: Women of Reason from Enlightenment to Romanticism*. New York. Palgrave Macmillan.

Eisner, Elliot. W. 2002. *The Arts and the Creation of Mind*. New York: Methuen.

Euripides. 1955. *Medea*. Translated by Rex Warner. In *Euripides I*. Chicago: University of Chicago Press.

——. 1972. *The Bacchae and Other Plays*. Translated by Phillip Vellacott. Baltimore: Penguin.

Faderman, Lillian. 1981. *Surpassing the Love of Men: Romantic Friendship and Love between Women from the Renaissance to the Present*. New York: William Morrow.

Fakinou, Eugenia. 1991. *The Seventh Garment*. Translated by Ed Emery. London: Serpent's Tail.

Farivar, Cyrus. 2011. *The Internet of Elsewhere: The Emergent Effects of a Wired World*. New Brunswick, NJ: Rutgers University Press.

Faulkner, William. 1951. *Absalom, Absalom*. New York: Random House.

Fitzgerald, F. Scott. [1925] 1953. *The Great Gatsby*. New York: Charles Scribner's Sons.

Forster, E. M. 1924. *A Passage to India*. New York: Harcourt.

——. 1951. *Two Cheers for Democracy*. New York: Harcourt.

——. 1971. *Maurice*. New York: Norton.

——. 1983. *The Hill of Devi and Other Indian Writings*. Edited by Elizabeth Heine. London: Edward Arnold.

Frantzen, Allen J. 1998. *Before the Closet: Same-Sex Love from* Beowulf *to* Angels in America. Chicago: University of Chicago Press.

Freud, Sigmund. 1957. "Mourning and Melancholia." In vol. 14 of *The Standard Edition of the Complete Psychological Works of Sigmund Freud*, edited by James Strachey, 243–58. London: Hogarth Press.

Furneaux, Holly. 2009. *Queer Dickens: Erotics, Families, Masculinities*. Oxford: Oxford University Press.

Fussell, Paul. 1975. *The Great War and Modern Memory*. London: Oxford University Press.

Gamson, Joshua. 2011. "The Unwatched Life Is Not Worth Living: The Elevation of the Ordinary in Celebrity Culture." *PMLA* 126, no. 4: 1061–69.

Gana, Nouri. 2011. *Signifying Loss: Toward a Poetics of Narrative Mourning*. Lewisburg, PA: Bucknell University Press.

Gandhi, Leela. 2006. *Affective Communities: Anticolonial Thought, Fin-de-Siècle Radicalism, and the Politics of Friendship*. Durham, NC: Duke University Press.

Gardner, Howard, and Katie Davis. 2013. *The App Generation: How Today's Youth Navigate Identity, Intimacy, and Imagination in a Digital World*. New Haven: Yale University Press.

Gaskell, Elizabeth. 1996. *Wives and Daughters*. London: Penguin.

Gerrig, Richard, and David N. Rupp. 2004. "Psychological Processes Underlying Literary Impact." *Poetics Today* 25, no. 2: 266–81.

Giddens, Anthony. 1992. *The Transformation of Intimacy: Sexuality, Love, and Eroticism in Modern Societies*. Stanford: Stanford University Press.

Girard, René. 2011. *Sacrifice*. Translated by Matthew Pattillo and David Dawson. East Lansing: Michigan State University Press.

Godbeer, Richard. 2009. *The Overflowing of Friendship: Love between Men and the Creation of the American Republic*. Baltimore: Johns Hopkins University Press.

Goldberg, Jonathan. 1992. *Sodometries: Renaissance Texts, Modern Sexualities*. Stanford: Stanford University Press.

Goldberg, Robert. 2006. "What Good Are Friends?" *St. John's Review* 64:73–99.

Gorgani, Fakhraddin. 2008. *Vis and Ramin*. Translated by Dick Davis. Washington, DC: Mage Publishers.

Gorman, James. 2012. "Ancient Bones Tell a Story of Compassion." *New York Times*, December 18, D1.

Gottschall, Jonathan. 2012. *The Storytelling Animal: How Stories Make Us Human*. Boston: Houghton Mifflin.

Gray, Thomas. 1973. *The Complete Poems of Thomas Gray*. London: Heinemann.

Greenberg, David. F. 1988. *The Construction of Homosexuality*. Chicago: University of Chicago Press.

Greene, Graham. 1955. *The Quiet American*. London: Heinemann.

Greif, Geoffrey L. 2009. *Buddy System: Understanding Male Friendships*. Oxford: Oxford University Press.

Grossman, David. 1988. *The Yellow Road*. Translated by Haim Watzman. New York: Farrar, Straus and Giroux.

Haggerty, George E. 1999. *Men in Love: Masculinity and Sexuality in the Eighteenth Century*. New York: Columbia University Press.

———. 2004. "Love and Loss." *GLQ: A Journal of Lesbian and Gay Studies* 10, no. 3: 385–405.

Halberstam, David. 2003. *The Teammates: A Portrait of a Friendship*. New York: Hyperion.

Halberstam, Judith. 2011. "Not So Lonesome Cowboys: The Queer Western." In *The Brokeback Book: From Story to Cultural Phenomenon*, ed. William R. Handley. Lincoln: University of Nebraska Press.

Hall, Radclyffe. 1956. *The Well of Loneliness*. New York: Random House.

Handley, William R. ed. 2011. *The Brokeback Book: From Story to Cultural Phenomenon*. Lincoln: University of Nebraska Press.

Hansen, Karen V. 1992. "'Our Eyes Behold Each Other': Masculinity and Intimate Friendship in Antebellum New England." In *Men's Friendship*, edited by Peter M. Nardi. Newbury Park, CA: Sage.

Harman, Oren. 2010. *The Price of Altruism: George Price and the Search for the Origins of Kindness*. New York: W.W. Norton.

Harrison, Robert Pogue. 2003. *The Dominion of the Dead*. Chicago: University of Chicago Press.

Haseldine, Julian. 1996. "Friendship, Equality, and Universal Harmony: The Universal and the Particular in Aelred of Rivaulx's *De Spiritali Amicitia*." In *Friendship East and West: Philosophical Perspectives*, edited by Oliver Leaman. Richmond, Surrey, UK: Curzon.

———. 1999. "Love, Separation and Male Friendship: Words and Actions in Saint Anselm's Letters to His Friends." In *Masculinity in Medieval Europe*, edited by Dawn M. Hadley. London: Longman.

Hegel, G. W. F. 1991. *Elements of the Philosophy of Right*. Translated by H. B. Nisbet. Cambridge: Cambridge University Press.

Heilke, Thomas. 2008. "Friendship in the Civic Order: A Reformation Absence." In *Friendship and Politics: Essays in Political Thought*, edited by John von Heyking and Richard Avramenko. Notre Dame, IN: University of Notre Dame Press.

Heller, Agnes. 1998. "The Beauty of Friendship." *South Atlantic Quarterly* 97, no. 1: 5–22.

Herdt, Gilbert. 1984. "Ritualized Homosexual Behavior in the Male Cults of Melanesia 1862–1983." In *Ritualized Homosexuality in Melanesia*, edited by Gilbert Herdt. Berkeley: University of California Press.

Herman, Gabriel. 1987. *Ritualized Friendship and the Greek City*. Cambridge: Cambridge University Press.

Hesiod. 1983. *Theogony, Works and Days, Shield*. Translated by Apostolos N. Athanasakis. Baltimore: Johns Hopkins University Press.

Herodotus. 1987. *The History*. Translated by David Grene. Chicago: University of Chicago Press.

Hines, Derrek. 2002. *Gilgamesh*. London: Chatto and Windus.

Hiss, Tony. 2010. *In Motion: The Experience of Travel*. New York: Knopf.

Hobbes, Thomas. 1983. *De Cive*. Edited by Howard Warrender. Oxford: Clarendon Press.

———. 1991. *Leviathan*. Cambridge: Cambridge University Press.

Hogan, Patrick Colm. 2010. "Literary Universals." In *Introduction to Cognitive Cultural Studies*, edited by Lisa Zunshine. Baltimore: Johns Hopkins University Press.

Hölderlin, Friedrich. 1967. *Poems and Fragments*. Translated by Michael Hamburger. Ann Arbor: University of Michigan Press.

Holst-Warhaft, Gail. 1992. *Dangerous Voices: Women's Laments and Greek Literature*. London: Routledge.

Homer. 1961. *The Odyssey*. Translated by Robert Fitzgerald. New York: Vintage Books.

———. 1978. *The Iliad*. Translated by A. T. Murray. Cambridge, MA: Loeb Classical Library, Harvard University Press.

———.1990. *The Iliad*. Translated by Robert Fagles. New York: Penguin.

Housman, A. E. 1965. *The Collected Poems of A. E. Housman*. New York: Holt, Rinehart, and Winston.

Huizinga, Johan. 1980. *Homo Ludens: A Study of the Play-Element in Culture*. London: Routledge.

Hunt, Lynn. 2007. *Inventing Human Rights: A History*. New York: W. W. Norton.

Hutter, Horst. 1978. *Politics as Friendship: The Origins of Classical Notions of Politics in the Theory and Practice of Friendship*. Waterloo, ON: Wilfrid Laurier University Press.

Hyatte, Reginald. 1994. *The Arts of Friendship: The Idealization of Friendship in Medieval and Early Renaissance Literature*. Leiden: Brill.

Jaeger, C. Stephen. 1999. *Ennobling Love: In Search of a Lost Sensibility*. Philadelphia: University of Pennsylvania Press.

James, Henry. 1971. *The American*. New York: Bantam Books.

Jamieson, Lynn. 1998. *Intimacy: Personal Relationships in Modern Societies*. Cambridge: Polity.

Jeffreys, Peter. 2005. *Eastern Questions: Hellenism and Orientalism in the Writings of E. M. Forster and C. P. Cavafy*. ELT Press of English Literature in Transition. Greensboro: University of North Carolina.

Johnston, Sarah Iles. 1999. *Restless Dead: Encounters between Living and Dead in Greece*. Berkeley: University of California Press.

Jurecic, Ann. 2012. *Illness as Narrative*. Pittsburgh: University of Pittsburgh Press.

Jusdanis, Gregory. 1987. *The Poetics of Cavafy: Textuality, Eroticism, History*. Princeton: Princeton University Press.

———. 2000. *The Necessary Nation*. Princeton: Princeton University Press.

———. 2010. *Fiction Agonistes: In Defense of Literature*. Stanford: Stanford University Press.

Kant, Immanuel. 2000. *The Critique of Judgment*. Translated by J. H. Bernard. Amherst, NY: Prometheus Books.

Kaplan, Danny. 2006. *The Men We Loved: Male Friendship and Nationalism in Israeli Culture*. New York: Berghahn Books.

Kaufmann, Jean-Claude. 2012. *Love Online*. Translated by David Macey. Cambridge: Polity.

Kazantzakis, Nikos. 1952. *Zorba the Greek*. Translated by Carl Wildman. New York: Simon and Schuster.

———. 1965. *Report to Greco*. Translated by Peter Bien. New York: Simon and Schuster.

———. 1973. *Vios kai Politeia tou Alexi Zorba*. Athens: Helen Kazantzakis.

Keats, John. 2001. *Complete Poems and Selected Letters of John Keats*. New York: Modern Library.

Keen, Maurice. 1984. *Chivalry*. New Haven: Yale University Press.

Keen, Suzanne. 2007. *Empathy and the Novel*. Oxford: Oxford University Press.

Keizer, Garret. 2012. *Privacy*. New York: Picador.

Kemp, Barry. 2012. *The City of Akhenaten and Nefertiti: Amarna and Its People*. London: Thames and Hudson.

Kennedy, Robinette. 1986. "Women's Friendship on Crete: A Psychological Perspective." In *Gender and Power in Rural Greece*, edited by Jill Dubisch. Princeton: Princeton University Press.

Kent, Dale. 2009. *Friendship, Love, and Trust in Renaissance Florence*. Cambridge: Harvard University Press.

Kierkegaard, Søren. 1995. *Works of Love*. Translated by Howard V. Hong and Edna H. Hong. Princeton: Princeton University Press.

Kimmel, Michael. 2008. *Guyland: The Perilous World Where Guys Become Men*. New York: Harper Collins.

Kirtsoglou, Elisabeth. 2004. *For the Love of Women: Gender, Identity, and Same-Sex Relations in a Greek Provincial Town*. London: Routledge.

Klein, Naomi. 2007. *The Shock Doctrine: The Rise of Disaster Capitalism*. Toronto: Knopf.

Knerr, Anthony. 1984. *Shelley's* Adonais*: A Critical Edition*. New York: Columbia University Press.

Koestenbaum, Wayne. 1989. *Double Talk: The Erotics of Male Literary Collaboration*. New York: Routledge.

Konner, Melvin. 2010. *The Evolution of Childhood: Relationships, Emotions, Mind*. Cambridge: Harvard University Press.

Konstan, David. 1997. *Friendship in the Classical World*. Cambridge: Cambridge University Press.

Kreitler, Hans, and Shulamith Kreitler. 1972. *Psychology of the Arts*. Durham, NC: Duke University Press.

Kübler-Ross, Elizabeth. 1969. *On Death and Dying*. New York: Macmillan.

Laforet, Carmen. 2007. *Nada*. Translated by Edith Grossman. New York: Modern Library.

Lanier, Jaron. 2010. *You Are Not a Gadget: A Manifesto*. New York: Knopf.

———. 2013. *Who Owns the Future?* New York: Simon and Schuster.

Lawrence, D. H. 1959. *Lady Chatterley's Lover*. New York: Modern Library.

———. 1966. *The White Peacock*. Carbondale: Southern Illinois University Press.

———. 1976. *Women in Love*. New York: Penguin.

Leib, Ethan J. 2011. *Friend v. Friend: The Transformation of Friendship—and What the Law Has to Do with It*. Oxford: Oxford University Press.

Leontsini, Eleni. 2013. "The Motive of Society: Aristotle on Civic Friendship, Justice, and Concord." *Res Publica* 19:12–35.

Lessing, Gotthold Ephraim. 2002. *Two Jewish Plays*. Translated by Noel Clark. London: Oberon Books.

Lévinas, Emmanuel. 1987. *Time and the Other and Additional Essays*. Translated by Richard A. Cohen. Pittsburgh: Duquesne University Press.

Levine, Robert. 2011. *Free Ride: How Digital Parasites Are Destroying the Culture Business and How the Culture Business Can Fight Back*. New York: Doubleday.

Lewis, C. S. 1988. *The Four Loves*. Orlando: Harcourt.

Lieberman, Matthew D. 2013. *Social: Why Our Brains Are Wired to Connect*. New York: Crown.

Lilly, Mark. 1993. *Gay Men's Literature in the Twentieth Century*. New York: New York University Press.

Lochman, Daniel, Maritere López, and Lorna Hudson, eds. 2010. *Discourses and Representations of Friendship in Early Modern Europe*. Farnham, UK: Ashgate.

Locke, John. 1960. *Two Treatises of Government*. Cambridge: Cambridge University Press.

——. 1995. *An Essay concerning Human Understanding*. Amherst, NY: Prometheus Books.

Llosa, Mario Vargas. 1982. *Aunt Julia and the Script Writer*. Translated by Helen R. Lane. New York: Avon Books.

Lovink, Geert. 2011. *Networks without a Cause: A Critique of Social Media*. Cambridge: Polity.

Luhmann, Niklas. 1986. *Love as Passion: The Codification of Intimacy*. Translated by Jeremy Gaines and Doris L. Jones. Cambridge: Harvard University Press.

Machiavelli, Niccolò. 1999. *The Prince*. Translated by George Bull. London: Penguin.

MacIntyre, Alasdair. 1981. *After Virtue: A Study of Moral Theory*. London: Duckworth.

Madison, James, Alexander Hamilton, and John Jay. 1987. *The Federalist Papers*. New York: Penguin.

Maeterlinck, Maurice. 1977. *Death*. Translated by Alexander Teixeira de Mattos. New York: Arno Press.

Magdalino, Paul. 1989. "Honor Among Romaioi: The Framework of Social Values in the World of Digenes Akritas and Kekaumenos" *Byzantine and Modern Greek Studies* 13, 183–218.

Mallon, Thomas. 2009. *Yours Ever: People and Their Letters*. New York: Pantheon.

Manoussakis, John Panteleimon. 2013. "Friendship in Late Antiquity: The Case of Gregory Nazianzen and Basil the Great." In *Ancient and Medieval Concepts of Friendship*, edited by S. Stern-Gillet and Gary Gurtler.

Márai, Sándor. 2002. *Embers*. Translated by Carol Brown Janeway. New York: Vintage International.

Marcus, Sharon. 2007. *Between Women: Friendship, Desire, and Marriage in Victorian England*. Princeton: Princeton University Press.

Marshall, James. 1976. *George and Martha: Rise and Shine*. Boston: Houghton Mifflin.

Mauss, Marcel. 1990. *The Gift: The Form and Reason for Exchange in Archaic Societies*. Translated by W. D. Halls. New York: Doubleday.

Mavor, Elizabeth. 1971. *The Ladies of Llangollen: A Study of Romantic Friendship*. Harmondsworth: Penguin.

McCloskey, Deirdre N. 2010. *Bourgeois Dignity: Why Economics Can't Explain the Modern World*. Chicago. University of Chicago Press.

McGowan, John. 1991. *Postmodernism and Its Critics*. Ithaca: Cornell University Press.

McGuire, Brian Patrick. 1988. *Friendship and Community: The Monastic Experience 350–1250*. Kalamazoo, MI: Cistercian Publications.

McLuhan, Marshall. 1964. *Understanding Media: The Extensions of Man*. New York: McGraw Hill.

Melville, Herman. 1956. *Moby-Dick or, The Whale*. Boston: Houghton Mifflin.

——. 1962. *Billy Budd, Sailor*. Edited by Harrison Hayford and Merton M. Sealts Jr. Chicago: University of Chicago Press.

Messent, Peter. 2009. *Mark Twain and Male Friendship*. Oxford: Oxford University Press.

Michaelis, David. 1983. *The Best of Friends: Profiles of Extraordinary Friendships*. New York: William Morrow.

Miller, Daniel. 2011. *Tales from Facebook*. Cambridge: Polity.

Miller, Madeline. 2012. *The Song of Achilles*. New York: Ecco.

Miller, Stuart. 1983. *Men and Friendship*. Boston: Houghton Mifflin.

Miller, Toby. 2007. *Cultural Citizenship: Cosmopolitanism, Consumerism*, and *Television in a Neoliberal Age*. Philadelphia: Temple University Press.

Milton, John. [1638]. 1983. *Milton's Lycidas: The Tradition and the Poem*. Edited by C. A. Patrides. Columbia: University of Missouri Press.

Montaigne, Michel de. 1958. *The Complete Essays of Montaigne*. Stanford: Stanford University Press.

Moritz, Karl Philipp. 2012. "An Attempt to Unify All the Fine Arts and Sciences under the Concept of *That Which Is Complete in Itself*." Translated by Elliott Schreiber. *PMLA* 127, no. 1: 94–100.

Moschus. 1912. "The Lament for Bion." In *The Greek Bucolic Poets*, translated by J. M. Edmonds. Cambridge: Harvard University Press.

Mozorov, Evgeny. 2011. *The Net Delusion: The Dark Side of Internet Freedom*. New York: Public Affairs.

Mullen, Margaret. 1997. *Theophylact of Ochrid: Reading the Letters of a Byzantine Arch bishop*. Birmingham, UK: Center for Byzantine, Ottoman, and Modern Greek Studies.

Mullett, M. E. 1988. "Byzantium: A Friendly Society?" *Past and Present* 118:3–24.

Munteanu, Dana LaCourse. 2012. *Tragic Pathos: Pity and Fear in Greek Philosophy and Literature*. Cambridge: Cambridge University Press.

Murray, Stephen O. 2000. *Homosexualities*. Chicago: University of Chicago Press.

Myrivilis, Stratis. 2003. *Life in the Tomb*. Translated by Peter Bien. River Vale, NJ: Cosmos Publishing.

Nagel, Thomas. 1970. *The Possibility of Altruism*. Oxford: Oxford University Press.

Nardelli, Jean-Fabrice. 2007. *Homosexuality and Liminality in Gilgamesh and Samuel*. Amsterdam: Hackert.

Nussbaum, Martha. C. 1997. *Cultivating Humanity: A Classical Defense of Reform in Liberal Education*. Cambridge. Harvard University Press.

——. 2001. *Upheavals of Thought: The Intelligence of Emotions*. Cambridge: Cambridge University Press.

Oliker, Stacey J. 1989. *Best Friends and Marriage: Exchange among Women*. Berkeley: University of California Press.

——. 1998. "The Modernization of Friendship: Individualism, Intimacy, and Gender in the Nineteenth Century." In *Placing Friendship in Context*, edited by Rebecca G. Adams and Graham Allan. Cambridge: Cambridge University Press.

Oulton, Carolyn W. de la L. 2007. *Romantic Friendship in Victorian Literature*. Aldershot, UK: Ashgate.

Pagel, Mark D. 2012. *Wired for Culture: Origins of the Human Social Mind*. New York: W. W. Norton.

Paine, Thomas. 1976. *Common Sense*. Edited by Isaac Kramnick. Harmondsworth, UK: Penguin.

Pakaluk, Michael, ed. 1991 *Other Selves: Philosophers on Friendship*. Indianapolis: Hackett Publishing.

Palumbo-Liu, David. 2012. *The Deliverance of Others: Reading Literature in a Global Age*. Durham, NC: Duke University Press.

Pangle, Loraine Smith. 2003. *Aristotle and the Philosophy of Friendship*. Cambridge: Cambridge University Press.

Papacharissi, Zizi A. 2010. *A Private Sphere: Democracy in the Digital Age*. Cambridge: Polity Press.

Papataxiarchis, Evthymios. 1991. "Friends of the Heart: Male Commensal Solidarity, Gender, and Kinship in Aegean Greece." In *Contested Identities: Gender and Kinship in Modern Greece*, edited by Peter Loizos and Evthymios Papataxiarchis. Princeton: Princeton University Press.

Parini, Jay. 2010. *The Passages of H. M.: A Novel of Herman Melville*. New York: Doubleday.

Parker-Pope, Tara. 2009. "What Are Friends For? A Longer Life?" *New York Times*, April 21, D1.

Passerini, Luisa. 1999. *Europe in Love, Love in Europe: Imagination and Politics between the Wars*. New York: New York University Press.

Peachin, Michael. 2001. "Friendship and Abuse at the Dinner Table." In "Aspects of Friendship in the Graeco-Roman World," edited by Michael Peachin, supplement, *Journal of Roman Archaeology*, no. 43.

Peebles, Stacey. 2011. *Welcome to the Suck: Narrating the American Soldier's Experience in Iraq*. Ithaca: Cornell University Press.

Pfeil, Fred. 1995. *White Guys: Studies in Postmodern Domination and Difference*. New York: Verso.

Phelan, James. 2005. *Living to Tell about It: A Rhetoric and Ethics of Character Narration*. Ithaca: Cornell University Press.

Pigliucci, Massimo. 2012. *Answers for Aristotle: How Science and Philosophy Can Lead Us to a More Meaningful Life*. New York: Basic Books.

Pinker, Steven. 2011. *The Better Angels of Our Nature: Why Violence Has Declined*. New York: Viking.

Plato. 1979. *Plato's Dialogue on Friendship: An Interpretation of the* Lysis *with a New Translation*. Translated by David Bolotin. Ithaca: Cornell University Press.

——. 1989. *Symposium*. Translated by Alexander Nehamas and Paul Woodruff. Indianapolis: Hackett Publishing.

Platt, Michael. 1998. "Montaigne, Of Friendship and On Tyranny." In *Freedom over Servitude: Montaigne, La Boétie, and On Voluntary Servitude*, edited by David Lewis Schaefer. Westport, CT: Greenwood Press.

Powers, Kevin. 2012. *The Yellow Birds*. New York: Little, Brown.

Price, A. W. 1989. *Love and Friendship in Plato and Aristotle*. Oxford: Oxford University Press.

Proulx, Annie. 2000. *Close Range: Wyoming Stories*. New York: Scribner.

Punday, Daniel. 2012. *Writing at the Limits: The Novel in the New Media Ecology*. Lincoln: University of Nebraska Press.

Putnam, Michael C. J. 1986. *Artifice and Eternity: Horace's Fourth Book of Odes*. Ithaca: Cornell University Press.

Putnam, Robert D. 2000. *Bowling Alone: The Collapse and Revival of American Community*. New York: Simon and Schuster.

Rader, Rosemary. 1983. *Breaking Boundaries: Male/Female Friendship in Early Christian Communities*. New York: Paulist Press.

Rahe, Paul. 1992. *Republics Ancient and Modern*. Chapel Hill: University of North Carolina Press.

Ramazani, Jahan. 1994. *Poetry of Mourning: The Modern Elegy from Hardy to Heaney*. Chicago: University of Chicago Press.

Rapp, Claudia. 1998. "Ritual Brotherhood in Byzantine Tradition." In *Traditio: Studies in Ancient and Medieval History, Thought, and Religion* 52: 285–326.

Ratcliffe, Sophie. 2008. *On Sympathy*. Oxford: Clarendon Press.

Rhodes, James M. 2008. "Platonic *Philia* and the Political Order." In *Friendship and Political Order: Essays in Political Thought*, edited by John von Heyking and Richard Avramenko. Notre Dame, IN: University of Notre Dame Press.

Rifkin, Jeremy. 2009. *The Empathic Civilization: The Race to Global Consciousness in a World in Crisis*. New York: Penguin.

Ritzenberg, Aaron. 2013. *The Sentimental Touch: The Language of Feeling in the Age of Managerialism*. New York: Fordham University Press.

Rosen, Michael. 2012. *Dignity: Its History and Meaning*. Cambridge: Harvard University Press.

Rosenberg, Tina. 2011. *Join the Club: How Peer Pressure Can Transform the World*. New York: W. W. Norton.

Rotundo, E. Anthony. 1993. *American Manhood: Transformations of Masculinity from the Revolution to the Modern Era*. New York: Basic Books.

Rubin, Lillian B. 1985. *Just Friends: The Role of Friendship in Our Lives*. New York: Harper and Row.

Ruggiero, Guido. 2007. *Machiavelli in Love: Sex, Self, and Society in the Italian Renaissance*. Baltimore: Johns Hopkins University Press.

Ruskin, John. 1893. *Selections from the Writings of John Ruskin*. 2nd ser. London: George Allen.

Russo, Vito. 1981. *The Celluloid Closet: Homosexuality in the Movies*. New York: Harper and Row.

Sacks, Peter M. 1985. *The English Elegy: Studies in the Genre from Spencer to Yeats*. Baltimore: Johns Hopkins University Press.

Salkever, Stephen. 2008. "Taking Friendship Seriously: Aristotle on the Place(s) of *Philia* in Human Life." In *Friendship and Political Order: Essays in Political Thought*, edited by John von Heyking and Richard Avramenko. Notre Dame, IN: University of Notre Dame Press.

Sargent, Winthrop. 1871. *The Life of Major John André*. New York: D. Appleton & Co.

Schaefer, David Lewis. 1998. "Introduction." In *Freedom over Servitude, Montaigne, La Boétie, and on Voluntary Servitude*. Westport, CT: Greenwood Press.

Schaeffer, Jean-Marie. 2010. *Why Fiction?* Translated by Dorrit Cohn. Lincoln: University of Nebraska Press.

Scheler, Max. 1970. *The Nature of Sympathy*. Translated by Peter Heath. Hamden, CT: Archon Books.

Schiller, Friedrich. 1996. *Don Carlos and Mary Stuart*. Translated by Hilary Collier Sy-Quia and Peter Oswald. Oxford: Oxford University Press.

Schweitzer, Ivy. 2006. *Perfecting Friendship: Politics and Affiliation in Early American Literature*. Chapel Hill: University of North Carolina Press.

Scott, Sarah. 1995. *Millenium Hall*. Edited by Gary Kelly. Peterborough, ON: Broadview Press.

Seabright, Paul. 2012. *The War of the Sexes: How Conflict and Cooperation Have Shaped Men and Women from Prehistory to the Present*. Princeton: Princeton University Press.

Seaford, Richard. 2004. *Money and the Early Greek Mind: Homer, Philosophy, Tragedy*. Cambridge: Cambridge University Press.

Sedgwick, Eve Kosofsky. 1985. *Between Men: English Literature and Male Homosocial Desire*. New York: Columbia University Press.

———. 1990. *Epistemology of the Closet*. Berkeley: University of California Press.

Seidler, Victor J. 1992. "Rejection, Vulnerability, and Friendship." In *Men's Friendship*, edited by Peter M. Nardi. Newbury Park, CA: Sage.

Sennett, Richard. 1974. *The Fall of Public Man*. New York: Vintage Books.

———. 2006. *The Culture of the New Capitalism*. New Haven: Yale University Press.

Shaftesbury, Third Earl of. 1999. *Characteristics of Men, Manners, Opinions, Times*. Edited by Lawrence E. Klein. Cambridge: Cambridge University Press.

Shannon, Laurie. 2002. *Sovereign Amity: Figures of Friendship in Shakespearean Context*. Chicago: University of Chicago Press.

Sharp, Ronald A. 1986. *Friendship and Literature: Spirit and Form*. Durham, NC: Duke University Press.

Shaw, David W. 1994. *Elegy and Paradox: Testing the Conventions*. Baltimore: Johns Hopkins University Press.

Shelley, Percy Bysshe. 1984. "Adonais: An Elegy on the Death of John Keats." In *Shelley's* Adonais: *A Critical Edition*, edited by Anthony Knerr. New York: Columbia University Press.

———. 1890. *A Defense of Poetry*. Edited by Albert S. Cook. Boston: Ginn & Co.

Sherrod, Drury. 1987. "The Bonds of Men: Problems and Possibilities in Close Male Relationships." In *The Making of Masculinities: The New Men's Studies*, edited by Harry Brod. Boston: Allen and Unwin.

Shirky, Clay. 2010. *Cognitive Surplus: Creativity and Generosity in a Connected Age*. New York: Penguin Press.

Siegel, Lee. 2008. *Against the Machine: Being Human in the Age of the Electronic Mob*. New York: Spiegel and Grau.

Silver, Allan. 1997. "Two Different Sorts of Commerce: Friendship and Strangership in Civil Society." In *Public and Private Thought and Practice: Perspectives on a Grand Dichotomy*, edited by Jeff Weintraub and Krishan Kumar. Chicago: University of Chicago Press.

Simmel, Georg. 1950. *The Sociology of Georg Simmel.* Edited and translated by Kurt H. Wolff. New York: Free Press.

———. 1990. *The Philosophy of Money.* Translated by Tom Bottomore and David Frisby. Routledge: London.

Smith, Adam. 1976. *The Theory of Moral Sentiments.* Indianapolis: Liberty Classics.

———. 1991. *The Wealth of Nations.* New York: Knopf.

Smith, Eric. 1977. *By Mourning Tongues: Studies in English Elegy.* Ipswich: Boydell Press.

Smith, Murray. 1995. *Engaging Characters: Fiction, Emotion, and the Cinema.* Oxford: Clarendon Press.

Smith-Rosenberg, Carol. 1975. "The Female World of Love and Ritual: Relations between Women in Nineteenth-Century America." *Signs* 1, no. 1: 1–29.

Sophocles. 1919. *Sophocles II.* Translated by F. Storr. New York: Loeb Classical Library, Putnam's.

Spain, Daphne. 1992. "The Spatial Foundations of Men's Friendships and Men's Power." In *Men's Friendship,* edited by Peter M. Nardi. Newbury Park, CA: Sage.

Spencer, Liz, and Ray Pahl. 2006. *Rethinking Friendship: Hidden Solidarities Today.* Princeton: Princeton University Press.

Steig, William. 1971. *Amos and Boris.* New York: Farrar, Straus and Giroux.

Steiner, Wendy. 2010. *The Real Real Thing: The Model in the Mirror of Art.* Chicago. University of Chicago Press.

Stone, Lawrence. 1977. *The Family, Sex, and Marriage in England 1500–1800.* New York: Harper and Row.

Stretter, Robert. 2003. "Rewriting Perfect Friendship in Chaucer's 'Knight's Tale' and Lydgate's 'Fabula Duorum Mercatorum.'" *Chaucer Review* 37, no. 3: 234–52.

Sullivan, Andrew. 1998. *Love Undetectable: Note on Friendship, Sex, and Survival.* New York: Knopf.

Swofford, Anthony. 2003. *Jarhead: A Marine's Chronicle of the Gulf War and Other Battles.* New York: Scribner.

Tacitus. 2008. *The Annals.* Translated by J. C. Yardley. Oxford: Oxford University Press.

Tadmor, Naomi. 2001. *Family and Friends in Eighteenth-Century England.* Cambridge: Cambridge University Press.

Taussig, Gurion. 2002. *Coleridge and the Idea of Friendship.* Newark: University of Delaware Press.

Taylor, Martin, ed. 1989. *Lads: Love Poetry of the Trenches.* London: Constable.

Tennyson, Lord Alfred. 2004. *In Memoriam.* Edited by Erik Gray. New York: W. W. Norton.

Terdiman, Richard. 2011. "Can We Read the Book of Love?" *PMLA* 126, no. 2: 472–82.

Theocritus. 1963. *The Idylls of Theocritus.* Translated by Barris Mills. West Lafayette, IN: Purdue University Press.

Thucydides. 1982. *The Peloponnesian War.* The Crawley Translation. Revised by T. E. Wick. New York: Modern Library.

Tinnefeld, Franz. 1973. "Freundschaft in den Briefen des Michael Psellos." *Jahrbuch der Österreichischen Byzantinistik* 22:151–68.

Tocqueville, Alexis de. 1969. *Democracy in America*. Translated by George Lawrence. New York: Harper.

Trivers, Robert. 2011. *The Folly of Fools: The Logic of Deceit and Self-Deception in Human Life*. New York: Basic Books.

Turkle, Sherry. 2011. *Alone Together: Why We Expect More from Technology and Less from Each Other*. New York: Basic Books.

Turner, Victor. 1967. *The Forest of Symbols: Aspects of Ndembu Ritual*. Ithaca: Cornell University Press.

——. 1969. *The Ritual Process: Structure and Anti-Structure*. Ithaca: Cornell University Press.

Twain, Mark. 2000. *The Adventures of Huckleberry Finn*. Edited by Susan K. Harris. Boston: Houghton Mifflin.

Tziovas, Dimitris. 2009. "From Being to Becoming: Reflections on the Enduring Popularity of Kazantzakis." *Byzantine and Modern Greek Studies* 33, no. 1: 83–91.

Van Dyke, Henry, ed. 1907. *Little Masterpieces of English Poetry by British and American Authors*. Vol. 6, *Elegies and Hymns*. New York: Doubleday.

Vermeule, Blakey. 2010. *Why Do We Care about Literary Characters?* Baltimore: Johns Hopkins University Press.

Vicinus, Martha. 2004. *Intimate Friends: Women Who Loved Women 1778–1928*. Chicago: University of Chicago Press.

Virgil. 1972. *The Aeneid of Virgil*. Translated by Allen Mandelbaum. New York: Bantam.

Vizyenos, Georgios. 1988. *My Mother's Sin and Other Stories*. Translated by William F. Wyatt Jr. Hanover, NH: University Press of New England.

Wade, Nicholas, 2011. "New View of How Humans Moved Away from Apes." *New York Times*, March 10, A3.

Wadell, Paul J. 1989. *Friendship and the Moral Life*. Notre Dame, IN: University of Notre Dame Press.

Walls, Neal. 2001. *Desire, Discord, and Death: Approaches to Ancient Near Eastern Myth*. Boston: American School of Oriental Research.

Walton, Kendall L. 1993. *Mimesis as Make-Believe: On the Foundations of the Representational Arts*. Cambridge: Harvard University Press.

Warren, Patricia Neil. 2011. "Real Cowboys and *Brokeback Mountain*." In *The Brokeback Book: From Story to Cultural Phenomenon*, ed. William R. Handley. Lincoln: University of Nebraska Press.

Waugh, Evelyn. 1960. *Brideshead Revisited*. London: Chapman and Hall.

Way, Niobe. 2011. *Deep Secrets: Boys' Friendships and the Crisis of Connection*. Cambridge: Harvard University Press.

White, Caroline. 1992. *Christian Friendship in the Fourth Century*. Cambridge: Cambridge University Press.

White, E. B. 1952. *Charlotte's Web*. New York: Harper and Brothers.

White, Stephen K. 1991. *Political Theory and Postmodernism*. Cambridge: Cambridge University Press.

Whitman, Walt. 1959. *Complete Poetry and Selected Prose*. Edited by James E. Miller Jr. Boston: Houghton Mifflin.

Williams, Tennessee. 1990. *Five O'Clock Angel: Letters of Tennessee Williams to Maria St. Just, 1948–1982*. New York: Penguin.

Williams, Walter L. 1992. "The Relationship between Male-Male Friendship and Male-Female Marriage." In *Men's Friendship*, edited by Peter M. Nardi. Newbury Park, CA: Sage.

Wolf, Christa. 1970. *The Quest for Christa T*. Translated by Christopher Middleton. New York. Farrar, Straus and Giroux.

Woolf, Virginia. 1927. *To the Lighthouse*. New York: Harcourt Brace Jovanovich.

Wright, Richard. 1937. *Black Boy*. New York: Harper and Row.

Xenophon. 1922. *Xenophon: Anabasis, Books IV–VII, Symposium and Apology*. Translated by Charleton L. Brownson and O. J. Todd. New York: Putnam's.

Yeats, W. B. 1983. *The Poems*. Edited by Richard J. Finneran. New York: Macmillan.

Yenor, Scott. 2003. "Locke and the Problem of Friendship in Modern Liberalism." In *Love and Friendship: Rethinking Politics and Affection in Modern Times*, edited by Eduardo A. Velásquez. Lanham, MD: Lexington Books.

Zahavi, Amotz, and Avishag Zahavi. 1997. *The Handicap Principle: A Missing Piece of Darwin's Puzzle*. New York: Oxford University Press.

Zelizer, Viviana A. 2005. *The Purchase of Intimacy*. Princeton: Princeton University Press.

Ziolkowski, Theodore. 2011. Gilgamesh *among Us: Modern Encounters with the Ancient Epic*. Ithaca: Cornell University Press.

Zunshine, Lisa. 2006. *Why We Read Fiction: Theory of Mind and the Novel*. Columbus: Ohio State University Press.

———. 2010. "Lying Bodies and the Enlightenment: Theory of Mind and Cultural Historicism." In *Introduction to Cognitive Cultural Studies*, edited by Lisa Zunshine. Baltimore: Johns Hopkins University Press.

Index